# Companion

# Companion

## *A Soulful Journey*

## Dristi

PARTRIDGE

**To order additional copies of this book, contact**
Partridge India
000 800 10062 62
orders.india@partridgepublishing.com

www.partridgepublishing.com/india

*To myself - you made it*

Why am I writing this?

When I started writing, I never imagined that I would actually publish a book. I've always wanted to try and help whomever I can. When I decided to publish my book sometime in September, I was warned by a friend that I will receive criticism and that if I'm not ready to face it, I shouldn't be publishing something so personal. I was pretty convinced that I should stop the process and just let this be private. Later that day when I was rethinking about this matter it dawned on me, that there are so many people out there, who feel the same way, and they hide behind anonymous names posting stories or shut down anyone who tries to ask or talk to them about what's wrong. If I can do even a little bit to change that, I'd want too. I don't care how much hate I receive, but even if one in a thousand can relate or feel better about him or herself because of me, that's just pure joy.

I am Dristi, isn't it surprising that an 18 year old is giving advice? Well, I believe age doesn't matter. There is no "age-limit" to publish a self-help book. Self-help is too overrated; so let's call this more like a guide or companion. Well I am certain most of you will be wondering why I wrote this? What would I have to say that famous psychologist and psychiatrist already haven't? But that's the difference, ~~I am not here to tell~~, I am here to share and be your companion thorough your journey.

I was hell-bent on publishing a book that I had been working on which I was unable to complete after reaching 10,000 words.

The thing is I don't want to leave a mark in this industry by writing a book which will one day turn into a movie (laughs) I don't want to be famous, not really. I just want to help, pure and simple help. I want to try and give the help I did not receive during my difficult times.

Lets get few things clear, you don't need to be depressed or have any mental illness to own this book, you just need to be human. As human beings we have tough days and we cannot cope with them at times and it can seem nearly impossible to do anything at all most of the times. This Companion will help you go through each day at a time, and you will also be able to note down your feelings and thoughts so that you are on track with your self. It might all not make sense at all- but it is essential to know and understand what you are feeling.

This is a book cum diary; I have tried to provide space like an actually diary designed for you so that you can put down your thoughts, emotions, schedules, to-do lists, etc. and stay connected with yourself.

My hardships got me here, even though they were tough and painful. There were days where I felt miserably low and gave up a few times and I still do, often.

Although I have the rest of my life ahead of me, as some of you might point out, that's too far away ahead to bother about now. I made it to today, I made it to complete a task that I took upon myself and that it is pretty good. The thing is we have downfalls, and most of the times we look at them and feel worse. The trick is, however, to turn that around. Try finding the bright side; for instance for me, it is this book. After everything happened, it resulted me to write and publish this- something that I am extremely proud of. We need to start treating our minds and hearts like little puppies, learning new tricks every time you achieve something, no matter how small or big. Just treat yourself! Everything you do is important and we don't really realize that. We let little things slide but don't the little things make the big thing?

'Why did you do it?" the therapist sighed.

"Because… because…" I replied, "You won't get it," I gasped

"At least try," she whispered

"It was the first Monday of January, there were five months left for graduation. I woke up at 06:47am with an unbearable pain in my soul. It was not the first time I experienced such pain, but it was greater than most days. I laid down lifelessly for a couple of minutes, till I lifted up my phone from the bedside table and stared monotonously at the time. At that very moment I felt blank- but I wasn't. There were a billion questions juggling my mind. The ones I usually ask myself on a daily basis but today, something felt different. The undying hope for my death seemed to be alive. Yes, suicide. It's not like I've never thought about it, it's crossed my mind a couple of times or maybe more than a couple, but I never really had the courage. I always thought about everyone who I'd be hurting by this drastic step. But that day, nothing and no one mattered. It was just me and the loudest voice in my head screeching… and that was it."

On 4th of Jan I was lying unconsciously on a hospital bed with a tube in my face trying to pump my stomach, and an IV drip on my arm for swallowing excessive pills.

Lets talk about something that people in general ignore or try to blindside, something that's a taboo. Let's talk about mental illness. We all have days when we are miserably low; some of us make that lowness a part of our daily routine. Mental illness is tricky to diagnose. It's not a sudden pain but a constant one.

Sometimes it takes a lifetime to even realize that something could possibly be wrong, maybe because we don't talk about it as much as we should. Maybe because we keep our therapy sessions and psychiatric appointments locked away in an overseas account that no one can find or trace.

I know the feeling of waking up every morning and feeling 'random.'

Every story towards mental illness starts differently it could start anyway, anyhow, anywhere. Mine started in four closed walls of my bathroom with a blade just like most of yours. I don't exactly remember the first time I harmed myself but I do remember why I did it and continued too.

I did it to feel, to feel something I understand. To feel a pain I could understand, pain and blood from the skin is so much easier to process than chaos inside your body, mind and soul. Its that relief I felt when I finally understood that pain. But that's not the pain we need to truly understand, that pain that strikes when your wrists distorted is not the pain you need to understand. You need to process the pain you are trying to run away from because remember, that pain is inside <u>you</u>, for how long will you run away from yourself? Until you finally end your life?

Well now that I am typing this, and if I read this somewhere I'd totally agree. It's so much easier to just end your life than to deal with that endless pain your heart's pumping into your bloodstream. But today if you ask me to consider suicide, I'll take a good look into the mirror and stare at myself blankly for a few seconds and remember all the little things I do or people do for me that create joy. I have always been so bitter because I always felt I never got the love I deserved, and somewhere I still do.

"Be the love you never received" –Rune Cazuli

First few steps to making yourself feel better according to me are acknowledging that something is wrong. You don't need to be mentally ill, you don't need to have severe depression or anxiety. You might even suffer from mental illness but you just don't know it.

Everyone has bad days, some more than others. Some more prolonged than others. That's beside the point.

## 1. Acknowledge something is **not** okay.

And that's okay, even the strongest people break down and that is totally fine. Breaking down is not a sign of weakness. Breaking down and crying doesn't make you a "girl" or a "baby." Showing emotions does not make you vulnerable it makes you human.

## 2. Share

Sometimes it helps to talk or write down what you're feeling.

Talking, in most cases is difficult and can make things worse, you need to talk to the right person who will understand and *empathize* not *sympathize*. Sometimes when you are in a vulnerable state of mind and you talk to someone and they don't say the thing you expect them to say, it might encourage you from not opening up to anyone at all.

It became difficult for me to open up to other people because I found everyone sympathizing and being pitiful. Many people seemed bored and fed up by listening to me endlessly go on and would respond ignorantly, which left me disheartened. The easiest way I found to pour out my feelings was through writing. You don't need to be the best at English or spellings. No one's testing your sentence structure or your vocabulary. When something inside you aches or even in a situation filled with joy, writing if your companion. If talking to others doesn't work, talk to yourself. Remember there are many different sides of you inside you, they will all guide you differently, the part that urges you to keep going and staying strong is the one you should listen to and try to enhance.

## 3. Other sources

Sometimes it becomes tedious and stressful to find the right words in these cases find an alternative. Search for a rhythm or lyrics that help you relate to your current status.

## 4. Stick to your source

Once you find your source, stick to it. Make sure it is handy or easily available to you when you need it. For instance, I was never too fond of penning it all down, so I use to type out my writings on my phone. On days when I felt too lethargic as if I could do nothing and absolutely not type/write out what was going on in my head, I'd record my voice so that it wasn't bottled up inside of me.

## 5. Downfall

Maybe at point after a while, you will feel alone. You might want to physically share your joy or pain with someone. But trust me, if your try and try to the fullest to help yourself nothing will stop you. You should be willing to help yourself, if you have purchased this book, this is a first step to helping yourself and loving yourself and I am proud of you for doing so.

P.S. make it a point to write your happy thoughts as well because when you look back at your words you shouldn't only find sadness.

If at all you aren't able to find something that relates, I hope my thoughts will:

Lets get really personal, I wrote a letter to my parents sometime in January when I was at a really low point in my life. Fortunately, I have gained a lot of strength on my own and have learnt that you have to be your "knight in shinning armor" and your own survivor to get through anything in life. It's easy to be dependent on others but that has its risks. When you are your own hero that's pure pride.

*Dear mum and dad,*

*I'd like to start by apologizing for my behavior lately, but trust me I can't help myself. I feel like I have no purpose in this world, I feel useless and empty. There are not enough words to describe how I feel.*

*I have tried to put myself back together but you really don't understand how hollow and shattered I feel from inside.*

*Some of you think I am doing all this because of a boy, but its not. I don't lie to you both. I try to tell you both everything. You guys know first love always hurts.*

*I wanted to write it to you both because I know you love me and you are worried about my well-being but I am just not okay. I don't want to be here any more. I feel my time is done. I feel I have experienced whatever life had to offer me. The only reason I am still here is cause I know dad will break down if anything happens to me. I saw him cry that day I popped those pills and my heart broke into a million more pieces.*

*With all of this going on coping with school is difficult, I feel so lost from inside that nothing is making sense and I just can't do anything. I am so scared I am going to not reach up to your expectations and disappoint you. I have been nice; I have been strong. It's gotten me nowhere so far. I am just fed up.*

*There's not much for me to say, nothing that you'd want to hear anyway you want your baby girl here but she doesn't want to be here. What do I do?*

*I feel like I have no energy left to fight, I have no more hope or faith left in me to do anything of such sort.*

*If I could just go away from here your burden would be so much lesser. You'd have to worry about one less person. All the troubles I am giving you would disappear with me but I am just scared with the pain I'd leave behind. That's why I am pushing you all away. That's why I keep performing these acts of self-harm hoping one day you all will get fed up and just leave and let me go away from this world in peace.*

*This might be too much to take in but it is what it is and I don't know what to do.*

*Love,*
*Dristi*

I wrote this letter to my parents almost a week after because I was still quite disturbed the same week I lost a few friends due to my "act" and gained a few. The next few months were so much easier with people around even though I keep telling you to be your own hero that doesn't mean you don't let people in, build walls and shut everyone out. Being your own hero is taking care of yourself when you most need it, being your own hero is been able to depend on yourself the most, being able to take care of yourself, being your own hero is being able to be there for yourself and putting yourself together when nobody else is

You know that feeling you get, when everything seems good after long and your life has never been better. We all have those moments most of the time in our lives. It is something we all long for with desperation, but when it comes, we don't cherish it as much as we should. We somehow still mange to be unhappy. Do you ever wonder why? I feel that we all are so use to the pain and sorrow in our lives that we forgot what happiness is or maybe now we are more comfortable being disturbed souls that being peaceful seems odd.

Sometimes we push happiness and love away, because we are afraid of being hurt and broken but darling, if you don't face heartbreak how will you face love? Your heart only breaks when you fall in love and let someone steel your heart; if you are heart broken do you stop loving? Just because of some incidents in your life you want to become a cold soul? I believe that there is someone out there, waiting for you maybe not as a lover, but as a friend or relative. You just need to try, and try harder till you find someone to mend your broken heart.

So look around, fall in love, have fun, have your heart broken, this is your life do what you can when you can, you don't know how long you're here. Every moment should be cherished, being sad or depressed isn't a bad thing but in those times don't forget your happiest times. Don't curse life or god, you make your own path, life is how it is because you chose to live that way, you chose to be happy, sad, worried, married, single, or anything else. It's your life, your choice, your wish and you owe no one, any explanation. Be you, be free, live your way cause there is no other better way.

There are something things you'll truly never let go off, your first kiss, your first love, and the first grave you cried on.

There are always going to be people in this world who let you down. You need to learn how to let it go. It will come to you when you least expect it. It can come from anywhere and anyone. It could be your family or your closest friend or a person you don't even know. That's the thing is, we make ourselves so vulnerable where when anyone says or does anything it can hurt us.

Do you ever look back at relationships and wonder why or how they ended? Do you sit and wonder what you could have done to keep it still going?

The paint underneath my finger nails, the paper cuts on my finger tips and all the hard work you put into that one piece, it's all worth it in the end.

Its so sad when everyone you love loses faith in you. They stop believing whatever you say and start being rude.

Maybe it's time that our society stopped pestering women to be more lady-like and avoid them from living their life. Maybe it's time we just let everyone be.

Maybe it's time we realize that a simple 'are you okay?' can save someone's life.

Maybe it's time we all start taking mental illnesses seriously.

Maybe it's time to make a lot of changes.

And believe when people say that the biggest smiles are the most wounded.

To women,

Why is it that if the girl with the heavier breasts and chubbier arms wears it, it's not appropriate? Why does our size have to define what we wear. Why is it that, if women go out in a tube top with her heavier breasts that she'll quickly be judged for being dressed in that manner.

Why is it that every single woman in any society especially Indian, has to critically analyze her own outfit before entering the public? Why is it not okay for women to show a little leg? Why our young girls quickly judged as the 'spoilt' and 'reckless' generation for being confident about themselves and what they wear. Why is it okay for old ladies to wear sarees and show their bare stomach, without being judged? Why does everyone think that when a girl dresses 'nice' its to impress someone, we just like to dress ourselves up for ourselves.

Why are girls suddenly not "home-ly" enough for going out drinking and having a good time. Why is it not okay for a girl to have a bunch of guy friends?

Why is it that we say we support feminism, but indeed, are the messed up society ourselves. We say we want equality, we say we want women to work but want our own daughter to be married at 24 and have a kid at 25. We say we want to live in a safe environment but we are the one tearing each other down, women tear down women.

Before we start the race for feminism and equality maybe we should ask women to respect each other and themselves. Maybe we should ask women to be nicer to each other. Maybe we should ask women not to judge another woman by her hair, outfit or anything else. If women don't stand together, we won't be strong enough and we'll always be dominated and trust me, it won't always be a man cause a woman can be a real bitch.

From one women to another

What happened to following your dreams and becoming the next Bill Gates or Steve Jobs. Why is everyone pushing themselves aside to please someone else?

Movies, late night drivers, staying in bed till noon, few sips of alcohol, street food.

Well I could go on, but these are all the things we crave and will remember for as long as we grow old and grey.

All these moments with the ones we love, family and friends, sometimes strangers that's all that's important.

We're not going to remember the expensive bag we once bought or the day we spent at the spa. We're going to remember the hours in school we didn't spend studying. We're going to remember the nights we ditched our significant other to chill with our chuddy-buddies.

So don't spend time trying to earn that extra cash to get a car, which will give you temporary happiness.

We'll that's all I have to say

It's so weird that people say they believe in giving second chances but they really don't. How an individual is so quickly judged by a few sets backs and is perceived to repeat the same mistakes again.

Since when did an act of suicide become an act of attention and not a cry for help.

It's true. Everyone leaves. Eventually. Even the people that swore won't leave, left. Because that's how life works the optimistic me believes that, when people leave better people walk in and that's the circle of life. How will you meet new people and expand your horizons by the same people.

But well, I believe, fuck, better people coming in, I had the best people and they left. I don't want anyone better now. I don't want to meet any more people cause I hate them. Give me back the ones I liked.

It all happened so soon
I'm still in denial
How long is this going to last
Are you really gone?
Will you never come back?
You won't drop your daughter to school on her first day?
You won't be here to teach her right and wrong?
You won't be here when a boy breaks her heart?
You know she needs you more than any of us do.
So please, come back? Would you?
You've been gone to long.

*In loving memory of my mamu*

I'm tearing myself apart to fix everyone else's wounds and I'm leaving my self bare

I stare at your image
Hoping you'd speak
One last time
I want to hear you creak
Seeing you there lay lifelessly
Kicked in with reality

Maybe I'm still in denial.
Hoping to see you smile
We knew you'd be here for a short period of time
But we weren't ready to let you go so soon
But I hope you're in a better place
And have some space
Know that we miss you
Know that we care
Forever in hearts
With love we say

*In loving memory of my mamu, I miss you everyday*

I don't want you to come on a knight and shinning armor and woo me but take care of my heart it is made of pieces of glass one crack can ruin the look of it and one drop can shatter it. Be careful, please?

She let her fears be the best of her and that ruined her

Let me be your high and low
Let me be your day and night
Let me be your rise and shine
As long as you'll be mine

I'm right here
Waiting for you
Can't you see me?
You're running behind everyone but me
Don't you know
No one will love you as much as me
Don't you know
The way I know you
No one will ever
Don't you know
How deep my love is for you
Even today
Don't you know
I'd take a bullet for you.

When you're on your lowest hour and the sadness kicks in and happiness drains out. When you feel like being productive but feel chained to your bed and your body's not willing to move a tissue. When you switch sides all night hoping to get some sleep. When you question your purpose on this earth and feel like have no reason to live that's depression and when this kicks in you're fucked.

Her heart throbbed when her phone rang and she saw his name flash repeatedly. Her face lit up with joy and her palms got all sweaty. She had a lasting glow on her face, which didn't rub of till reality caught up with her.

He followed her around begging her to take him back. But she knew she couldn't cause she had finally moved on even though a part of her will always love him, she loved herself enough to walk away from something that broke her one too many times.

There was something about her smile that lit the room up & something about her sadness that brought tears in everyone's eye. There was something so special about her but not everyone could see it. She enjoyed every bit of what she did and one day she stopped. She stopped it all. Her liveliness slowly began to fade. Something inevitable happened that completely changed her and she could never be the same again. She tried but to an extent to when she had no more strength and effort left in her. She gave in, she was done trying.

Maybe one day I'll shut my eyes and just relax. I won't think about the horrors of life, I won't think about the past or the future, I won't think about him, all I'll do is live in the present be in the moment & relax. Someday.

She shut her eyes hoping to feel nothing. She shut her eyes and felt sadness rushing through her veins. She could feel herself drowning helplessly, she tried splashing around trying to hold her head above water to breathe, but after a little effort she saw no point and she let go. She let her heaviness of her sadness let her sink to the bottom of the ocean and give up.

She ran towards him as tears rolled down her cheeks. She hugged him tightly and just stayed in his arms.

He didn't move a muscle because he sensed something was wrong. As she pulled herself back she said, "Maybe a hug is all we need to fix ourselves. Not just any hug, a heartfelt hug from a loved one. A hug that will put all my pieces back together. A hug from a person who, I know can fix me. You're my person, you fix me"

I'm hollow. I'm empty. I'm broken. I'm breaking. My 100 pieces are becoming a 1000 and my 1000 pieces are becoming a million and soon they'll all just disappear like sawdust into oblivion, and take me away forever, for good.

I looked at myself in the mirror today for a few minutes, then I shut my eyes and tried to recall my face, I pictured my self sad and I thought, you are and you become what you think of yourself, isn't it? I had no reason to be sad about but I still pictured myself in sorrow. Sometimes when in a young age as teenagers mostly, we go through a lot of stress and other things, some of us remain scarred for life and are never able to leave the maze of pain. Its like a load on our shoulders and we feel that we will never be able to overcome it, so we imagine ourselves helpless and lonely and that's the only part of ourselves that we can see. Even in happy times somehow we bring up our sorrow, one can call it an art or a talent of being unhappy.

Sometimes we just don't understand people whom we think we do. Sometimes we feel that feelings don't change. That, that one person will always be there for you that he or she will never go away or change. Sometimes someone we love the most can go away for good or another reason we just have to be strong and supportive. You might have cried the night but did you get what you cried, for in morning? No right? But it's okay. Cause sometimes we cry to lighten ourselves. It's a good thing, crying doesn't mean you're weak. It just shows that you can handle yourself

It's not been very long since we've met.

It's just been two summers and one Christmas dinner.

Sleeping quietly in Papas arms, hoping Santa would fill those stockings full.

Then came snow and then came New Year, valentine proving it the worst year.

Spring and summer past by.

I waited on Christmas to feel complete for New Year and it happened again.

Another spring, another summer and another Christmas dinner without you dear.

Where you disappeared.

No one seems to know.

Did you meet angels that I don't know?

All I need is, a shoulder to cry on, someone who can hug me with lots of love. Words saying, "it will all be okay, your not alone" just someone who cares, someone who'll listen, and truly be there, someone who'll never leave. That someone's a dream and always remain one.

No. It's not easy to forgive and not at all to forget. It's not my brain; it's my heart, my soul that's wounded. It's a thing you try so hard to forget but you don't, you just keeping thinking about it. It's like when your parents tell you not to do something and you want to do it even more then.

The person you learn to love and trust, breaks you all over again

I want a day without tears, without sadness, without memories and without loneliness. I want a day of happiness.

When you just sit back and realize how fast time passes, how things change and people grow. How priorities change but in the end there's always a lesson.

It's not easy to give up on something you love, on something that was such an important part of your life. But you have too, eventually.

It's like I can't feel myself breath anymore all I have is bones, flesh and a broken heart.

Try making the most of your life; I know all the times you fall it's hard to get back on your feet but its not impossible.

It's how strong we are and it all goes to the people who stand by us and give us the strength to move on and fight.

I need you to be my strength when I'm weak. I need to be there whether I need you or not. I need you to understand cause I know you've gone through worse. I need you to be there in the worst scenarios cause when I say go or bye or I don't need you, those are the times I need you the most.

We all try to find our way to love. Some of us can never get it right, some of us rush into it. It's never going to be the way we imagined it or perfect, we still have to embrace it.

Not everyone is true. Not everyone will love you the way you love them. Not everyone will care like you do. Not everyone will make you feel as important as you make him or her feel. Not everybody will have that space in their heart that you have for them. But sometimes, you fail to do all these things. Sometimes you are just too scared sometimes you don't know what you feel, sometimes there is a lot going on in your unconscious mind, which disturbs you. Sometimes the person you always understood fails to understand you and then all you have is yourself.

You break. You break and you feel unfixable. Like the whole world is against you and nobody likes you. So you push everyone away cause you feel unfixable and devastated. After pushing them away some don't give up but the rest do but when they all lose hope all you have is yourself

So everyone's out there Instagraming how happy their relationship is and how long they've spent together. And I'm here, alone, listening to music and missing you so much and wishing we could rewind and go back to how we were, deeply in love. We could go back to all that, where we'd do anything to meet each other. What happened to all that? How can it all just disappear in a blink of an eye? It all happened so soon, it's so hard to process. Was it always supposed to be this way? Why didn't we just let it be. And even if we got back together why break up then. I was so sure that this was going to last longer. I was sure this was a sure thing, that we were real. That everything that happened between us was real. And that "distance" would never break that and us was the last thing I thought that would break us.

Relationships, it hurts most when they end. It pains within, you feel numb and helpless, you try everything to get back together after sometime you realize "I'm the only one trying" that's when you stop or at least try too. That's when you actually realize it's over but you just don't want to believe it, until you are humiliated and shattered further. When you can literally feel so anesthetic that you blank out and disappear from the world then you go do something crazy to feel something again.

That's when you realize love, is something so sharp that it's going to hurt no matter what. Love is so deep that only a lot of digging can get it out. Love is something that can bring the worst or best out of you. Love is irresistible. Love has no respect, it is demeaning, and that's when you stop believing in love and it takes one person to make all this happen. One heart break, hundreds of pieces and a thousand of tears.

When you grow old and look back on your life what will you have left?

The memories, the people whom you knew, the people who were your friends and maybe some who still our. You'll remember the stupid pranks and the late night conversations. You'll remember the thousands of pictures you'll took, you might even have some of them. You'll remember the times you'll danced like maniacs. When you think of school, you'll remember the teachers whom you drove crazy, you'll remember the name calling, you'll remember the secret paring among students. All those events you took part in and how amazing they all were. When you look back at your life your not going to remember whom you hated so much and the negativity. You'll remember the good things.

So, go. Go take risks, have fun give yourself something to remember about, no matter how small or how big. I'm not asking you to jump off a cliff but laugh a little more, cry a little less and love to your fullest. Stay positive and keep going, when your old and sitting in your rocking chair doing nothing, remember all these years and have no regrets at all.

You move/shift, for various reasons and you see the world. You move away from your comfort zone. Your little bubble breaks, you attend a different school/college, you meet new people and then understand that the place you've stayed the longest and spent your childhood in will always be home and the people there will always be your people, no matter how much you hated then once. You realize and see the types of people around. You also understand that things can change in a fraction of a second first you were there and now your here. It's never going to be easy, it might not even be joyful, but it'll be a lesson

Nothing is permanent; some of us learn it the hard way.

Try. But try to an extend where your self respect is still intact

Love, is just an over exaggeration of the Shakespeare era-when it existed.

Why is it all so easy and romantic in TV shows and movies. Why can't that be reality? Wouldn't it be easier for everyone? If a fat girl dates a jock and beauty queen dates a nerd. It all seems so perfect there, where it all isn't even true. But the made up version gives hope and longing. Why does it all have to be so difficult. Why does love have to come with pain.

Have you ever just burst into tears looking at an old photo or an old video? Why?

Why did you cry?

You miss it? Do something about it.

Think for a moment. What do you do the whole day? Work? Does it give you happiness? No? Then what does? Your family?

Note how much time you spend with your family and at work. See the difference?

As humans we tend to run after money and let our mood and happiness depend on that. We forget what family, togetherness and love means. Think about a situation with your family, your smiling? Now think about the most expensive thing you've ever bought, feel anything?

We hurt the people we love unknowingly which makes them distant. You have a family you love, take a step or two, don't let everyone go their separate ways. We are all in this together, let's show.

Let's not have any regret. You never know how long someone's going to be there.

I bent down to pick up the pieces on the floor
I got up and saw them missing from my soul
I let you in to my heart, and home
Now we don't even talk no more

People say "let go" or "forget about it" or "move on" I want to ask this to everyone who sometime in their life has told someone to let go, take a minute think, do you an old memory, photography, lost lover, family member or anything or anyone like that in your head whom you always think about and get sad or feel something you only feel when you think about them or see that photograph? So darling, it's easy to say "let go" but do we do it ourselves?

The truth is, something's or people are just impossible to forget about, they will always be present in your unconscious mind. You may feel that you have forgotten, but you never actually do, if you revisit a place you had been with them, it all comes back and you freeze for a second all the memories, you feel it all. That's it, those are the things we can never let go off. Because life is so challenging we try to treasure as many moments and moments we can, because in the end that's all we are going to have left.

We stay up thinking about out failed relationships, the tests we didn't pass, the people we disappointed, the people that left us. But do we ever stay up thinking about the great relationships we have going on, the tests we passed wonderfully, the people who love us no matter what and are still here beside us?

It's hard to let someone in but it's harder to let go

You still manage to break my heart every night right before bed.

It all falls apart when logic takes over love.

Only if we'd stay together, you could've seen. Together, we are invincible

Stranded in an empty land
Hoping for a helping hand
Lost in the middle of nowhere
Do you see me there?
The skies are crying
But the trees are drying
The earths shrinking
And everyone's drinking
I came to you with a little hope
You told me to cope
How do I cope without you dear
I cried with a tear

So whom do I call at night when I'm afraid and lose sleep. Whom do I text the first thing in the morning. Whom do I call to share something exciting with. Whom do I send a picture to when I'm feeling pretty.

You've gone and you've take the biggest part of me with you. And I've never felt more incomplete. It's like there's a hole in my body and I can feel the breeze pass to and fro.

It's not as easy as it seems. You might bump into a stranger who is grumpy, smiling or in tears. But you judge them with what you see on the outside not on the inside. You don't know what they are going through, someone could have the biggest smile, and be shattered from inside or could genuinely be happy. You'd never know if you never try, right? Take an initiative and ask someone how they are doing, it might truly make their whole day or give them momentary joy, that someone cares. It might be someone you work with, or someone that works for you. No person is too big or too small, this is us, being human and spreading humanitarian. Your step to humanity is just 4 words away "how are you doing?"

Things don't always turn out the way you want them too, because if they it, what's the challenge?

If we all got whatever we wanted, we'd just wish for more, would we be content?

We might

I said I'd always be there, I am here.
You said you'd never leave even in the heaviest breeze
But it just took a little sneeze to get you off my feet
Now it's snowing and raining all at once
The fogs blurring my vision
Are you here?
I'm knee deep, covered in snow, hoping for sun to show

Are you a person who over thinks, every single scenario? Sometimes you over think things without even realizing and you tend to see the worst cases rather than the best. It's unimaginable how we always prepare ourselves for the worst but still manage to get hurt, cause the truth is we prepare ourselves but we never actually imagine it to happen. Secretly we want the best out of everything, they say what you believe usually happens, is it because we believe and think of the worst that's what happens?

What's the point of being in a class which has no unity? What's the point of 'friendship' when it's not even true? They say high school is suppose to be the most memorable years of our lives, they say the friends you make in high school last forever. What's forever? What's a friend? Is a friend someone who saves you when your drowning and won't mind sinking in with you, or is a friend someone who will push you inside the water and walk away.

We all experience good and bad times no doubt. But it's always good to have someone right by your side helping you cope.

Thank you for being my someone

Have you felt this alone that even if a 1000 people stood beside you it wouldn't matter cause there are just a few selected people whom you'd want there. Have you felt so broken that you can hear the pieces of your heart fall to the pit of your stomach? Have you felt so sad, that you question your presence on the planet?

The worst off all is feeling it all together, and the people who can handle themselves at that moment, they, are the true heroes.

They describe a girls beauty by her hair, her eyes, her smile.
But maybe if you look past that you'll see where real beauty lies.

Do you every feel used. Do you feel like the people around you just are just here because they want something from you?

Do you ever feel like no one is every going to care about you? Do you ever feel like an alien to the universe? Like a completely different person, whose never going to fit in. No matter what you do, people are always going to judge you and try to find a motive behind your kindness.

People are always going to use you and make you feel like shit when you've always tried to be there without expecting anything in return. But what's the use?

When you fall, you fall because gravity what's to give you a hug so tight that you stand back up and fight.

See past your disabilities, only then your abilities will shine.

It's about the little things;
The random hugs
A sudden phone call
A sweet message
Stupid conversations
That's what adds up to your memory, not the gifts or how many hours a week
you work

What defines us as people? The way we look? The way we dress? The friends we have? The way we talk? Our behavior or the brand of clothes we wear?

In my opinion, nowadays branded clothes have became a necessity and not as a style statement but as a character statement. We don't dress according to comfort, instead we dress according to the label, popularity and price. The world has become different, we live in a universe where many people choose their friends according to the way they are marque. But what people really don't understand is that, that you are supposed to define the brand and make it look priceless.

Are you your label?

I feel like I'm drowning into the deep blue ocean, I'm not even trying to save myself, my arms and legs feel numb, I can't breath, my lungs are going to collapse because of the water, my hearts going to stop beating, my skin will lose its beauty, my lips will turn blue. I don't want to be tangled in the weeds waiting to be eaten by some water creature. After all this time I waited for you I still feel you're the only one, a fisherman in the sea with a net who catches me. That's all I need, I need you to save me

For that time. That moment, you seemed like your old self again. The person who meant the world to me. Who'd be there for me no matter what? When did you change? Is it that easy for people to change? I know you have different priorities now but do i even make the top 5 on the list now?

Every year, month, day, date, time or moment has a meaning to someone or the other. It could be someone's birthday, the year you lost a loved one, the month you graduated, the day you reunited with your lover or an old friend. Each time set has a different significance to all of us. Some of us remember the exact moment it happened, some forget. It actually depends on how much you chose to remember and the importance of that time, now.

It baffles me to see 'couple' posts on social media, teenagers going around dating and using the term forever and love.

It's weird how we deeply care for someone whom we've meet 17 minutes ago and ignore the people who have taken care of us for 17 years. How can we predict 'forever' when we can't guarantee our on life span?

I want to swim in the sea and be lost with the waves. That seems much better than what I feel right now.

"If it's meant to be, it will happen. But that doesn't mean you won't have to work for it."

I read this today, and I thought to myself, when do you stop? When do you stop working. When do you know you've worked hard enough and you should just stop. How much is too much? How much is enough?

Do you just stare at something and disappear. Your soul drowns and you start to feel hollow, like there's nothing inside you. Nothing left, no more. As if everyone's picked up pieces of you and just vanished into oblivion. That's what destroys us, slowly, the hollowness the emptiness the loneliness.

Do you ever feel abandoned, like no one in this world wants you. Have you ever felt that if you die tomorrow it wouldn't matter much to anyone. If something ever happened to you, you won't be the reason for someone to lose sleep at night or stay hungry. Do you just feel so alone that even if you disappear no one would really realize. Do you lay in bed thinking about all the people that matter to you and question your importance in their life?

Don't ask me what's wrong cause I don't know myself. Don't ask me to fix you when I'm in pieces. Don't ask me to hold you cause I'm numb. Don't ask me to smile cause it'll be meaningless. Just stay here; next to me and I'll hopefully be alright.

Is it weird that after all these months I still miss you like I use to. Is it weird that it still feels like yesterday we walked out of each other's lives? Is it weird that still writes things about you. Is it weird that I think about you more than I think about anyone else? Is it weird that you still mean the world to me like you use to. Is it weird that you are the first person I want to call when something's good or bad?

Is it weird that I still love you after all these months, even though we're not together anymore?

Love cannot be understood or bought. It's felt. You can fall in love anytime with anyone. You can't go looking for love-love comes looking for you.

Sometimes it's easier said than done. Isn't it?

It's easy to say "get up and live," after something tragic.

It's easy to say, "oh so what? You'll find someone better" to someone who's just been dumped.

Next time you say something like that put yourself in that person's position what would you want to hear?

Say that.

You don't look at me the way you use to and it breaks me.

Maybe it is better to let go. Maybe it will save you all the pain.

Hope.

The worst thing to do is hope. Why? Hope gives you a false expectation. Which when not met, shatters you completely. People might argue that hope is needed to see the positive side in things, but when there's nothing positive to see, what are you 'hoping' to find?

There's nothing you can say or do that'll make me love you less. You can keep breaking my heart a thousand times. But when you need me I'll be there in a heartbeat. The thing is, I'm not yet ready to give up on us and maybe I never will be

There are some of us who feel trapped in our mind and some feel free.
Some whose thoughts control them while others who control their thoughts.
The world is filled with people who are going through things

See through that eye make up. See through that dark liner. See those sad eyes.

High school is about the drama, the politics, the newbies, the name-calling, the first kiss, the crazy nights, the long conversation, the stress, the memories, the laughter, the tears, the pranks and everything much more.

They say when you go to college, it's a completely new beginning; true. But when you walk into the future you don't necessarily forget your past, it's always a part of you, good or bad.

Your scars don't break you, they make you.

The worlds always going to hurt, love yourself first

It a mystery how we can fall in and out of love so quickly, it takes a glimpse for a heart to melt and seconds to break. Love will never be understood love is different. You can find love in family and friends, you can sense love in someone helping you, and you can show love by helping someone. Love can never be measured, love cannot be bought or sold, love is unpredictable and unimaginable. It can happen to anyone, anywhere. That's what makes love so special and painful at the same time.

Its important to be in touch with yourself and your feelings. It's very easy for stress to turn into anxiety or depression. Most of us don't even take account of it until its too late.

# Habit Tracker

**Month:**

|  | 1st | 2nd | 3rd | 4th | 5th |  |
|---|---|---|---|---|---|---|
| Sleep |  |  |  |  |  |  |
| Caffeine |  |  |  |  |  |  |
| Alcohol |  |  |  |  |  |  |
| Cigarettes |  |  |  |  |  |  |
| Exercise |  |  |  |  |  |  |
|  | 6th | 7th | 8th | 9th | 10th |  |
| Sleep |  |  |  |  |  |  |
| Caffeine |  |  |  |  |  |  |
| Alcohol |  |  |  |  |  |  |
| Cigarettes |  |  |  |  |  |  |
| Exercise |  |  |  |  |  |  |
|  | 11th | 12th | 13th | 14th | 15th |  |
| Sleep |  |  |  |  |  |  |
| Caffeine |  |  |  |  |  |  |
| Alcohol |  |  |  |  |  |  |
| Cigarettes |  |  |  |  |  |  |
| Exercise |  |  |  |  |  |  |
|  | 16th | 17th | 18th | 19th | 20th |  |
| Sleep |  |  |  |  |  |  |
| Caffeine |  |  |  |  |  |  |
| Alcohol |  |  |  |  |  |  |
| Cigarettes |  |  |  |  |  |  |
| Exercise |  |  |  |  |  |  |
|  | 21th | 22th | 23th | 24th | 25th |  |
| Sleep |  |  |  |  |  |  |
| Caffeine |  |  |  |  |  |  |
| Alcohol |  |  |  |  |  |  |
| Cigarettes |  |  |  |  |  |  |
| Exercise |  |  |  |  |  |  |
|  | 26th | 27th | 28th | 29th | 30th | 31st |
| Sleep |  |  |  |  |  |  |
| Caffeine |  |  |  |  |  |  |
| Alcohol |  |  |  |  |  |  |
| Cigarettes |  |  |  |  |  |  |
| Exercise |  |  |  |  |  |  |

# Emotion tracker

*How are you felling today? It is important to be in touch with yourself and your emotions.*

| | Anger | Hurt/Pain | Disappointment | Upset | Happy | Blah! | Lazy |
|---|---|---|---|---|---|---|---|
| 1st | | | | | | | |
| 2nd | | | | | | | |
| 3rd | | | | | | | |
| 4th | | | | | | | |
| 5th | | | | | | | |
| 6th | | | | | | | |
| 7th | | | | | | | |
| 8th | | | | | | | |
| 9th | | | | | | | |
| 10th | | | | | | | |
| 11th | | | | | | | |
| 12th | | | | | | | |
| 13th | | | | | | | |
| 14th | | | | | | | |
| 15th | | | | | | | |
| 16th | | | | | | | |
| 17th | | | | | | | |
| 18th | | | | | | | |
| 19th | | | | | | | |
| 20th | | | | | | | |
| 21st | | | | | | | |
| 22nd | | | | | | | |
| 23rd | | | | | | | |
| 24th | | | | | | | |
| 25th | | | | | | | |
| 26th | | | | | | | |
| 27th | | | | | | | |
| 28th | | | | | | | |
| 29th | | | | | | | |
| 30th | | | | | | | |
| 31st | | | | | | | |

|        | Guilt | Anxious | Sadness | Shame | Guilt | Worthless |
|--------|-------|---------|---------|-------|-------|-----------|
| 1st    |       |         |         |       |       |           |
| 2nd    |       |         |         |       |       |           |
| 3rd    |       |         |         |       |       |           |
| 4th    |       |         |         |       |       |           |
| 5th    |       |         |         |       |       |           |
| 6th    |       |         |         |       |       |           |
| 7th    |       |         |         |       |       |           |
| 8th    |       |         |         |       |       |           |
| 9th    |       |         |         |       |       |           |
| 10th   |       |         |         |       |       |           |
| 11th   |       |         |         |       |       |           |
| 12th   |       |         |         |       |       |           |
| 13th   |       |         |         |       |       |           |
| 14th   |       |         |         |       |       |           |
| 15th   |       |         |         |       |       |           |
| 16th   |       |         |         |       |       |           |
| 17th   |       |         |         |       |       |           |
| 18th   |       |         |         |       |       |           |
| 19th   |       |         |         |       |       |           |
| 20th   |       |         |         |       |       |           |
| 21st   |       |         |         |       |       |           |
| 22nd   |       |         |         |       |       |           |
| 23rd   |       |         |         |       |       |           |
| 24th   |       |         |         |       |       |           |
| 25th   |       |         |         |       |       |           |
| 26th   |       |         |         |       |       |           |
| 27th   |       |         |         |       |       |           |
| 28th   |       |         |         |       |       |           |
| 29th   |       |         |         |       |       |           |
| 30th   |       |         |         |       |       |           |
| 31st   |       |         |         |       |       |           |

# Food Tracker

| | Healthy food | Junk food | Both | Didn't eat ☹ |
|---|---|---|---|---|
| 1st | | | | |
| 2nd | | | | |
| 3rd | | | | |
| 4th | | | | |
| 5th | | | | |
| 6th | | | | |
| 7th | | | | |
| 8th | | | | |
| 9th | | | | |
| 10th | | | | |
| 11th | | | | |
| 12th | | | | |
| 13th | | | | |
| 14th | | | | |
| 15th | | | | |
| 16th | | | | |
| 17th | | | | |
| 18th | | | | |
| 19th | | | | |
| 20th | | | | |
| 21st | | | | |
| 22nd | | | | |
| 23rd | | | | |
| 24th | | | | |
| 25th | | | | |
| 26th | | | | |
| 27th | | | | |
| 28th | | | | |
| 29th | | | | |
| 30th | | | | |
| 31st | | | | |

# Weight Tracker

**Month:**

| | Kgs/lbs | | Kgs/lbs |
|---|---|---|---|
| 1st | | 16th | |
| 2nd | | 17th | |
| 3rd | | 18th | |
| 4th | | 19th | |
| 5th | | 20th | |
| 6th | | 21st | |
| 7th | | 22nd | |
| 8th | | 23rd | |
| 9th | | 24th | |
| 10th | | 25th | |
| 11th | | 26th | |
| 12th | | 27th | |
| 13th | | 28th | |
| 14th | | 29th | |
| 15th | | 30th | |
| | | 31st | |

# Journal

Good Morning Sunshine!

Lets start the beginning of the month by noting down our details, so this way we can track changes every month

Age:
Weight:
Height:
Date of last menstrual cycle and time frame:

Did you...

o Get out of bed, woke        o Brush you teeth        o Eat breakfast
  up at:                        o Take a shower          o Take your meds
o Smile

Every little task is important sometimes we forget the silliest things so lets make a to-do list to keep track!

To-do list:

Good afternoon!

Did you...

o Eat lunch                    o Finish your tasks?

Good evening love, how's your day so far?

Did you...

o Eat snacks                   o Finish all that you had on    o Eat dinner
o Have a good day                your to do list              o Sleep early
o Have a bad day

Good night and sleep well

Good Morning Sunshine!

Lets start the beginning of the month by noting down our details, so this way we can track changes every month

Age:
Weight:
Height:
Date of last menstrual cycle and time frame:

Did you…

- o Get out of bed, woke
  up at:
- o Smile
- o Brush you teeth
- o Take a shower
- o Eat breakfast
- o Take your meds

Every little task is important sometimes we forget the silliest things so lets make a to-do list to keep track!

To-do list:

Good afternoon!

Did you…

- o Eat lunch
- o Finish your tasks?

Good evening love, how's your day so far?

Did you…

- o Eat snacks
- o Have a good day
- o Have a bad day
- o Finish all that you had on
  your to do list
- o Eat dinner
- o Sleep early

Good night and sleep well

dd/mm/yy

Good Morning Sunshine!

Lets start the beginning of the month by noting down our details, so this way we can track changes every month

Age:
Weight:
Height:
Date of last menstrual cycle and time frame:

Did you…

- o Get out of bed, woke up at:
- o Smile
- o Brush you teeth
- o Take a shower
- o Eat breakfast
- o Take your meds

Every little task is important sometimes we forget the silliest things so lets make a to-do list to keep track!

To-do list:

Good afternoon!

Did you…

- o Eat lunch
- o Finish your tasks?

Good evening love, how's your day so far?

Did you…

- o Eat snacks
- o Have a good day
- o Have a bad day
- o Finish all that you had on your to do list
- o Eat dinner
- o Sleep early

Good night and sleep well

Good Morning Sunshine!

Lets start the beginning of the month by noting down our details, so this way we can track changes every month

Age:
Weight:
Height:
Date of last menstrual cycle and time frame:

Did you…

- o Get out of bed, woke up at:
- o Smile
- o Brush you teeth
- o Take a shower
- o Eat breakfast
- o Take your meds

Every little task is important sometimes we forget the silliest things so lets make a to-do list to keep track!

To-do list:

Good afternoon!

Did you…

- o Eat lunch
- o Finish your tasks?

Good evening love, how's your day so far?

Did you…

- o Eat snacks
- o Have a good day
- o Have a bad day
- o Finish all that you had on your to do list
- o Eat dinner
- o Sleep early

Good night and sleep well

Good Morning Sunshine!

Lets start the beginning of the month by noting down our details, so this way we can track changes every month

Age:
Weight:
Height:
Date of last menstrual cycle and time frame:

Did you...

o Get out of bed, woke       o Brush you teeth          o Eat breakfast
   up at:                    o Take a shower            o Take your meds
o Smile

Every little task is important sometimes we forget the silliest things so lets make a to-do list to keep track!

To-do list:

Good afternoon!

Did you...

o Eat lunch              o Finish your tasks?

Good evening love, how's your day so far?

Did you...

o Eat snacks             o Finish all that you had on    o Eat dinner
o Have a good day           your to do list               o Sleep early
o Have a bad day

Good night and sleep well

Good Morning Sunshine!

Lets start the beginning of the month by noting down our details, so this way we can track changes every month

Age:
Weight:
Height:
Date of last menstrual cycle and time frame:

Did you…

- o Get out of bed, woke up at:
- o Smile
- o Brush you teeth
- o Take a shower
- o Eat breakfast
- o Take your meds

Every little task is important sometimes we forget the silliest things so lets make a to-do list to keep track!

To-do list:

Good afternoon!

Did you…

- o Eat lunch
- o Finish your tasks?

Good evening love, how's your day so far?

Did you…

- o Eat snacks
- o Have a good day
- o Have a bad day
- o Finish all that you had on your to do list
- o Eat dinner
- o Sleep early

Good night and sleep well

Good Morning Sunshine!

Lets start the beginning of the month by noting down our details, so this way we can track changes every month

Age:
Weight:
Height:
Date of last menstrual cycle and time frame:

Did you…

| | | |
|---|---|---|
| o Get out of bed, woke up at: | o Brush you teeth | o Eat breakfast |
| o Smile | o Take a shower | o Take your meds |

Every little task is important sometimes we forget the silliest things so lets make a to-do list to keep track!

To-do list:

Good afternoon!

Did you…

o Eat lunch          o Finish your tasks?

Good evening love, how's your day so far?

Did you…

| | | |
|---|---|---|
| o Eat snacks | o Finish all that you had on | o Eat dinner |
| o Have a good day | your to do list | o Sleep early |
| o Have a bad day | | |

Good night and sleep well

Good Morning Sunshine!

Lets start the beginning of the month by noting down our details, so this way we can track changes every month

Age:
Weight:
Height:
Date of last menstrual cycle and time frame:

Did you…

o Get out of bed, woke    o Brush you teeth    o Eat breakfast
   up at:    o Take a shower    o Take your meds
o Smile

Every little task is important sometimes we forget the silliest things so lets make a to-do list to keep track!

To-do list:

Good afternoon!

Did you…

o Eat lunch    o Finish your tasks?

Good evening love, how's your day so far?

Did you…

o Eat snacks    o Finish all that you had on    o Eat dinner
o Have a good day       your to do list    o Sleep early
o Have a bad day

Good night and sleep well

Good Morning Sunshine!

Lets start the beginning of the month by noting down our details, so this way we can track changes every month

Age:
Weight:
Height:
Date of last menstrual cycle and time frame:

Did you…

o Get out of bed, woke    o Brush you teeth    o Eat breakfast
   up at:                o Take a shower    o Take your meds
o Smile

Every little task is important sometimes we forget the silliest things so lets make a to-do list to keep track!

To-do list:

Good afternoon!

Did you…

o Eat lunch                 o Finish your tasks?

Good evening love, how's your day so far?

Did you…

o Eat snacks          o Finish all that you had on   o Eat dinner
o Have a good day       your to do list           o Sleep early
o Have a bad day

Good night and sleep well

Good Morning Sunshine!

Lets start the beginning of the month by noting down our details, so this way we can track changes every month

Age:
Weight:
Height:
Date of last menstrual cycle and time frame:

Did you...

o Get out of bed, woke          o Brush you teeth          o Eat breakfast
   up at:                       o Take a shower            o Take your meds
o Smile

Every little task is important sometimes we forget the silliest things so lets make a to-do list to keep track!

To-do list:

Good afternoon!

Did you...

o Eat lunch                o Finish your tasks?

Good evening love, how's your day so far?

Did you...

o Eat snacks              o Finish all that you had on    o Eat dinner
o Have a good day            your to do list             o Sleep early
o Have a bad day

Good night and sleep well

Good Morning Sunshine!

Lets start the beginning of the month by noting down our details, so this way we can track changes every month

Age:
Weight:
Height:
Date of last menstrual cycle and time frame:

Did you…

o Get out of bed, woke      o Brush you teeth        o Eat breakfast
   up at:                   o Take a shower          o Take your meds
o Smile

Every little task is important sometimes we forget the silliest things so lets make a to-do list to keep track!

To-do list:

Good afternoon!

Did you…

o Eat lunch                 o Finish your tasks?

Good evening love, how's your day so far?

Did you…

o Eat snacks                o Finish all that you had on   o Eat dinner
o Have a good day              your to do list              o Sleep early
o Have a bad day

Good night and sleep well

Good Morning Sunshine!

Lets start the beginning of the month by noting down our details, so this way we can track changes every month

Age:
Weight:
Height:
Date of last menstrual cycle and time frame:

Did you...

o Get out of bed, woke        o Brush you teeth        o Eat breakfast
  up at:                      o Take a shower          o Take your meds
o Smile

Every little task is important sometimes we forget the silliest things so lets make a to-do list to keep track!

To-do list:

Good afternoon!

Did you...

o Eat lunch                o Finish your tasks?

Good evening love, how's your day so far?

Did you...

o Eat snacks              o Finish all that you had on    o Eat dinner
o Have a good day            your to do list             o Sleep early
o Have a bad day

Good night and sleep well

Good Morning Sunshine!

Lets start the beginning of the month by noting down our details, so this way we can track changes every month

Age:
Weight:
Height:
Date of last menstrual cycle and time frame:

Did you…

- o Get out of bed, woke up at:
- o Smile
- o Brush you teeth
- o Take a shower
- o Eat breakfast
- o Take your meds

Every little task is important sometimes we forget the silliest things so lets make a to-do list to keep track!

To-do list:

Good afternoon!

Did you…

- o Eat lunch
- o Finish your tasks?

Good evening love, how's your day so far?

Did you…

- o Eat snacks
- o Have a good day
- o Have a bad day
- o Finish all that you had on your to do list
- o Eat dinner
- o Sleep early

Good night and sleep well

Good Morning Sunshine!

Lets start the beginning of the month by noting down our details, so this way we can track changes every month

Age:
Weight:
Height:
Date of last menstrual cycle and time frame:

Did you...

o Get out of bed, woke       o Brush you teeth         o Eat breakfast
   up at:                    o Take a shower           o Take your meds
o Smile

Every little task is important sometimes we forget the silliest things so lets make a to-do list to keep track!

To-do list:

Good afternoon!

Did you...

o Eat lunch                  o Finish your tasks?

Good evening love, how's your day so far?

Did you...

o Eat snacks                 o Finish all that you had on   o Eat dinner
o Have a good day               your to do list            o Sleep early
o Have a bad day

Good night and sleep well

Good Morning Sunshine!

Lets start the beginning of the month by noting down our details, so this way we can track changes every month

Age:
Weight:
Height:
Date of last menstrual cycle and time frame:

Did you...

o Get out of bed, woke      o Brush you teeth        o Eat breakfast
  up at:                    o Take a shower          o Take your meds
o Smile

Every little task is important sometimes we forget the silliest things so lets make a to-do list to keep track!

To-do list:

Good afternoon!

Did you...

o Eat lunch               o Finish your tasks?

Good evening love, how's your day so far?

Did you...

o Eat snacks              o Finish all that you had on   o Eat dinner
o Have a good day           your to do list              o Sleep early
o Have a bad day

Good night and sleep well

Good Morning Sunshine!

Lets start the beginning of the month by noting down our details, so this way we can track changes every month

Age:
Weight:
Height:
Date of last menstrual cycle and time frame:

Did you…

- o Get out of bed, woke up at:
- o Smile
- o Brush you teeth
- o Take a shower
- o Eat breakfast
- o Take your meds

Every little task is important sometimes we forget the silliest things so lets make a to-do list to keep track!

To-do list:

Good afternoon!

Did you…

- o Eat lunch
- o Finish your tasks?

Good evening love, how's your day so far?

Did you…

- o Eat snacks
- o Have a good day
- o Have a bad day
- o Finish all that you had on your to do list
- o Eat dinner
- o Sleep early

Good night and sleep well

Good Morning Sunshine!

Lets start the beginning of the month by noting down our details, so this way we can track changes every month

Age:
Weight:
Height:
Date of last menstrual cycle and time frame:

Did you…

o Get out of bed, woke      o Brush you teeth        o Eat breakfast
   up at:                   o Take a shower          o Take your meds
o Smile

Every little task is important sometimes we forget the silliest things so lets make a to-do list to keep track!

To-do list:

Good afternoon!

Did you…

o Eat lunch                 o Finish your tasks?

Good evening love, how's your day so far?

Did you…

o Eat snacks                o Finish all that you had on   o Eat dinner
o Have a good day              your to do list             o Sleep early
o Have a bad day

Good night and sleep well

Good Morning Sunshine!

Lets start the beginning of the month by noting down our details, so this way we can track changes every month

Age:
Weight:
Height:
Date of last menstrual cycle and time frame:

Did you...

o Get out of bed, woke          o Brush you teeth          o Eat breakfast
   up at:                           o Take a shower            o Take your meds
o Smile

Every little task is important sometimes we forget the silliest things so lets make a to-do list to keep track!

To-do list:

Good afternoon!

Did you...

o Eat lunch                     o Finish your tasks?

Good evening love, how's your day so far?

Did you...

o Eat snacks                    o Finish all that you had on     o Eat dinner
o Have a good day                  your to do list                o Sleep early
o Have a bad day

Good night and sleep well

Good Morning Sunshine!

Lets start the beginning of the month by noting down our details, so this way we can track changes every month

Age:
Weight:
Height:
Date of last menstrual cycle and time frame:

Did you…

o Get out of bed, woke
  up at:
o Smile

o Brush you teeth
o Take a shower

o Eat breakfast
o Take your meds

Every little task is important sometimes we forget the silliest things so lets make a to-do list to keep track!

To-do list:

Good afternoon!

Did you…

o Eat lunch

o Finish your tasks?

Good evening love, how's your day so far?

Did you…

o Eat snacks
o Have a good day
o Have a bad day

o Finish all that you had on
  your to do list

o Eat dinner
o Sleep early

Good night and sleep well

Good Morning Sunshine!

Lets start the beginning of the month by noting down our details, so this way we can track changes every month

Age:
Weight:
Height:
Date of last menstrual cycle and time frame:

Did you…

o Get out of bed, woke       o Brush you teeth          o Eat breakfast
   up at:                    o Take a shower            o Take your meds
o Smile

Every little task is important sometimes we forget the silliest things so lets make a to-do list to keep track!

To-do list:

Good afternoon!

Did you…

o Eat lunch                  o Finish your tasks?

Good evening love, how's your day so far?

Did you…

o Eat snacks                 o Finish all that you had on    o Eat dinner
o Have a good day               your to do list              o Sleep early
o Have a bad day

Good night and sleep well

Good Morning Sunshine!

Lets start the beginning of the month by noting down our details, so this way we can track changes every month

Age:
Weight:
Height:
Date of last menstrual cycle and time frame:

Did you...

o Get out of bed, woke          o Brush you teeth          o Eat breakfast
   up at:                       o Take a shower            o Take your meds
o Smile

Every little task is important sometimes we forget the silliest things so lets make a to-do list to keep track!

To-do list:

Good afternoon!

Did you...

o Eat lunch                o Finish your tasks?

Good evening love, how's your day so far?

Did you...

o Eat snacks               o Finish all that you had on   o Eat dinner
o Have a good day             your to do list             o Sleep early
o Have a bad day

Good night and sleep well

Good Morning Sunshine!

Lets start the beginning of the month by noting down our details, so this way we can track changes every month

Age:
Weight:
Height:
Date of last menstrual cycle and time frame:

Did you...

o Get out of bed, woke      o Brush you teeth      o Eat breakfast
   up at:                   o Take a shower        o Take your meds
o Smile

Every little task is important sometimes we forget the silliest things so lets make a to-do list to keep track!

To-do list:

Good afternoon!

Did you...

o Eat lunch              o Finish your tasks?

Good evening love, how's your day so far?

Did you...

o Eat snacks            o Finish all that you had on    o Eat dinner
o Have a good day          your to do list             o Sleep early
o Have a bad day

Good night and sleep well

Good Morning Sunshine!

Lets start the beginning of the month by noting down our details, so this way we can track changes every month

Age:
Weight:
Height:
Date of last menstrual cycle and time frame:

Did you…

o Get out of bed, woke          o Brush you teeth          o Eat breakfast
  up at:                        o Take a shower            o Take your meds
o Smile

Every little task is important sometimes we forget the silliest things so lets make a to-do list to keep track!

To-do list:

Good afternoon!

Did you…

o Eat lunch                     o Finish your tasks?

Good evening love, how's your day so far?

Did you…

o Eat snacks                    o Finish all that you had on    o Eat dinner
o Have a good day                 your to do list               o Sleep early
o Have a bad day

Good night and sleep well

Good Morning Sunshine!

Lets start the beginning of the month by noting down our details, so this way we can track changes every month

Age:
Weight:
Height:
Date of last menstrual cycle and time frame:

Did you...

o Get out of bed, woke          o Brush you teeth          o Eat breakfast
  up at:                          o Take a shower            o Take your meds
o Smile

Every little task is important sometimes we forget the silliest things so lets make a to-do list to keep track!

To-do list:

Good afternoon!

Did you...

o Eat lunch                          o Finish your tasks?

Good evening love, how's your day so far?

Did you...

o Eat snacks                        o Finish all that you had on      o Eat dinner
o Have a good day              your to do list                    o Sleep early
o Have a bad day

Good night and sleep well

Good Morning Sunshine!

Lets start the beginning of the month by noting down our details, so this way we can track changes every month

Age:
Weight:
Height:
Date of last menstrual cycle and time frame:

Did you…

- o Get out of bed, woke up at:
- o Smile
- o Brush you teeth
- o Take a shower
- o Eat breakfast
- o Take your meds

Every little task is important sometimes we forget the silliest things so lets make a to-do list to keep track!

To-do list:

Good afternoon!

Did you…

- o Eat lunch
- o Finish your tasks?

Good evening love, how's your day so far?

Did you…

- o Eat snacks
- o Have a good day
- o Have a bad day
- o Finish all that you had on your to do list
- o Eat dinner
- o Sleep early

Good night and sleep well

Good Morning Sunshine!

Lets start the beginning of the month by noting down our details, so this way we can track changes every month

Age:
Weight:
Height:
Date of last menstrual cycle and time frame:

Did you…

o Get out of bed, woke    o Brush you teeth    o Eat breakfast
   up at:    o Take a shower    o Take your meds
o Smile

Every little task is important sometimes we forget the silliest things so lets make a to-do list to keep track!

To-do list:

Good afternoon!

Did you…

o Eat lunch      o Finish your tasks?

Good evening love, how's your day so far?

Did you…

o Eat snacks    o Finish all that you had on    o Eat dinner
o Have a good day      your to do list    o Sleep early
o Have a bad day

Good night and sleep well

Good Morning Sunshine!

Lets start the beginning of the month by noting down our details, so this way we can track changes every month

Age:
Weight:
Height:
Date of last menstrual cycle and time frame:

Did you…

o Get out of bed, woke        o Brush you teeth        o Eat breakfast
   up at:                     o Take a shower          o Take your meds
o Smile

Every little task is important sometimes we forget the silliest things so lets make a to-do list to keep track!

To-do list:

Good afternoon!

Did you…

 o Eat lunch                  o Finish your tasks?

Good evening love, how's your day so far?

Did you…

o Eat snacks                  o Finish all that you had on    o Eat dinner
o Have a good day                your to do list              o Sleep early
o Have a bad day

Good night and sleep well

Good Morning Sunshine!

Lets start the beginning of the month by noting down our details, so this way we can track changes every month

Age:
Weight:
Height:
Date of last menstrual cycle and time frame:

Did you…

o Get out of bed, woke        o Brush you teeth        o Eat breakfast
   up at:                     o Take a shower          o Take your meds
o Smile

Every little task is important sometimes we forget the silliest things so lets make a to-do list to keep track!

To-do list:

Good afternoon!

Did you…

o Eat lunch              o Finish your tasks?

Good evening love, how's your day so far?

Did you…

o Eat snacks             o Finish all that you had on    o Eat dinner
o Have a good day           your to do list             o Sleep early
o Have a bad day

Good night and sleep well

Good Morning Sunshine!

Lets start the beginning of the month by noting down our details, so this way we can track changes every month

Age:
Weight:
Height:
Date of last menstrual cycle and time frame:

Did you…

o Get out of bed, woke     o Brush you teeth     o Eat breakfast
  up at:                   o Take a shower       o Take your meds
o Smile

Every little task is important sometimes we forget the silliest things so lets make a to-do list to keep track!

To-do list:

Good afternoon!

Did you…

o Eat lunch                o Finish your tasks?

Good evening love, how's your day so far?

Did you…

o Eat snacks               o Finish all that you had on    o Eat dinner
o Have a good day            your to do list               o Sleep early
o Have a bad day

Good night and sleep well

dd/mm/yy

Good Morning Sunshine!

Lets start the beginning of the month by noting down our details, so this way we can track changes every month

Age:
Weight:
Height:
Date of last menstrual cycle and time frame:

Did you…

o Get out of bed, woke      o Brush you teeth      o Eat breakfast
   up at:                   o Take a shower        o Take your meds
o Smile

Every little task is important sometimes we forget the silliest things so lets make a to-do list to keep track!

To-do list:

Good afternoon!

Did you…

o Eat lunch                o Finish your tasks?

Good evening love, how's your day so far?

Did you…

o Eat snacks               o Finish all that you had on    o Eat dinner
o Have a good day             your to do list              o Sleep early
o Have a bad day

Good night and sleep well

Good Morning Sunshine!

Lets start the beginning of the month by noting down our details, so this way we can track changes every month

Age:
Weight:
Height:
Date of last menstrual cycle and time frame:

Did you...

o Get out of bed, woke      o Brush you teeth       o Eat breakfast
   up at:                     o Take a shower         o Take your meds
o Smile

Every little task is important sometimes we forget the silliest things so lets make a to-do list to keep track!

To-do list:

Good afternoon!

Did you...

o Eat lunch                o Finish your tasks?

Good evening love, how's your day so far?

Did you...

o Eat snacks               o Finish all that you had on   o Eat dinner
o Have a good day            your to do list            o Sleep early
o Have a bad day

Good night and sleep well

# This Month...

o I tried something new by…

o I helped somebody by…

o I become a better person by…

o I lost ____ kgs by…

o I gained ____kgs by…

o

o

o

# Habit Tracker

**Month:**

|  | 1st | 2nd | 3rd | 4th | 5th |  |
|---|---|---|---|---|---|---|
| Sleep |  |  |  |  |  |  |
| Caffeine |  |  |  |  |  |  |
| Alcohol |  |  |  |  |  |  |
| Cigarettes |  |  |  |  |  |  |
| Exercise |  |  |  |  |  |  |
|  | 6th | 7th | 8th | 9th | 10th |  |
| Sleep |  |  |  |  |  |  |
| Caffeine |  |  |  |  |  |  |
| Alcohol |  |  |  |  |  |  |
| Cigarettes |  |  |  |  |  |  |
| Exercise |  |  |  |  |  |  |
|  | 11th | 12th | 13th | 14th | 15th |  |
| Sleep |  |  |  |  |  |  |
| Caffeine |  |  |  |  |  |  |
| Alcohol |  |  |  |  |  |  |
| Cigarettes |  |  |  |  |  |  |
| Exercise |  |  |  |  |  |  |
|  | 16th | 17th | 18th | 19th | 20th |  |
| Sleep |  |  |  |  |  |  |
| Caffeine |  |  |  |  |  |  |
| Alcohol |  |  |  |  |  |  |
| Cigarettes |  |  |  |  |  |  |
| Exercise |  |  |  |  |  |  |
|  | 21th | 22th | 23th | 24th | 25th |  |
| Sleep |  |  |  |  |  |  |
| Caffeine |  |  |  |  |  |  |
| Alcohol |  |  |  |  |  |  |
| Cigarettes |  |  |  |  |  |  |
| Exercise |  |  |  |  |  |  |
|  | 26th | 27th | 28th | 29th | 30th | 31st |
| Sleep |  |  |  |  |  |  |
| Caffeine |  |  |  |  |  |  |
| Alcohol |  |  |  |  |  |  |
| Cigarettes |  |  |  |  |  |  |
| Exercise |  |  |  |  |  |  |

# Emotion tracker

*How are you felling today? It is important to be in touch with yourself and your emotions.*

| | Anger | Hurt/Pain | Disappointment | Upset | Happy | Blah! | Lazy |
|---|---|---|---|---|---|---|---|
| 1st | | | | | | | |
| 2nd | | | | | | | |
| 3rd | | | | | | | |
| 4th | | | | | | | |
| 5th | | | | | | | |
| 6th | | | | | | | |
| 7th | | | | | | | |
| 8th | | | | | | | |
| 9th | | | | | | | |
| 10th | | | | | | | |
| 11th | | | | | | | |
| 12th | | | | | | | |
| 13th | | | | | | | |
| 14th | | | | | | | |
| 15th | | | | | | | |
| 16th | | | | | | | |
| 17th | | | | | | | |
| 18th | | | | | | | |
| 19th | | | | | | | |
| 20th | | | | | | | |
| 21st | | | | | | | |
| 22nd | | | | | | | |
| 23rd | | | | | | | |
| 24th | | | | | | | |
| 25th | | | | | | | |
| 26th | | | | | | | |
| 27th | | | | | | | |
| 28th | | | | | | | |
| 29th | | | | | | | |
| 30th | | | | | | | |
| 31st | | | | | | | |

|  | Guilt | Anxious | Sadness | Shame | Guilt | Worthless |
|------|-------|---------|---------|-------|-------|-----------|
| 1st |  |  |  |  |  |  |
| 2nd |  |  |  |  |  |  |
| 3rd |  |  |  |  |  |  |
| 4th |  |  |  |  |  |  |
| 5th |  |  |  |  |  |  |
| 6th |  |  |  |  |  |  |
| 7th |  |  |  |  |  |  |
| 8th |  |  |  |  |  |  |
| 9th |  |  |  |  |  |  |
| 10th |  |  |  |  |  |  |
| 11th |  |  |  |  |  |  |
| 12th |  |  |  |  |  |  |
| 13th |  |  |  |  |  |  |
| 14th |  |  |  |  |  |  |
| 15th |  |  |  |  |  |  |
| 16th |  |  |  |  |  |  |
| 17th |  |  |  |  |  |  |
| 18th |  |  |  |  |  |  |
| 19th |  |  |  |  |  |  |
| 20th |  |  |  |  |  |  |
| 21st |  |  |  |  |  |  |
| 22nd |  |  |  |  |  |  |
| 23rd |  |  |  |  |  |  |
| 24th |  |  |  |  |  |  |
| 25th |  |  |  |  |  |  |
| 26th |  |  |  |  |  |  |
| 27th |  |  |  |  |  |  |
| 28th |  |  |  |  |  |  |
| 29th |  |  |  |  |  |  |
| 30th |  |  |  |  |  |  |
| 31st |  |  |  |  |  |  |

# Food Tracker

| | Healthy food | Junk food | Both | Didn't eat ☹ |
|---|---|---|---|---|
| 1st | | | | |
| 2nd | | | | |
| 3rd | | | | |
| 4th | | | | |
| 5th | | | | |
| 6th | | | | |
| 7th | | | | |
| 8th | | | | |
| 9th | | | | |
| 10th | | | | |
| 11th | | | | |
| 12th | | | | |
| 13th | | | | |
| 14th | | | | |
| 15th | | | | |
| 16th | | | | |
| 17th | | | | |
| 18th | | | | |
| 19th | | | | |
| 20th | | | | |
| 21st | | | | |
| 22nd | | | | |
| 23rd | | | | |
| 24th | | | | |
| 25th | | | | |
| 26th | | | | |
| 27th | | | | |
| 28th | | | | |
| 29th | | | | |
| 30th | | | | |
| 31st | | | | |

# Weight Tracker

**Month:**

| | Kgs/lbs | | Kgs/lbs |
|---|---|---|---|
| 1st | | 16th | |
| 2nd | | 17th | |
| 3rd | | 18th | |
| 4th | | 19th | |
| 5th | | 20th | |
| 6th | | 21st | |
| 7th | | 22nd | |
| 8th | | 23rd | |
| 9th | | 24th | |
| 10th | | 25th | |
| 11th | | 26th | |
| 12th | | 27th | |
| 13th | | 28th | |
| 14th | | 29th | |
| 15th | | 30th | |
| | | 31st | |

# Journal

Good Morning Sunshine!

Lets start the beginning of the month by noting down our details, so this way we can track changes every month

Age:
Weight:
Height:
Date of last menstrual cycle and time frame:

Did you…

| | | |
|---|---|---|
| o Get out of bed, woke up at: | o Brush you teeth | o Eat breakfast |
| o Smile | o Take a shower | o Take your meds |

Every little task is important sometimes we forget the silliest things so lets make a to-do list to keep track!

To-do list:

Good afternoon!

Did you…

o Eat lunch          o Finish your tasks?

Good evening love, how's your day so far?

Did you…

| | | |
|---|---|---|
| o Eat snacks | o Finish all that you had on | o Eat dinner |
| o Have a good day | your to do list | o Sleep early |
| o Have a bad day | | |

Good night and sleep well

Good Morning Sunshine!

Lets start the beginning of the month by noting down our details, so this way we can track changes every month

Age:
Weight:
Height:
Date of last menstrual cycle and time frame:

Did you...

o Get out of bed, woke      o Brush you teeth         o Eat breakfast
  up at:                          o Take a shower            o Take your meds
o Smile

Every little task is important sometimes we forget the silliest things so lets make a to-do list to keep track!

To-do list:

Good afternoon!

Did you...

o Eat lunch                o Finish your tasks?

Good evening love, how's your day so far?

Did you...

o Eat snacks               o Finish all that you had on    o Eat dinner
o Have a good day            your to do list              o Sleep early
o Have a bad day

Good night and sleep well

Good Morning Sunshine!

Lets start the beginning of the month by noting down our details, so this way we can track changes every month

Age:
Weight:
Height:
Date of last menstrual cycle and time frame:

Did you…

o Get out of bed, woke      o Brush you teeth       o Eat breakfast
   up at:                    o Take a shower          o Take your meds
o Smile

Every little task is important sometimes we forget the silliest things so lets make a to-do list to keep track!

To-do list:

Good afternoon!

Did you…

o Eat lunch              o Finish your tasks?

Good evening love, how's your day so far?

Did you…

o Eat snacks             o Finish all that you had on    o Eat dinner
o Have a good day           your to do list              o Sleep early
o Have a bad day

Good night and sleep well

Good Morning Sunshine!

Lets start the beginning of the month by noting down our details, so this way we can track changes every month

Age:
Weight:
Height:
Date of last menstrual cycle and time frame:

Did you…

o Get out of bed, woke    o Brush you teeth        o Eat breakfast
   up at:                 o Take a shower          o Take your meds
o Smile

Every little task is important sometimes we forget the silliest things so lets make a to-do list to keep track!

To-do list:

Good afternoon!

Did you…

o Eat lunch              o Finish your tasks?

Good evening love, how's your day so far?

Did you…

o Eat snacks             o Finish all that you had on   o Eat dinner
o Have a good day           your to do list              o Sleep early
o Have a bad day

Good night and sleep well

dd/mm/yy

Good Morning Sunshine!

Lets start the beginning of the month by noting down our details, so this way we can track changes every month

Age:
Weight:
Height:
Date of last menstrual cycle and time frame:

Did you…

- Get out of bed, woke up at:
- Smile
- Brush you teeth
- Take a shower
- Eat breakfast
- Take your meds

Every little task is important sometimes we forget the silliest things so lets make a to-do list to keep track!

To-do list:

Good afternoon!

Did you…

- Eat lunch
- Finish your tasks?

Good evening love, how's your day so far?

Did you…

- Eat snacks
- Have a good day
- Have a bad day
- Finish all that you had on your to do list
- Eat dinner
- Sleep early

Good night and sleep well

Good Morning Sunshine!

Lets start the beginning of the month by noting down our details, so this way we can track changes every month

Age:
Weight:
Height:
Date of last menstrual cycle and time frame:

Did you…

o Get out of bed, woke       o Brush you teeth        o Eat breakfast
   up at:                    o Take a shower          o Take your meds
o Smile

Every little task is important sometimes we forget the silliest things so lets make a to-do list to keep track!

To-do list:

Good afternoon!

Did you…

o Eat lunch                  o Finish your tasks?

Good evening love, how's your day so far?

Did you…

o Eat snacks                 o Finish all that you had on    o Eat dinner
o Have a good day               your to do list             o Sleep early
o Have a bad day

Good night and sleep well

Good Morning Sunshine!

Lets start the beginning of the month by noting down our details, so this way we can track changes every month

Age:
Weight:
Height:
Date of last menstrual cycle and time frame:

Did you…

| | | |
|---|---|---|
| o Get out of bed, woke up at: | o Brush you teeth | o Eat breakfast |
| o Smile | o Take a shower | o Take your meds |

Every little task is important sometimes we forget the silliest things so lets make a to-do list to keep track!

To-do list:

Good afternoon!

Did you…

| | |
|---|---|
| o Eat lunch | o Finish your tasks? |

Good evening love, how's your day so far?

Did you…

| | | |
|---|---|---|
| o Eat snacks | o Finish all that you had on your to do list | o Eat dinner |
| o Have a good day | | o Sleep early |
| o Have a bad day | | |

Good night and sleep well

Good Morning Sunshine!

Lets start the beginning of the month by noting down our details, so this way we can track changes every month

Age:
Weight:
Height:
Date of last menstrual cycle and time frame:

Did you…

o Get out of bed, woke     o Brush you teeth        o Eat breakfast
   up at:                  o Take a shower          o Take your meds
o Smile

Every little task is important sometimes we forget the silliest things so lets make a to-do list to keep track!

To-do list:

Good afternoon!

Did you…

o Eat lunch               o Finish your tasks?

Good evening love, how's your day so far?

Did you…

o Eat snacks              o Finish all that you had on   o Eat dinner
o Have a good day            your to do list              o Sleep early
o Have a bad day

Good night and sleep well

Good Morning Sunshine!

Lets start the beginning of the month by noting down our details, so this way we can track changes every month

Age:
Weight:
Height:
Date of last menstrual cycle and time frame:

Did you…

- o Get out of bed, woke up at:
- o Smile
- o Brush you teeth
- o Take a shower
- o Eat breakfast
- o Take your meds

Every little task is important sometimes we forget the silliest things so lets make a to-do list to keep track!

To-do list:

Good afternoon!

Did you…

- o Eat lunch
- o Finish your tasks?

Good evening love, how's your day so far?

Did you…

- o Eat snacks
- o Have a good day
- o Have a bad day
- o Finish all that you had on your to do list
- o Eat dinner
- o Sleep early

Good night and sleep well

Good Morning Sunshine!

Lets start the beginning of the month by noting down our details, so this way we can track changes every month

Age:
Weight:
Height:
Date of last menstrual cycle and time frame:

Did you…

o Get out of bed, woke      o Brush you teeth          o Eat breakfast
   up at:              o Take a shower            o Take your meds
o Smile

Every little task is important sometimes we forget the silliest things so lets make a to-do list to keep track!

To-do list:

Good afternoon!

Did you…

o Eat lunch                o Finish your tasks?

Good evening love, how's your day so far?

Did you…

o Eat snacks               o Finish all that you had on    o Eat dinner
o Have a good day              your to do list               o Sleep early
o Have a bad day

Good night and sleep well

Good Morning Sunshine!

Lets start the beginning of the month by noting down our details, so this way we can track changes every month

Age:
Weight:
Height:
Date of last menstrual cycle and time frame:

Did you...

o Get out of bed, woke        o Brush you teeth        o Eat breakfast
   up at:                     o Take a shower          o Take your meds
o Smile

Every little task is important sometimes we forget the silliest things so lets make a to-do list to keep track!

To-do list:

Good afternoon!

Did you...

o Eat lunch                   o Finish your tasks?

Good evening love, how's your day so far?

Did you...

o Eat snacks                  o Finish all that you had on    o Eat dinner
o Have a good day                your to do list              o Sleep early
o Have a bad day

Good night and sleep well

Good Morning Sunshine!

Lets start the beginning of the month by noting down our details, so this way we can track changes every month

Age:
Weight:
Height:
Date of last menstrual cycle and time frame:

Did you…

o Get out of bed, woke          o Brush you teeth          o Eat breakfast
  up at:                           o Take a shower            o Take your meds
o Smile

Every little task is important sometimes we forget the silliest things so lets make a to-do list to keep track!

To-do list:

Good afternoon!

Did you…

o Eat lunch                     o Finish your tasks?

Good evening love, how's your day so far?

Did you…

o Eat snacks                    o Finish all that you had on    o Eat dinner
o Have a good day                 your to do list             o Sleep early
o Have a bad day

Good night and sleep well

Good Morning Sunshine!

Lets start the beginning of the month by noting down our details, so this way we can track changes every month

Age:
Weight:
Height:
Date of last menstrual cycle and time frame:

Did you…

o Get out of bed, woke    o Brush you teeth    o Eat breakfast
  up at:                  o Take a shower      o Take your meds
o Smile

Every little task is important sometimes we forget the silliest things so lets make a to-do list to keep track!

To-do list:

Good afternoon!

Did you…

o Eat lunch              o Finish your tasks?

Good evening love, how's your day so far?

Did you…

o Eat snacks             o Finish all that you had on   o Eat dinner
o Have a good day          your to do list             o Sleep early
o Have a bad day

Good night and sleep well

dd/mm/yy

Good Morning Sunshine!

Lets start the beginning of the month by noting down our details, so this way we can track changes every month

Age:
Weight:
Height:
Date of last menstrual cycle and time frame:

Did you...

o Get out of bed, woke          o Brush you teeth          o Eat breakfast
   up at:                       o Take a shower            o Take your meds
o Smile

Every little task is important sometimes we forget the silliest things so lets make a to-do list to keep track!

To-do list:

Good afternoon!

Did you...

o Eat lunch                o Finish your tasks?

Good evening love, how's your day so far?

Did you...

o Eat snacks               o Finish all that you had on    o Eat dinner
o Have a good day             your to do list              o Sleep early
o Have a bad day

Good night and sleep well

Good Morning Sunshine!

Lets start the beginning of the month by noting down our details, so this way we can track changes every month

Age:
Weight:
Height:
Date of last menstrual cycle and time frame:

Did you…

- o Get out of bed, woke up at:
- o Smile
- o Brush you teeth
- o Take a shower
- o Eat breakfast
- o Take your meds

Every little task is important sometimes we forget the silliest things so lets make a to-do list to keep track!

To-do list:

Good afternoon!

Did you…

- o Eat lunch
- o Finish your tasks?

Good evening love, how's your day so far?

Did you…

- o Eat snacks
- o Have a good day
- o Have a bad day
- o Finish all that you had on your to do list
- o Eat dinner
- o Sleep early

Good night and sleep well

Good Morning Sunshine!

Lets start the beginning of the month by noting down our details, so this way we can track changes every month

Age:
Weight:
Height:
Date of last menstrual cycle and time frame:

Did you…

o Get out of bed, woke     o Brush you teeth        o Eat breakfast
   up at:                  o Take a shower          o Take your meds
o Smile

Every little task is important sometimes we forget the silliest things so lets make a to-do list to keep track!

To-do list:

Good afternoon!

Did you…

o Eat lunch              o Finish your tasks?

Good evening love, how's your day so far?

Did you…

o Eat snacks             o Finish all that you had on    o Eat dinner
o Have a good day           your to do list               o Sleep early
o Have a bad day

Good night and sleep well

Good Morning Sunshine!

Lets start the beginning of the month by noting down our details, so this way we can track changes every month

Age:
Weight:
Height:
Date of last menstrual cycle and time frame:

Did you...

o Get out of bed, woke      o Brush you teeth        o Eat breakfast
   up at:                   o Take a shower          o Take your meds
o Smile

Every little task is important sometimes we forget the silliest things so lets make a to-do list to keep track!

To-do list:

Good afternoon!

Did you...

o Eat lunch                 o Finish your tasks?

Good evening love, how's your day so far?

Did you...

o Eat snacks                o Finish all that you had on   o Eat dinner
o Have a good day              your to do list             o Sleep early
o Have a bad day

Good night and sleep well

Good Morning Sunshine!

Lets start the beginning of the month by noting down our details, so this way we can track changes every month

Age:
Weight:
Height:
Date of last menstrual cycle and time frame:

Did you…

o Get out of bed, woke          o Brush you teeth          o Eat breakfast
   up at:          o Take a shower          o Take your meds
o Smile

Every little task is important sometimes we forget the silliest things so lets make a to-do list to keep track!

To-do list:

Good afternoon!

Did you…

o Eat lunch          o Finish your tasks?

Good evening love, how's your day so far?

Did you…

o Eat snacks          o Finish all that you had on          o Eat dinner
o Have a good day             your to do list          o Sleep early
o Have a bad day

Good night and sleep well

Good Morning Sunshine!

Lets start the beginning of the month by noting down our details, so this way we can track changes every month

Age:
Weight:
Height:
Date of last menstrual cycle and time frame:

Did you…

- o Get out of bed, woke up at:
- o Smile
- o Brush you teeth
- o Take a shower
- o Eat breakfast
- o Take your meds

Every little task is important sometimes we forget the silliest things so lets make a to-do list to keep track!

To-do list:

Good afternoon!

Did you…

- o Eat lunch
- o Finish your tasks?

Good evening love, how's your day so far?

Did you…

- o Eat snacks
- o Have a good day
- o Have a bad day
- o Finish all that you had on your to do list
- o Eat dinner
- o Sleep early

Good night and sleep well

dd/mm/yy

Good Morning Sunshine!

Lets start the beginning of the month by noting down our details, so this way we can track changes every month

Age:
Weight:
Height:
Date of last menstrual cycle and time frame:

Did you…

- o Get out of bed, woke up at:
- o Smile
- o Brush you teeth
- o Take a shower
- o Eat breakfast
- o Take your meds

Every little task is important sometimes we forget the silliest things so lets make a to-do list to keep track!

To-do list:

Good afternoon!

Did you…

- o Eat lunch
- o Finish your tasks?

Good evening love, how's your day so far?

Did you…

- o Eat snacks
- o Have a good day
- o Have a bad day
- o Finish all that you had on your to do list
- o Eat dinner
- o Sleep early

Good night and sleep well

Good Morning Sunshine!

Lets start the beginning of the month by noting down our details, so this way we can track changes every month

Age:
Weight:
Height:
Date of last menstrual cycle and time frame:

Did you…

o Get out of bed, woke          o Brush you teeth          o Eat breakfast
  up at:                           o Take a shower            o Take your meds
o Smile

Every little task is important sometimes we forget the silliest things so lets make a to-do list to keep track!

To-do list:

Good afternoon!

Did you…

o Eat lunch                  o Finish your tasks?

Good evening love, how's your day so far?

Did you…

o Eat snacks                o Finish all that you had on    o Eat dinner
o Have a good day             your to do list                o Sleep early
o Have a bad day

Good night and sleep well

Good Morning Sunshine!

Lets start the beginning of the month by noting down our details, so this way we can track changes every month

Age:
Weight:
Height:
Date of last menstrual cycle and time frame:

Did you...

o Get out of bed, woke          o Brush you teeth          o Eat breakfast
  up at:                        o Take a shower            o Take your meds
o Smile

Every little task is important sometimes we forget the silliest things so lets make a to-do list to keep track!

To-do list:

Good afternoon!

Did you...

o Eat lunch                    o Finish your tasks?

Good evening love, how's your day so far?

Did you...

o Eat snacks                   o Finish all that you had on    o Eat dinner
o Have a good day                your to do list            o Sleep early
o Have a bad day

Good night and sleep well

Good Morning Sunshine!

Lets start the beginning of the month by noting down our details, so this way we can track changes every month

Age:
Weight:
Height:
Date of last menstrual cycle and time frame:

Did you…

o Get out of bed, woke    o Brush you teeth       o Eat breakfast
   up at:                 o Take a shower          o Take your meds
o Smile

Every little task is important sometimes we forget the silliest things so lets make a to-do list to keep track!

To-do list:

Good afternoon!

Did you…

o Eat lunch                o Finish your tasks?

Good evening love, how's your day so far?

Did you…

o Eat snacks               o Finish all that you had on   o Eat dinner
o Have a good day             your to do list             o Sleep early
o Have a bad day

Good night and sleep well

Good Morning Sunshine!

Lets start the beginning of the month by noting down our details, so this way we can track changes every month

Age:
Weight:
Height:
Date of last menstrual cycle and time frame:

Did you...

o Get out of bed, woke      o Brush you teeth       o Eat breakfast
  up at:                          o Take a shower          o Take your meds
o Smile

Every little task is important sometimes we forget the silliest things so lets make a to-do list to keep track!

To-do list:

Good afternoon!

Did you...

o Eat lunch                  o Finish your tasks?

Good evening love, how's your day so far?

Did you...

o Eat snacks                 o Finish all that you had on    o Eat dinner
o Have a good day              your to do list              o Sleep early
o Have a bad day

Good night and sleep well

Good Morning Sunshine!

Lets start the beginning of the month by noting down our details, so this way we can track changes every month

Age:
Weight:
Height:
Date of last menstrual cycle and time frame:

Did you…

o Get out of bed, woke      o Brush you teeth      o Eat breakfast
   up at:                           o Take a shower      o Take your meds
o Smile

Every little task is important sometimes we forget the silliest things so lets make a to-do list to keep track!

To-do list:

Good afternoon!

Did you…

o Eat lunch                  o Finish your tasks?

Good evening love, how's your day so far?

Did you…

o Eat snacks           o Finish all that you had on      o Eat dinner
o Have a good day        your to do list             o Sleep early
o Have a bad day

Good night and sleep well

Good Morning Sunshine!

Lets start the beginning of the month by noting down our details, so this way we can track changes every month

Age:
Weight:
Height:
Date of last menstrual cycle and time frame:

Did you...

o Get out of bed, woke      o Brush you teeth       o Eat breakfast
   up at:                   o Take a shower          o Take your meds
o Smile

Every little task is important sometimes we forget the silliest things so lets make a to-do list to keep track!

To-do list:

Good afternoon!

Did you...

o Eat lunch              o Finish your tasks?

Good evening love, how's your day so far?

Did you...

o Eat snacks            o Finish all that you had on   o Eat dinner
o Have a good day          your to do list             o Sleep early
o Have a bad day

Good night and sleep well

Good Morning Sunshine!

Lets start the beginning of the month by noting down our details, so this way we can track changes every month

Age:
Weight:
Height:
Date of last menstrual cycle and time frame:

Did you…

o Get out of bed, woke      o Brush you teeth          o Eat breakfast
   up at:                   o Take a shower            o Take your meds
o Smile

Every little task is important sometimes we forget the silliest things so lets make a to-do list to keep track!

To-do list:

Good afternoon!

Did you…

o Eat lunch                 o Finish your tasks?

Good evening love, how's your day so far?

Did you…

o Eat snacks               o Finish all that you had on   o Eat dinner
o Have a good day             your to do list             o Sleep early
o Have a bad day

Good night and sleep well

Good Morning Sunshine!

Lets start the beginning of the month by noting down our details, so this way we can track changes every month

Age:
Weight:
Height:
Date of last menstrual cycle and time frame:

Did you…

o Get out of bed, woke        o Brush you teeth        o Eat breakfast
   up at:                             o Take a shower        o Take your meds
o Smile

Every little task is important sometimes we forget the silliest things so lets make a to-do list to keep track!

To-do list:

Good afternoon!

Did you…

o Eat lunch                   o Finish your tasks?

Good evening love, how's your day so far?

Did you…

o Eat snacks                  o Finish all that you had on    o Eat dinner
o Have a good day               your to do list          o Sleep early
o Have a bad day

Good night and sleep well

Good Morning Sunshine!

Lets start the beginning of the month by noting down our details, so this way we can track changes every month

Age:
Weight:
Height:
Date of last menstrual cycle and time frame:

Did you…

- o Get out of bed, woke up at:
- o Smile
- o Brush you teeth
- o Take a shower
- o Eat breakfast
- o Take your meds

Every little task is important sometimes we forget the silliest things so lets make a to-do list to keep track!

To-do list:

Good afternoon!

Did you…

- o Eat lunch
- o Finish your tasks?

Good evening love, how's your day so far?

Did you…

- o Eat snacks
- o Have a good day
- o Have a bad day
- o Finish all that you had on your to do list
- o Eat dinner
- o Sleep early

Good night and sleep well

Good Morning Sunshine!

Lets start the beginning of the month by noting down our details, so this way we can track changes every month

Age:
Weight:
Height:
Date of last menstrual cycle and time frame:

Did you…

o Get out of bed, woke    o Brush you teeth       o Eat breakfast
   up at:                 o Take a shower         o Take your meds
o Smile

Every little task is important sometimes we forget the silliest things so lets make a to-do list to keep track!

To-do list:

Good afternoon!

Did you…

o Eat lunch              o Finish your tasks?

Good evening love, how's your day so far?

Did you…

o Eat snacks             o Finish all that you had on   o Eat dinner
o Have a good day           your to do list            o Sleep early
o Have a bad day

Good night and sleep well

Good Morning Sunshine!

Lets start the beginning of the month by noting down our details, so this way we can track changes every month

Age:
Weight:
Height:
Date of last menstrual cycle and time frame:

Did you…

o Get out of bed, woke     o Brush you teeth     o Eat breakfast
  up at:                   o Take a shower       o Take your meds
o Smile

Every little task is important sometimes we forget the silliest things so lets make a to-do list to keep track!

To-do list:

Good afternoon!

Did you…

o Eat lunch               o Finish your tasks?

Good evening love, how's your day so far?

Did you…

o Eat snacks              o Finish all that you had on   o Eat dinner
o Have a good day           your to do list              o Sleep early
o Have a bad day

Good night and sleep well

# This Month...

o I tried something new by…

o I helped somebody by…

o I become a better person by…

o I lost ____ kgs by…

o I gained ____kgs by…

o

o

o

# Habit Tracker

**Month:**

|  | 1st | 2nd | 3rd | 4th | 5th |  |
|---|---|---|---|---|---|---|
| Sleep |  |  |  |  |  |  |
| Caffeine |  |  |  |  |  |  |
| Alcohol |  |  |  |  |  |  |
| Cigarettes |  |  |  |  |  |  |
| Exercise |  |  |  |  |  |  |
|  | 6th | 7th | 8th | 9th | 10th |  |
| Sleep |  |  |  |  |  |  |
| Caffeine |  |  |  |  |  |  |
| Alcohol |  |  |  |  |  |  |
| Cigarettes |  |  |  |  |  |  |
| Exercise |  |  |  |  |  |  |
|  | 11th | 12th | 13th | 14th | 15th |  |
| Sleep |  |  |  |  |  |  |
| Caffeine |  |  |  |  |  |  |
| Alcohol |  |  |  |  |  |  |
| Cigarettes |  |  |  |  |  |  |
| Exercise |  |  |  |  |  |  |
|  | 16th | 17th | 18th | 19th | 20th |  |
| Sleep |  |  |  |  |  |  |
| Caffeine |  |  |  |  |  |  |
| Alcohol |  |  |  |  |  |  |
| Cigarettes |  |  |  |  |  |  |
| Exercise |  |  |  |  |  |  |
|  | 21th | 22th | 23th | 24th | 25th |  |
| Sleep |  |  |  |  |  |  |
| Caffeine |  |  |  |  |  |  |
| Alcohol |  |  |  |  |  |  |
| Cigarettes |  |  |  |  |  |  |
| Exercise |  |  |  |  |  |  |
|  | 26th | 27th | 28th | 29th | 30th | 31st |
| Sleep |  |  |  |  |  |  |
| Caffeine |  |  |  |  |  |  |
| Alcohol |  |  |  |  |  |  |
| Cigarettes |  |  |  |  |  |  |
| Exercise |  |  |  |  |  |  |

# Emotion tracker

*How are you felling today? It is important to be in touch with yourself and your emotions.*

| | Anger | Hurt/Pain | Disappointment | Upset | Happy | Blah! | Lazy |
|---|---|---|---|---|---|---|---|
| 1st | | | | | | | |
| 2nd | | | | | | | |
| 3rd | | | | | | | |
| 4th | | | | | | | |
| 5th | | | | | | | |
| 6th | | | | | | | |
| 7th | | | | | | | |
| 8th | | | | | | | |
| 9th | | | | | | | |
| 10th | | | | | | | |
| 11th | | | | | | | |
| 12th | | | | | | | |
| 13th | | | | | | | |
| 14th | | | | | | | |
| 15th | | | | | | | |
| 16th | | | | | | | |
| 17th | | | | | | | |
| 18th | | | | | | | |
| 19th | | | | | | | |
| 20th | | | | | | | |
| 21st | | | | | | | |
| 22nd | | | | | | | |
| 23rd | | | | | | | |
| 24th | | | | | | | |
| 25th | | | | | | | |
| 26th | | | | | | | |
| 27th | | | | | | | |
| 28th | | | | | | | |
| 29th | | | | | | | |
| 30th | | | | | | | |
| 31st | | | | | | | |

|        | Guilt | Anxious | Sadness | Shame | Guilt | Worthless |
|--------|-------|---------|---------|-------|-------|-----------|
| 1st    |       |         |         |       |       |           |
| 2nd    |       |         |         |       |       |           |
| 3rd    |       |         |         |       |       |           |
| 4th    |       |         |         |       |       |           |
| 5th    |       |         |         |       |       |           |
| 6th    |       |         |         |       |       |           |
| 7th    |       |         |         |       |       |           |
| 8th    |       |         |         |       |       |           |
| 9th    |       |         |         |       |       |           |
| 10th   |       |         |         |       |       |           |
| 11th   |       |         |         |       |       |           |
| 12th   |       |         |         |       |       |           |
| 13th   |       |         |         |       |       |           |
| 14th   |       |         |         |       |       |           |
| 15th   |       |         |         |       |       |           |
| 16th   |       |         |         |       |       |           |
| 17th   |       |         |         |       |       |           |
| 18th   |       |         |         |       |       |           |
| 19th   |       |         |         |       |       |           |
| 20th   |       |         |         |       |       |           |
| 21st   |       |         |         |       |       |           |
| 22nd   |       |         |         |       |       |           |
| 23rd   |       |         |         |       |       |           |
| 24th   |       |         |         |       |       |           |
| 25th   |       |         |         |       |       |           |
| 26th   |       |         |         |       |       |           |
| 27th   |       |         |         |       |       |           |
| 28th   |       |         |         |       |       |           |
| 29th   |       |         |         |       |       |           |
| 30th   |       |         |         |       |       |           |
| 31st   |       |         |         |       |       |           |

# Food Tracker

| | Healthy food | Junk food | Both | Didn't eat ☹ |
|---|---|---|---|---|
| 1st | | | | |
| 2nd | | | | |
| 3rd | | | | |
| 4th | | | | |
| 5th | | | | |
| 6th | | | | |
| 7th | | | | |
| 8th | | | | |
| 9th | | | | |
| 10th | | | | |
| 11th | | | | |
| 12th | | | | |
| 13th | | | | |
| 14th | | | | |
| 15th | | | | |
| 16th | | | | |
| 17th | | | | |
| 18th | | | | |
| 19th | | | | |
| 20th | | | | |
| 21st | | | | |
| 22nd | | | | |
| 23rd | | | | |
| 24th | | | | |
| 25th | | | | |
| 26th | | | | |
| 27th | | | | |
| 28th | | | | |
| 29th | | | | |
| 30th | | | | |
| 31st | | | | |

# Weight Tracker

**Month:**

| | Kgs/lbs | | Kgs/lbs |
|---|---|---|---|
| 1st | | 16th | |
| 2nd | | 17th | |
| 3rd | | 18th | |
| 4th | | 19th | |
| 5th | | 20th | |
| 6th | | 21st | |
| 7th | | 22nd | |
| 8th | | 23rd | |
| 9th | | 24th | |
| 10th | | 25th | |
| 11th | | 26th | |
| 12th | | 27th | |
| 13th | | 28th | |
| 14th | | 29th | |
| 15th | | 30th | |
| | | 31st | |

# Journal

Good Morning Sunshine!

Lets start the beginning of the month by noting down our details, so this way we can track changes every month

Age:
Weight:
Height:
Date of last menstrual cycle and time frame:

Did you...

- o Get out of bed, woke up at:
- o Smile
- o Brush you teeth
- o Take a shower
- o Eat breakfast
- o Take your meds

Every little task is important sometimes we forget the silliest things so lets make a to-do list to keep track!

To-do list:

Good afternoon!

Did you...

- o Eat lunch
- o Finish your tasks?

Good evening love, how's your day so far?

Did you...

- o Eat snacks
- o Have a good day
- o Have a bad day
- o Finish all that you had on your to do list
- o Eat dinner
- o Sleep early

Good night and sleep well

Good Morning Sunshine!

Lets start the beginning of the month by noting down our details, so this way we can track changes every month

Age:
Weight:
Height:
Date of last menstrual cycle and time frame:

Did you...

o Get out of bed, woke      o Brush you teeth          o Eat breakfast
   up at:                   o Take a shower            o Take your meds
o Smile

Every little task is important sometimes we forget the silliest things so lets make a to-do list to keep track!

To-do list:

Good afternoon!

Did you...

o Eat lunch                 o Finish your tasks?

Good evening love, how's your day so far?

Did you...

o Eat snacks                o Finish all that you had on   o Eat dinner
o Have a good day              your to do list              o Sleep early
o Have a bad day

Good night and sleep well

Good Morning Sunshine!

Lets start the beginning of the month by noting down our details, so this way we can track changes every month

Age:
Weight:
Height:
Date of last menstrual cycle and time frame:

Did you...

o Get out of bed, woke        o Brush you teeth          o Eat breakfast
   up at:                      o Take a shower            o Take your meds
o Smile

Every little task is important sometimes we forget the silliest things so lets make a to-do list to keep track!

To-do list:




Good afternoon!

Did you...

o Eat lunch                    o Finish your tasks?

Good evening love, how's your day so far?

Did you...

o Eat snacks                   o Finish all that you had on    o Eat dinner
o Have a good day                 your to do list              o Sleep early
o Have a bad day

Good night and sleep well

Good Morning Sunshine!

Lets start the beginning of the month by noting down our details, so this way we can track changes every month

Age:
Weight:
Height:
Date of last menstrual cycle and time frame:

Did you...

o Get out of bed, woke      o Brush you teeth          o Eat breakfast
   up at:                   o Take a shower            o Take your meds
o Smile

Every little task is important sometimes we forget the silliest things so lets make a to-do list to keep track!

To-do list:

Good afternoon!

Did you...

o Eat lunch               o Finish your tasks?

Good evening love, how's your day so far?

Did you...

o Eat snacks              o Finish all that you had on   o Eat dinner
o Have a good day            your to do list             o Sleep early
o Have a bad day

Good night and sleep well

Good Morning Sunshine!

Lets start the beginning of the month by noting down our details, so this way we can track changes every month

Age:
Weight:
Height:
Date of last menstrual cycle and time frame:

Did you…

- o Get out of bed, woke up at:
- o Smile
- o Brush you teeth
- o Take a shower
- o Eat breakfast
- o Take your meds

Every little task is important sometimes we forget the silliest things so lets make a to-do list to keep track!

To-do list:

Good afternoon!

Did you…

- o Eat lunch
- o Finish your tasks?

Good evening love, how's your day so far?

Did you…

- o Eat snacks
- o Have a good day
- o Have a bad day
- o Finish all that you had on your to do list
- o Eat dinner
- o Sleep early

Good night and sleep well

Good Morning Sunshine!

Lets start the beginning of the month by noting down our details, so this way we can track changes every month

Age:
Weight:
Height:
Date of last menstrual cycle and time frame:

Did you…

o Get out of bed, woke          o Brush you teeth          o Eat breakfast
  up at:          o Take a shower          o Take your meds
o Smile

Every little task is important sometimes we forget the silliest things so lets make a to-do list to keep track!

To-do list:

Good afternoon!

Did you…

o Eat lunch          o Finish your tasks?

Good evening love, how's your day so far?

Did you…

o Eat snacks          o Finish all that you had on          o Eat dinner
o Have a good day            your to do list          o Sleep early
o Have a bad day

Good night and sleep well

Good Morning Sunshine!

Lets start the beginning of the month by noting down our details, so this way we can track changes every month

Age:
Weight:
Height:
Date of last menstrual cycle and time frame:

Did you…

o Get out of bed, woke      o Brush you teeth        o Eat breakfast
   up at:                   o Take a shower          o Take your meds
o Smile

Every little task is important sometimes we forget the silliest things so lets make a to-do list to keep track!

To-do list:

Good afternoon!

Did you…

o Eat lunch                 o Finish your tasks?

Good evening love, how's your day so far?

Did you…

o Eat snacks                o Finish all that you had on   o Eat dinner
o Have a good day              your to do list             o Sleep early
o Have a bad day

Good night and sleep well

Good Morning Sunshine!

Lets start the beginning of the month by noting down our details, so this way we can track changes every month

Age:
Weight:
Height:
Date of last menstrual cycle and time frame:

Did you...

o Get out of bed, woke    o Brush you teeth      o Eat breakfast
   up at:                 o Take a shower        o Take your meds
o Smile

Every little task is important sometimes we forget the silliest things so lets make a to-do list to keep track!

To-do list:

Good afternoon!

Did you...

o Eat lunch               o Finish your tasks?

Good evening love, how's your day so far?

Did you...

o Eat snacks              o Finish all that you had on   o Eat dinner
o Have a good day            your to do list            o Sleep early
o Have a bad day

Good night and sleep well

Good Morning Sunshine!

Lets start the beginning of the month by noting down our details, so this way we can track changes every month

Age:
Weight:
Height:
Date of last menstrual cycle and time frame:

Did you…

o Get out of bed, woke          o Brush you teeth          o Eat breakfast
   up at:                        o Take a shower            o Take your meds
o Smile

Every little task is important sometimes we forget the silliest things so lets make a to-do list to keep track!

To-do list:

Good afternoon!

Did you…

o Eat lunch                    o Finish your tasks?

Good evening love, how's your day so far?

Did you…

o Eat snacks                 o Finish all that you had on   o Eat dinner
o Have a good day              your to do list              o Sleep early
o Have a bad day

Good night and sleep well

dd/mm/yy

Good Morning Sunshine!

Lets start the beginning of the month by noting down our details, so this way we can track changes every month

Age:
Weight:
Height:
Date of last menstrual cycle and time frame:

Did you…

o Get out of bed, woke    o Brush you teeth       o Eat breakfast
  up at:                  o Take a shower         o Take your meds
o Smile

Every little task is important sometimes we forget the silliest things so lets make a to-do list to keep track!

To-do list:

Good afternoon!

Did you…

o Eat lunch              o Finish your tasks?

Good evening love, how's your day so far?

Did you…

o Eat snacks             o Finish all that you had on    o Eat dinner
o Have a good day          your to do list              o Sleep early
o Have a bad day

Good night and sleep well

Good Morning Sunshine!

Lets start the beginning of the month by noting down our details, so this way we can track changes every month

Age:
Weight:
Height:
Date of last menstrual cycle and time frame:

Did you…

o Get out of bed, woke        o Brush you teeth        o Eat breakfast
   up at:                     o Take a shower          o Take your meds
o Smile

Every little task is important sometimes we forget the silliest things so lets make a to-do list to keep track!

To-do list:

Good afternoon!

Did you…

o Eat lunch                   o Finish your tasks?

Good evening love, how's your day so far?

Did you…

o Eat snacks                  o Finish all that you had on    o Eat dinner
o Have a good day                your to do list              o Sleep early
o Have a bad day

Good night and sleep well

Good Morning Sunshine!

Lets start the beginning of the month by noting down our details, so this way we can track changes every month

Age:
Weight:
Height:
Date of last menstrual cycle and time frame:

Did you...

- o Get out of bed, woke up at:
- o Smile
- o Brush you teeth
- o Take a shower
- o Eat breakfast
- o Take your meds

Every little task is important sometimes we forget the silliest things so lets make a to-do list to keep track!

To-do list:

Good afternoon!

Did you...

- o Eat lunch
- o Finish your tasks?

Good evening love, how's your day so far?

Did you...

- o Eat snacks
- o Have a good day
- o Have a bad day
- o Finish all that you had on your to do list
- o Eat dinner
- o Sleep early

Good night and sleep well

Good Morning Sunshine!

Lets start the beginning of the month by noting down our details, so this way we can track changes every month

Age:
Weight:
Height:
Date of last menstrual cycle and time frame:

Did you…

o Get out of bed, woke    o Brush you teeth    o Eat breakfast
   up at:                o Take a shower    o Take your meds
o Smile

Every little task is important sometimes we forget the silliest things so lets make a to-do list to keep track!

To-do list:

Good afternoon!

Did you…

o Eat lunch             o Finish your tasks?

Good evening love, how's your day so far?

Did you…

o Eat snacks       o Finish all that you had on   o Eat dinner
o Have a good day     your to do list          o Sleep early
o Have a bad day

Good night and sleep well

Good Morning Sunshine!

Lets start the beginning of the month by noting down our details, so this way we can track changes every month

Age:
Weight:
Height:
Date of last menstrual cycle and time frame:

Did you…

o Get out of bed, woke    o Brush you teeth    o Eat breakfast
  up at:                   o Take a shower      o Take your meds
o Smile

Every little task is important sometimes we forget the silliest things so lets make a to-do list to keep track!

To-do list:

Good afternoon!

Did you…

o Eat lunch              o Finish your tasks?

Good evening love, how's your day so far?

Did you…

o Eat snacks             o Finish all that you had on   o Eat dinner
o Have a good day          your to do list              o Sleep early
o Have a bad day

Good night and sleep well

Good Morning Sunshine!

Lets start the beginning of the month by noting down our details, so this way we can track changes every month

Age:
Weight:
Height:
Date of last menstrual cycle and time frame:

Did you...

- o Get out of bed, woke    o Brush you teeth       o Eat breakfast
  up at:                    o Take a shower         o Take your meds
- o Smile

Every little task is important sometimes we forget the silliest things so lets make a to-do list to keep track!

To-do list:

Good afternoon!

Did you...

- o Eat lunch                o Finish your tasks?

Good evening love, how's your day so far?

Did you...

- o Eat snacks               o Finish all that you had on   o Eat dinner
- o Have a good day            your to do list              o Sleep early
- o Have a bad day

Good night and sleep well

Good Morning Sunshine!

Lets start the beginning of the month by noting down our details, so this way we can track changes every month

Age:
Weight:
Height:
Date of last menstrual cycle and time frame:

Did you…

o Get out of bed, woke        o Brush you teeth        o Eat breakfast
   up at:                               o Take a shower          o Take your meds
o Smile

Every little task is important sometimes we forget the silliest things so lets make a to-do list to keep track!

To-do list:

Good afternoon!

Did you…

o Eat lunch                    o Finish your tasks?

Good evening love, how's your day so far?

Did you…

o Eat snacks               o Finish all that you had on    o Eat dinner
o Have a good day            your to do list               o Sleep early
o Have a bad day

Good night and sleep well

Good Morning Sunshine!

Lets start the beginning of the month by noting down our details, so this way we can track changes every month

Age:
Weight:
Height:
Date of last menstrual cycle and time frame:

Did you…

- o Get out of bed, woke up at:
- o Smile
- o Brush you teeth
- o Take a shower
- o Eat breakfast
- o Take your meds

Every little task is important sometimes we forget the silliest things so lets make a to-do list to keep track!

To-do list:

Good afternoon!

Did you…

- o Eat lunch
- o Finish your tasks?

Good evening love, how's your day so far?

Did you…

- o Eat snacks
- o Have a good day
- o Have a bad day
- o Finish all that you had on your to do list
- o Eat dinner
- o Sleep early

Good night and sleep well

Good Morning Sunshine!

Lets start the beginning of the month by noting down our details, so this way we can track changes every month

Age:
Weight:
Height:
Date of last menstrual cycle and time frame:

Did you…

o Get out of bed, woke     o Brush you teeth         o Eat breakfast
  up at:                   o Take a shower           o Take your meds
o Smile

Every little task is important sometimes we forget the silliest things so lets make a to-do list to keep track!

To-do list:

Good afternoon!

Did you…

o Eat lunch                o Finish your tasks?

Good evening love, how's your day so far?

Did you…

o Eat snacks               o Finish all that you had on   o Eat dinner
o Have a good day            your to do list             o Sleep early
o Have a bad day

Good night and sleep well

Good Morning Sunshine!

Lets start the beginning of the month by noting down our details, so this way we can track changes every month

Age:
Weight:
Height:
Date of last menstrual cycle and time frame:

Did you…

- o Get out of bed, woke up at:
- o Smile
- o Brush you teeth
- o Take a shower
- o Eat breakfast
- o Take your meds

Every little task is important sometimes we forget the silliest things so lets make a to-do list to keep track!

To-do list:

Good afternoon!

Did you…

- o Eat lunch
- o Finish your tasks?

Good evening love, how's your day so far?

Did you…

- o Eat snacks
- o Have a good day
- o Have a bad day
- o Finish all that you had on your to do list
- o Eat dinner
- o Sleep early

Good night and sleep well

dd/mm/yy

Good Morning Sunshine!

Lets start the beginning of the month by noting down our details, so this way we can track changes every month

Age:
Weight:
Height:
Date of last menstrual cycle and time frame:

Did you...

- o Get out of bed, woke up at:
- o Smile
- o Brush you teeth
- o Take a shower
- o Eat breakfast
- o Take your meds

Every little task is important sometimes we forget the silliest things so lets make a to-do list to keep track!

To-do list:

Good afternoon!

Did you...

- o Eat lunch
- o Finish your tasks?

Good evening love, how's your day so far?

Did you...

- o Eat snacks
- o Have a good day
- o Have a bad day
- o Finish all that you had on your to do list
- o Eat dinner
- o Sleep early

Good night and sleep well

Good Morning Sunshine!

Lets start the beginning of the month by noting down our details, so this way we can track changes every month

Age:
Weight:
Height:
Date of last menstrual cycle and time frame:

Did you…

- o Get out of bed, woke up at:
- o Smile
- o Brush you teeth
- o Take a shower
- o Eat breakfast
- o Take your meds

Every little task is important sometimes we forget the silliest things so lets make a to-do list to keep track!

To-do list:




Good afternoon!

Did you…

- o Eat lunch
- o Finish your tasks?

Good evening love, how's your day so far?

Did you…

- o Eat snacks
- o Have a good day
- o Have a bad day
- o Finish all that you had on your to do list
- o Eat dinner
- o Sleep early

Good night and sleep well

Good Morning Sunshine!

Lets start the beginning of the month by noting down our details, so this way we can track changes every month

Age:
Weight:
Height:
Date of last menstrual cycle and time frame:

Did you…

o Get out of bed, woke      o Brush you teeth       o Eat breakfast
   up at:                   o Take a shower         o Take your meds
o Smile

Every little task is important sometimes we forget the silliest things so lets make a to-do list to keep track!

To-do list:

Good afternoon!

Did you…

o Eat lunch              o Finish your tasks?

Good evening love, how's your day so far?

Did you…

o Eat snacks             o Finish all that you had on    o Eat dinner
o Have a good day           your to do list              o Sleep early
o Have a bad day

Good night and sleep well

dd/mm/yy

Good Morning Sunshine!

Lets start the beginning of the month by noting down our details, so this way we can track changes every month

Age:
Weight:
Height:
Date of last menstrual cycle and time frame:

Did you…

- o Get out of bed, woke
  up at:
- o Smile
- o Brush you teeth
- o Take a shower
- o Eat breakfast
- o Take your meds

Every little task is important sometimes we forget the silliest things so lets make a to-do list to keep track!

To-do list:

Good afternoon!

Did you…

- o Eat lunch
- o Finish your tasks?

Good evening love, how's your day so far?

Did you…

- o Eat snacks
- o Have a good day
- o Have a bad day
- o Finish all that you had on
  your to do list
- o Eat dinner
- o Sleep early

Good night and sleep well

dd/mm/yy

Good Morning Sunshine!

Lets start the beginning of the month by noting down our details, so this way we can track changes every month

Age:
Weight:
Height:
Date of last menstrual cycle and time frame:

Did you...

o Get out of bed, woke    o Brush you teeth       o Eat breakfast
  up at:                  o Take a shower         o Take your meds
o Smile

Every little task is important sometimes we forget the silliest things so lets make a to-do list to keep track!

To-do list:

Good afternoon!

Did you...

o Eat lunch              o Finish your tasks?

Good evening love, how's your day so far?

Did you...

o Eat snacks             o Finish all that you had on   o Eat dinner
o Have a good day          your to do list              o Sleep early
o Have a bad day

Good night and sleep well

Good Morning Sunshine!

Lets start the beginning of the month by noting down our details, so this way we can track changes every month

Age:
Weight:
Height:
Date of last menstrual cycle and time frame:

Did you…

- o Get out of bed, woke up at:
- o Smile
- o Brush you teeth
- o Take a shower
- o Eat breakfast
- o Take your meds

Every little task is important sometimes we forget the silliest things so lets make a to-do list to keep track!

To-do list:

Good afternoon!

Did you…

- o Eat lunch
- o Finish your tasks?

Good evening love, how's your day so far?

Did you…

- o Eat snacks
- o Have a good day
- o Have a bad day
- o Finish all that you had on your to do list
- o Eat dinner
- o Sleep early

Good night and sleep well

Good Morning Sunshine!

Lets start the beginning of the month by noting down our details, so this way we can track changes every month

Age:
Weight:
Height:
Date of last menstrual cycle and time frame:

Did you…

o Get out of bed, woke    o Brush you teeth       o Eat breakfast
   up at:                 o Take a shower         o Take your meds
o Smile

Every little task is important sometimes we forget the silliest things so lets make a to-do list to keep track!

To-do list:

Good afternoon!

Did you…

o Eat lunch               o Finish your tasks?

Good evening love, how's your day so far?

Did you…

o Eat snacks              o Finish all that you had on    o Eat dinner
o Have a good day            your to do list              o Sleep early
o Have a bad day

Good night and sleep well

Good Morning Sunshine!

Lets start the beginning of the month by noting down our details, so this way we can track changes every month

Age:
Weight:
Height:
Date of last menstrual cycle and time frame:

Did you...

- o Get out of bed, woke    o Brush you teeth      o Eat breakfast
  up at:                   o Take a shower        o Take your meds
- o Smile

Every little task is important sometimes we forget the silliest things so lets make a to-do list to keep track!

To-do list:

Good afternoon!

Did you...

- o Eat lunch              o Finish your tasks?

Good evening love, how's your day so far?

Did you...

- o Eat snacks             o Finish all that you had on   o Eat dinner
- o Have a good day           your to do list              o Sleep early
- o Have a bad day

Good night and sleep well

Good Morning Sunshine!

Lets start the beginning of the month by noting down our details, so this way we can track changes every month

Age:
Weight:
Height:
Date of last menstrual cycle and time frame:

Did you...

| | | |
|---|---|---|
| o Get out of bed, woke up at: | o Brush you teeth | o Eat breakfast |
| | o Take a shower | o Take your meds |
| o Smile | | |

Every little task is important sometimes we forget the silliest things so lets make a to-do list to keep track!

To-do list:

Good afternoon!

Did you...

o Eat lunch            o Finish your tasks?

Good evening love, how's your day so far?

Did you...

| | | |
|---|---|---|
| o Eat snacks | o Finish all that you had on | o Eat dinner |
| o Have a good day | your to do list | o Sleep early |
| o Have a bad day | | |

Good night and sleep well

Good Morning Sunshine!

Lets start the beginning of the month by noting down our details, so this way we can track changes every month

Age:
Weight:
Height:
Date of last menstrual cycle and time frame:

Did you…

- o Get out of bed, woke up at:
- o Smile
- o Brush you teeth
- o Take a shower
- o Eat breakfast
- o Take your meds

Every little task is important sometimes we forget the silliest things so lets make a to-do list to keep track!

To-do list:

Good afternoon!

Did you…

- o Eat lunch
- o Finish your tasks?

Good evening love, how's your day so far?

Did you…

- o Eat snacks
- o Have a good day
- o Have a bad day
- o Finish all that you had on your to do list
- o Eat dinner
- o Sleep early

Good night and sleep well

Good Morning Sunshine!

Lets start the beginning of the month by noting down our details, so this way we can track changes every month

Age:
Weight:
Height:
Date of last menstrual cycle and time frame:

Did you…

o Get out of bed, woke          o Brush you teeth          o Eat breakfast
   up at:          o Take a shower          o Take your meds
o Smile

Every little task is important sometimes we forget the silliest things so lets make a to-do list to keep track!

To-do list:

Good afternoon!

Did you…

o Eat lunch          o Finish your tasks?

Good evening love, how's your day so far?

Did you…

o Eat snacks          o Finish all that you had on          o Eat dinner
o Have a good day             your to do list          o Sleep early
o Have a bad day

Good night and sleep well

Good Morning Sunshine!

Lets start the beginning of the month by noting down our details, so this way we can track changes every month

Age:
Weight:
Height:
Date of last menstrual cycle and time frame:

Did you…

o Get out of bed, woke    o Brush you teeth       o Eat breakfast
  up at:                  o Take a shower         o Take your meds
o Smile

Every little task is important sometimes we forget the silliest things so lets make a to-do list to keep track!

To-do list:

Good afternoon!

Did you…

o Eat lunch              o Finish your tasks?

Good evening love, how's your day so far?

Did you…

o Eat snacks             o Finish all that you had on   o Eat dinner
o Have a good day          your to do list             o Sleep early
o Have a bad day

Good night and sleep well

# This Month...

o I tried something new by...


o I helped somebody by...


o I become a better person by...


o I lost ____ kgs by...


o I gained ____kgs by...

o

o

o

# Habit Tracker

**Month:**

|  | 1st | 2nd | 3rd | 4th | 5th |  |
|---|---|---|---|---|---|---|
| Sleep |  |  |  |  |  |  |
| Caffeine |  |  |  |  |  |  |
| Alcohol |  |  |  |  |  |  |
| Cigarettes |  |  |  |  |  |  |
| Exercise |  |  |  |  |  |  |
|  | 6th | 7th | 8th | 9th | 10th |  |
| Sleep |  |  |  |  |  |  |
| Caffeine |  |  |  |  |  |  |
| Alcohol |  |  |  |  |  |  |
| Cigarettes |  |  |  |  |  |  |
| Exercise |  |  |  |  |  |  |
|  | 11th | 12th | 13th | 14th | 15th |  |
| Sleep |  |  |  |  |  |  |
| Caffeine |  |  |  |  |  |  |
| Alcohol |  |  |  |  |  |  |
| Cigarettes |  |  |  |  |  |  |
| Exercise |  |  |  |  |  |  |
|  | 16th | 17th | 18th | 19th | 20th |  |
| Sleep |  |  |  |  |  |  |
| Caffeine |  |  |  |  |  |  |
| Alcohol |  |  |  |  |  |  |
| Cigarettes |  |  |  |  |  |  |
| Exercise |  |  |  |  |  |  |
|  | 21th | 22th | 23th | 24th | 25th |  |
| Sleep |  |  |  |  |  |  |
| Caffeine |  |  |  |  |  |  |
| Alcohol |  |  |  |  |  |  |
| Cigarettes |  |  |  |  |  |  |
| Exercise |  |  |  |  |  |  |
|  | 26th | 27th | 28th | 29th | 30th | 31st |
| Sleep |  |  |  |  |  |  |
| Caffeine |  |  |  |  |  |  |
| Alcohol |  |  |  |  |  |  |
| Cigarettes |  |  |  |  |  |  |
| Exercise |  |  |  |  |  |  |

# Emotion tracker

*How are you felling today? It is important to be in touch with yourself and your emotions.*

| | Anger | Hurt/Pain | Disappointment | Upset | Happy | Blah! | Lazy |
|---|---|---|---|---|---|---|---|
| 1st | | | | | | | |
| 2nd | | | | | | | |
| 3rd | | | | | | | |
| 4th | | | | | | | |
| 5th | | | | | | | |
| 6th | | | | | | | |
| 7th | | | | | | | |
| 8th | | | | | | | |
| 9th | | | | | | | |
| 10th | | | | | | | |
| 11th | | | | | | | |
| 12th | | | | | | | |
| 13th | | | | | | | |
| 14th | | | | | | | |
| 15th | | | | | | | |
| 16th | | | | | | | |
| 17th | | | | | | | |
| 18th | | | | | | | |
| 19th | | | | | | | |
| 20th | | | | | | | |
| 21st | | | | | | | |
| 22nd | | | | | | | |
| 23rd | | | | | | | |
| 24th | | | | | | | |
| 25th | | | | | | | |
| 26th | | | | | | | |
| 27th | | | | | | | |
| 28th | | | | | | | |
| 29th | | | | | | | |
| 30th | | | | | | | |
| 31st | | | | | | | |

| | Guilt | Anxious | Sadness | Shame | Guilt | Worthless |
|---|---|---|---|---|---|---|
| 1st | | | | | | |
| 2nd | | | | | | |
| 3rd | | | | | | |
| 4th | | | | | | |
| 5th | | | | | | |
| 6th | | | | | | |
| 7th | | | | | | |
| 8th | | | | | | |
| 9th | | | | | | |
| 10th | | | | | | |
| 11th | | | | | | |
| 12th | | | | | | |
| 13th | | | | | | |
| 14th | | | | | | |
| 15th | | | | | | |
| 16th | | | | | | |
| 17th | | | | | | |
| 18th | | | | | | |
| 19th | | | | | | |
| 20th | | | | | | |
| 21st | | | | | | |
| 22nd | | | | | | |
| 23rd | | | | | | |
| 24th | | | | | | |
| 25th | | | | | | |
| 26th | | | | | | |
| 27th | | | | | | |
| 28th | | | | | | |
| 29th | | | | | | |
| 30th | | | | | | |
| 31st | | | | | | |

# Food Tracker

| | Healthy food | Junk food | Both | Didn't eat ☹ |
|---|---|---|---|---|
| 1st | | | | |
| 2nd | | | | |
| 3rd | | | | |
| 4th | | | | |
| 5th | | | | |
| 6th | | | | |
| 7th | | | | |
| 8th | | | | |
| 9th | | | | |
| 10th | | | | |
| 11th | | | | |
| 12th | | | | |
| 13th | | | | |
| 14th | | | | |
| 15th | | | | |
| 16th | | | | |
| 17th | | | | |
| 18th | | | | |
| 19th | | | | |
| 20th | | | | |
| 21st | | | | |
| 22nd | | | | |
| 23rd | | | | |
| 24th | | | | |
| 25th | | | | |
| 26th | | | | |
| 27th | | | | |
| 28th | | | | |
| 29th | | | | |
| 30th | | | | |
| 31st | | | | |

# Weight Tracker

**Month:**

|  | Kgs/lbs |  | Kgs/lbs |
|---|---|---|---|
| 1st |  | 16th |  |
| 2nd |  | 17th |  |
| 3rd |  | 18th |  |
| 4th |  | 19th |  |
| 5th |  | 20th |  |
| 6th |  | 21st |  |
| 7th |  | 22nd |  |
| 8th |  | 23rd |  |
| 9th |  | 24th |  |
| 10th |  | 25th |  |
| 11th |  | 26th |  |
| 12th |  | 27th |  |
| 13th |  | 28th |  |
| 14th |  | 29th |  |
| 15th |  | 30th |  |
|  |  | 31st |  |

# Journal

dd/mm/yy

Good Morning Sunshine!

Lets start the beginning of the month by noting down our details, so this way we can track changes every month

Age:
Weight:
Height:
Date of last menstrual cycle and time frame:

Did you…

- o Get out of bed, woke up at:
- o Smile
- o Brush you teeth
- o Take a shower
- o Eat breakfast
- o Take your meds

Every little task is important sometimes we forget the silliest things so lets make a to-do list to keep track!

To-do list:

Good afternoon!

Did you…

- o Eat lunch
- o Finish your tasks?

Good evening love, how's your day so far?

Did you…

- o Eat snacks
- o Have a good day
- o Have a bad day
- o Finish all that you had on your to do list
- o Eat dinner
- o Sleep early

Good night and sleep well

Good Morning Sunshine!

Lets start the beginning of the month by noting down our details, so this way we can track changes every month

Age:
Weight:
Height:
Date of last menstrual cycle and time frame:

Did you...

o Get out of bed, woke          o Brush you teeth          o Eat breakfast
   up at:                       o Take a shower            o Take your meds
o Smile

Every little task is important sometimes we forget the silliest things so lets make a to-do list to keep track!

To-do list:

Good afternoon!

Did you...

o Eat lunch                     o Finish your tasks?

Good evening love, how's your day so far?

Did you...

o Eat snacks                    o Finish all that you had on    o Eat dinner
o Have a good day                  your to do list              o Sleep early
o Have a bad day

Good night and sleep well

Good Morning Sunshine!

Lets start the beginning of the month by noting down our details, so this way we can track changes every month

Age:
Weight:
Height:
Date of last menstrual cycle and time frame:

Did you...

o Get out of bed, woke        o Brush you teeth        o Eat breakfast
   up at:                          o Take a shower         o Take your meds
o Smile

Every little task is important sometimes we forget the silliest things so lets make a to-do list to keep track!

To-do list:

Good afternoon!

Did you...

o Eat lunch                   o Finish your tasks?

Good evening love, how's your day so far?

Did you...

o Eat snacks                  o Finish all that you had on   o Eat dinner
o Have a good day                your to do list              o Sleep early
o Have a bad day

Good night and sleep well

Good Morning Sunshine!

Lets start the beginning of the month by noting down our details, so this way we can track changes every month

Age:
Weight:
Height:
Date of last menstrual cycle and time frame:

Did you...

o Get out of bed, woke      o Brush you teeth       o Eat breakfast
   up at:                   o Take a shower         o Take your meds
o Smile

Every little task is important sometimes we forget the silliest things so lets make a to-do list to keep track!

To-do list:

Good afternoon!

Did you...

o Eat lunch               o Finish your tasks?

Good evening love, how's your day so far?

Did you...

o Eat snacks              o Finish all that you had on    o Eat dinner
o Have a good day            your to do list              o Sleep early
o Have a bad day

Good night and sleep well

Good Morning Sunshine!

Lets start the beginning of the month by noting down our details, so this way we can track changes every month

Age:
Weight:
Height:
Date of last menstrual cycle and time frame:

Did you...

- o Get out of bed, woke
  up at:
- o Smile

- o Brush you teeth
- o Take a shower

- o Eat breakfast
- o Take your meds

Every little task is important sometimes we forget the silliest things so lets make a to-do list to keep track!

To-do list:

Good afternoon!

Did you...

- o Eat lunch

- o Finish your tasks?

Good evening love, how's your day so far?

Did you...

- o Eat snacks
- o Have a good day
- o Have a bad day

- o Finish all that you had on
  your to do list

- o Eat dinner
- o Sleep early

Good night and sleep well

Good Morning Sunshine!

Lets start the beginning of the month by noting down our details, so this way we can track changes every month

Age:
Weight:
Height:
Date of last menstrual cycle and time frame:

Did you...

o Get out of bed, woke          o Brush you teeth          o Eat breakfast
   up at:                       o Take a shower            o Take your meds
o Smile

Every little task is important sometimes we forget the silliest things so lets make a to-do list to keep track!

To-do list:



Good afternoon!

Did you...

o Eat lunch                     o Finish your tasks?

Good evening love, how's your day so far?

Did you...

o Eat snacks                    o Finish all that you had on    o Eat dinner
o Have a good day                  your to do list              o Sleep early
o Have a bad day

Good night and sleep well

Good Morning Sunshine!

Lets start the beginning of the month by noting down our details, so this way we can track changes every month

Age:
Weight:
Height:
Date of last menstrual cycle and time frame:

Did you...

o Get out of bed, woke     o Brush you teeth          o Eat breakfast
  up at:                   o Take a shower            o Take your meds
o Smile

Every little task is important sometimes we forget the silliest things so lets make a to-do list to keep track!

To-do list:

Good afternoon!

Did you...

o Eat lunch               o Finish your tasks?

Good evening love, how's your day so far?

Did you...

o Eat snacks              o Finish all that you had on    o Eat dinner
o Have a good day           your to do list               o Sleep early
o Have a bad day

Good night and sleep well

Good Morning Sunshine!

Lets start the beginning of the month by noting down our details, so this way we can track changes every month

Age:
Weight:
Height:
Date of last menstrual cycle and time frame:

Did you…

o Get out of bed, woke      o Brush you teeth       o Eat breakfast
   up at:                  o Take a shower         o Take your meds
o Smile

Every little task is important sometimes we forget the silliest things so lets make a to-do list to keep track!

To-do list:

Good afternoon!

Did you…

o Eat lunch              o Finish your tasks?

Good evening love, how's your day so far?

Did you…

o Eat snacks             o Finish all that you had on   o Eat dinner
o Have a good day           your to do list            o Sleep early
o Have a bad day

Good night and sleep well

Good Morning Sunshine!

Lets start the beginning of the month by noting down our details, so this way we can track changes every month

Age:
Weight:
Height:
Date of last menstrual cycle and time frame:

Did you…

- o Get out of bed, woke up at:
- o Smile
- o Brush you teeth
- o Take a shower
- o Eat breakfast
- o Take your meds

Every little task is important sometimes we forget the silliest things so lets make a to-do list to keep track!

To-do list:

Good afternoon!

Did you…

- o Eat lunch
- o Finish your tasks?

Good evening love, how's your day so far?

Did you…

- o Eat snacks
- o Have a good day
- o Have a bad day
- o Finish all that you had on your to do list
- o Eat dinner
- o Sleep early

Good night and sleep well

Good Morning Sunshine!

Lets start the beginning of the month by noting down our details, so this way we can track changes every month

Age:
Weight:
Height:
Date of last menstrual cycle and time frame:

Did you…

o Get out of bed, woke    o Brush you teeth    o Eat breakfast
   up at:    o Take a shower    o Take your meds
o Smile

Every little task is important sometimes we forget the silliest things so lets make a to-do list to keep track!

To-do list:

Good afternoon!

Did you…

o Eat lunch    o Finish your tasks?

Good evening love, how's your day so far?

Did you…

o Eat snacks    o Finish all that you had on    o Eat dinner
o Have a good day      your to do list    o Sleep early
o Have a bad day

Good night and sleep well

Good Morning Sunshine!

Lets start the beginning of the month by noting down our details, so this way we can track changes every month

Age:
Weight:
Height:
Date of last menstrual cycle and time frame:

Did you...

o Get out of bed, woke    o Brush you teeth       o Eat breakfast
  up at:                  o Take a shower         o Take your meds
o Smile

Every little task is important sometimes we forget the silliest things so lets make a to-do list to keep track!

To-do list:

Good afternoon!

Did you...

o Eat lunch               o Finish your tasks?

Good evening love, how's your day so far?

Did you...

o Eat snacks              o Finish all that you had on   o Eat dinner
o Have a good day           your to do list             o Sleep early
o Have a bad day

Good night and sleep well

Good Morning Sunshine!

Lets start the beginning of the month by noting down our details, so this way we can track changes every month

Age:
Weight:
Height:
Date of last menstrual cycle and time frame:

Did you...

o Get out of bed, woke     o Brush you teeth        o Eat breakfast
   up at:                  o Take a shower          o Take your meds
o Smile

Every little task is important sometimes we forget the silliest things so lets make a to-do list to keep track!

To-do list:

Good afternoon!

Did you...

o Eat lunch                o Finish your tasks?

Good evening love, how's your day so far?

Did you...

o Eat snacks               o Finish all that you had on    o Eat dinner
o Have a good day             your to do list               o Sleep early
o Have a bad day

Good night and sleep well

Good Morning Sunshine!

Lets start the beginning of the month by noting down our details, so this way we can track changes every month

Age:
Weight:
Height:
Date of last menstrual cycle and time frame:

Did you…

- Get out of bed, woke up at:
- Smile

- Brush you teeth
- Take a shower

- Eat breakfast
- Take your meds

Every little task is important sometimes we forget the silliest things so lets make a to-do list to keep track!

To-do list:

Good afternoon!

Did you…

- Eat lunch

- Finish your tasks?

Good evening love, how's your day so far?

Did you…

- Eat snacks
- Have a good day
- Have a bad day

- Finish all that you had on your to do list

- Eat dinner
- Sleep early

Good night and sleep well

Good Morning Sunshine!

Lets start the beginning of the month by noting down our details, so this way we can track changes every month

Age:
Weight:
Height:
Date of last menstrual cycle and time frame:

Did you…

- o Get out of bed, woke up at:
- o Smile
- o Brush you teeth
- o Take a shower
- o Eat breakfast
- o Take your meds

Every little task is important sometimes we forget the silliest things so lets make a to-do list to keep track!

To-do list:

Good afternoon!

Did you…

- o Eat lunch
- o Finish your tasks?

Good evening love, how's your day so far?

Did you…

- o Eat snacks
- o Have a good day
- o Have a bad day
- o Finish all that you had on your to do list
- o Eat dinner
- o Sleep early

Good night and sleep well

Good Morning Sunshine!

Lets start the beginning of the month by noting down our details, so this way we can track changes every month

Age:
Weight:
Height:
Date of last menstrual cycle and time frame:

Did you...

o Get out of bed, woke      o Brush you teeth        o Eat breakfast
   up at:                   o Take a shower          o Take your meds
o Smile

Every little task is important sometimes we forget the silliest things so lets make a to-do list to keep track!

To-do list:

Good afternoon!

Did you...

o Eat lunch              o Finish your tasks?

Good evening love, how's your day so far?

Did you...

o Eat snacks             o Finish all that you had on    o Eat dinner
o Have a good day           your to do list               o Sleep early
o Have a bad day

Good night and sleep well

Good Morning Sunshine!

Lets start the beginning of the month by noting down our details, so this way we can track changes every month

Age:
Weight:
Height:
Date of last menstrual cycle and time frame:

Did you...

o Get out of bed, woke      o Brush you teeth        o Eat breakfast
   up at:                   o Take a shower          o Take your meds
o Smile

Every little task is important sometimes we forget the silliest things so lets make a to-do list to keep track!

To-do list:

Good afternoon!

Did you...

o Eat lunch                 o Finish your tasks?

Good evening love, how's your day so far?

Did you...

o Eat snacks                o Finish all that you had on    o Eat dinner
o Have a good day              your to do list               o Sleep early
o Have a bad day

Good night and sleep well

Good Morning Sunshine!

Lets start the beginning of the month by noting down our details, so this way we can track changes every month

Age:
Weight:
Height:
Date of last menstrual cycle and time frame:

Did you…

o Get out of bed, woke      o Brush you teeth        o Eat breakfast
  up at:                              o Take a shower          o Take your meds
o Smile

Every little task is important sometimes we forget the silliest things so lets make a to-do list to keep track!

To-do list:

Good afternoon!

Did you…

o Eat lunch                    o Finish your tasks?

Good evening love, how's your day so far?

Did you…

o Eat snacks              o Finish all that you had on   o Eat dinner
o Have a good day            your to do list          o Sleep early
o Have a bad day

Good night and sleep well

Good Morning Sunshine!

Lets start the beginning of the month by noting down our details, so this way we can track changes every month

Age:
Weight:
Height:
Date of last menstrual cycle and time frame:

Did you…

o Get out of bed, woke    o Brush you teeth    o Eat breakfast
   up at:    o Take a shower    o Take your meds
o Smile

Every little task is important sometimes we forget the silliest things so lets make a to-do list to keep track!

To-do list:

Good afternoon!

Did you…

o Eat lunch    o Finish your tasks?

Good evening love, how's your day so far?

Did you…

o Eat snacks    o Finish all that you had on    o Eat dinner
o Have a good day      your to do list    o Sleep early
o Have a bad day

Good night and sleep well

Good Morning Sunshine!

Lets start the beginning of the month by noting down our details, so this way we can track changes every month

Age:
Weight:
Height:
Date of last menstrual cycle and time frame:

Did you…

- o Get out of bed, woke up at:
- o Smile
- o Brush you teeth
- o Take a shower
- o Eat breakfast
- o Take your meds

Every little task is important sometimes we forget the silliest things so lets make a to-do list to keep track!

To-do list:

Good afternoon!

Did you…

- o Eat lunch
- o Finish your tasks?

Good evening love, how's your day so far?

Did you…

- o Eat snacks
- o Have a good day
- o Have a bad day
- o Finish all that you had on your to do list
- o Eat dinner
- o Sleep early

Good night and sleep well

Good Morning Sunshine!

Lets start the beginning of the month by noting down our details, so this way we can track changes every month

Age:
Weight:
Height:
Date of last menstrual cycle and time frame:

Did you...

o Get out of bed, woke      o Brush you teeth      o Eat breakfast
   up at:      o Take a shower      o Take your meds
o Smile

Every little task is important sometimes we forget the silliest things so lets make a to-do list to keep track!

To-do list:

Good afternoon!

Did you...

o Eat lunch                o Finish your tasks?

Good evening love, how's your day so far?

Did you...

o Eat snacks          o Finish all that you had on    o Eat dinner
o Have a good day        your to do list              o Sleep early
o Have a bad day

Good night and sleep well

Good Morning Sunshine!

Lets start the beginning of the month by noting down our details, so this way we can track changes every month

Age:
Weight:
Height:
Date of last menstrual cycle and time frame:

Did you…

o Get out of bed, woke      o Brush you teeth       o Eat breakfast
   up at:                   o Take a shower         o Take your meds
o Smile

Every little task is important sometimes we forget the silliest things so lets make a to-do list to keep track!

To-do list:

Good afternoon!

Did you…

o Eat lunch                o Finish your tasks?

Good evening love, how's your day so far?

Did you…

o Eat snacks               o Finish all that you had on    o Eat dinner
o Have a good day             your to do list              o Sleep early
o Have a bad day

Good night and sleep well

Good Morning Sunshine!

Lets start the beginning of the month by noting down our details, so this way we can track changes every month

Age:
Weight:
Height:
Date of last menstrual cycle and time frame:

Did you…

o Get out of bed, woke     o Brush you teeth     o Eat breakfast
   up at:                  o Take a shower       o Take your meds
o Smile

Every little task is important sometimes we forget the silliest things so lets make a to-do list to keep track!

To-do list:

Good afternoon!

Did you…

o Eat lunch          o Finish your tasks?

Good evening love, how's your day so far?

Did you…

o Eat snacks          o Finish all that you had on     o Eat dinner
o Have a good day        your to do list              o Sleep early
o Have a bad day

Good night and sleep well

Good Morning Sunshine!

Lets start the beginning of the month by noting down our details, so this way we can track changes every month

Age:
Weight:
Height:
Date of last menstrual cycle and time frame:

Did you...

o Get out of bed, woke      o Brush you teeth         o Eat breakfast
  up at:               o Take a shower           o Take your meds
o Smile

Every little task is important sometimes we forget the silliest things so lets make a to-do list to keep track!

To-do list:

Good afternoon!

Did you...

o Eat lunch                 o Finish your tasks?

Good evening love, how's your day so far?

Did you...

o Eat snacks                o Finish all that you had on   o Eat dinner
o Have a good day             your to do list         o Sleep early
o Have a bad day

Good night and sleep well

Good Morning Sunshine!

Lets start the beginning of the month by noting down our details, so this way we can track changes every month

Age:
Weight:
Height:
Date of last menstrual cycle and time frame:

Did you…

o Get out of bed, woke        o Brush you teeth        o Eat breakfast
   up at:        o Take a shower        o Take your meds
o Smile

Every little task is important sometimes we forget the silliest things so lets make a to-do list to keep track!

To-do list:




Good afternoon!

Did you…

o Eat lunch        o Finish your tasks?

Good evening love, how's your day so far?

Did you…

o Eat snacks        o Finish all that you had on        o Eat dinner
o Have a good day           your to do list        o Sleep early
o Have a bad day

Good night and sleep well

Good Morning Sunshine!

Lets start the beginning of the month by noting down our details, so this way we can track changes every month

Age:
Weight:
Height:
Date of last menstrual cycle and time frame:

Did you…

o Get out of bed, woke    o Brush you teeth       o Eat breakfast
  up at:                  o Take a shower         o Take your meds
o Smile

Every little task is important sometimes we forget the silliest things so lets make a to-do list to keep track!

To-do list:

Good afternoon!

Did you…

o Eat lunch              o Finish your tasks?

Good evening love, how's your day so far?

Did you…

o Eat snacks             o Finish all that you had on   o Eat dinner
o Have a good day          your to do list              o Sleep early
o Have a bad day

Good night and sleep well

Good Morning Sunshine!

Lets start the beginning of the month by noting down our details, so this way we can track changes every month

Age:
Weight:
Height:
Date of last menstrual cycle and time frame:

Did you…

o Get out of bed, woke    o Brush you teeth     o Eat breakfast
   up at:              o Take a shower     o Take your meds
o Smile

Every little task is important sometimes we forget the silliest things so lets make a to-do list to keep track!

To-do list:

Good afternoon!

Did you…

o Eat lunch             o Finish your tasks?

Good evening love, how's your day so far?

Did you…

o Eat snacks         o Finish all that you had on   o Eat dinner
o Have a good day       your to do list          o Sleep early
o Have a bad day

Good night and sleep well

Good Morning Sunshine!

Lets start the beginning of the month by noting down our details, so this way we can track changes every month

Age:
Weight:
Height:
Date of last menstrual cycle and time frame:

Did you…

o Get out of bed, woke        o Brush you teeth        o Eat breakfast
   up at:                     o Take a shower          o Take your meds
o Smile

Every little task is important sometimes we forget the silliest things so lets make a to-do list to keep track!

To-do list:

Good afternoon!

Did you…

o Eat lunch                   o Finish your tasks?

Good evening love, how's your day so far?

Did you…

o Eat snacks                  o Finish all that you had on    o Eat dinner
o Have a good day                your to do list               o Sleep early
o Have a bad day

Good night and sleep well

Good Morning Sunshine!

Lets start the beginning of the month by noting down our details, so this way we can track changes every month

Age:
Weight:
Height:
Date of last menstrual cycle and time frame:

Did you…

o Get out of bed, woke      o Brush you teeth        o Eat breakfast
   up at:                   o Take a shower          o Take your meds
o Smile

Every little task is important sometimes we forget the silliest things so lets make a to-do list to keep track!

To-do list:

Good afternoon!

Did you…

o Eat lunch                o Finish your tasks?

Good evening love, how's your day so far?

Did you…

o Eat snacks               o Finish all that you had on    o Eat dinner
o Have a good day             your to do list               o Sleep early
o Have a bad day

Good night and sleep well

Good Morning Sunshine!

Lets start the beginning of the month by noting down our details, so this way we can track changes every month

Age:
Weight:
Height:
Date of last menstrual cycle and time frame:

Did you…

o Get out of bed, woke        o Brush you teeth        o Eat breakfast
  up at:                      o Take a shower          o Take your meds
o Smile

Every little task is important sometimes we forget the silliest things so lets make a to-do list to keep track!

To-do list:

Good afternoon!

Did you…

o Eat lunch              o Finish your tasks?

Good evening love, how's your day so far?

Did you…

o Eat snacks             o Finish all that you had on    o Eat dinner
o Have a good day          your to do list               o Sleep early
o Have a bad day

Good night and sleep well

Good Morning Sunshine!

Lets start the beginning of the month by noting down our details, so this way we can track changes every month

Age:
Weight:
Height:
Date of last menstrual cycle and time frame:

Did you...

o Get out of bed, woke          o Brush you teeth          o Eat breakfast
   up at:                          o Take a shower          o Take your meds
o Smile

Every little task is important sometimes we forget the silliest things so lets make a to-do list to keep track!

To-do list:

Good afternoon!

Did you...

o Eat lunch                    o Finish your tasks?

Good evening love, how's your day so far?

Did you...

o Eat snacks              o Finish all that you had on    o Eat dinner
o Have a good day          your to do list              o Sleep early
o Have a bad day

Good night and sleep well

Good Morning Sunshine!

Lets start the beginning of the month by noting down our details, so this way we can track changes every month

Age:
Weight:
Height:
Date of last menstrual cycle and time frame:

Did you…

o Get out of bed, woke          o Brush you teeth          o Eat breakfast
   up at:                                 o Take a shower            o Take your meds
o Smile

Every little task is important sometimes we forget the silliest things so lets make a to-do list to keep track!

To-do list:

Good afternoon!

Did you…

o Eat lunch                          o Finish your tasks?

Good evening love, how's your day so far?

Did you…

o Eat snacks                        o Finish all that you had on    o Eat dinner
o Have a good day              your to do list                        o Sleep early
o Have a bad day

Good night and sleep well

# This Month...

o I tried something new by...

o I helped somebody by...

o I become a better person by...

o I lost ____ kgs by...

o I gained ____kgs by...

o

o

o

# Habit Tracker

**Month:**

|            | 1st  | 2nd  | 3rd  | 4th  | 5th  |     |
|------------|------|------|------|------|------|-----|
| Sleep      |      |      |      |      |      |     |
| Caffeine   |      |      |      |      |      |     |
| Alcohol    |      |      |      |      |      |     |
| Cigarettes |      |      |      |      |      |     |
| Exercise   |      |      |      |      |      |     |
|            | 6th  | 7th  | 8th  | 9th  | 10th |     |
| Sleep      |      |      |      |      |      |     |
| Caffeine   |      |      |      |      |      |     |
| Alcohol    |      |      |      |      |      |     |
| Cigarettes |      |      |      |      |      |     |
| Exercise   |      |      |      |      |      |     |
|            | 11th | 12th | 13th | 14th | 15th |     |
| Sleep      |      |      |      |      |      |     |
| Caffeine   |      |      |      |      |      |     |
| Alcohol    |      |      |      |      |      |     |
| Cigarettes |      |      |      |      |      |     |
| Exercise   |      |      |      |      |      |     |
|            | 16th | 17th | 18th | 19th | 20th |     |
| Sleep      |      |      |      |      |      |     |
| Caffeine   |      |      |      |      |      |     |
| Alcohol    |      |      |      |      |      |     |
| Cigarettes |      |      |      |      |      |     |
| Exercise   |      |      |      |      |      |     |
|            | 21th | 22th | 23th | 24th | 25th |     |
| Sleep      |      |      |      |      |      |     |
| Caffeine   |      |      |      |      |      |     |
| Alcohol    |      |      |      |      |      |     |
| Cigarettes |      |      |      |      |      |     |
| Exercise   |      |      |      |      |      |     |
|            | 26th | 27th | 28th | 29th | 30th | 31st |
| Sleep      |      |      |      |      |      |     |
| Caffeine   |      |      |      |      |      |     |
| Alcohol    |      |      |      |      |      |     |
| Cigarettes |      |      |      |      |      |     |
| Exercise   |      |      |      |      |      |     |

# Emotion tracker

*How are you felling today? It is important to be in touch with yourself and your emotions.*

|       | Anger | Hurt/Pain | Disappointment | Upset | Happy | Blah! | Lazy |
|-------|-------|-----------|----------------|-------|-------|-------|------|
| 1st   |       |           |                |       |       |       |      |
| 2nd   |       |           |                |       |       |       |      |
| 3rd   |       |           |                |       |       |       |      |
| 4th   |       |           |                |       |       |       |      |
| 5th   |       |           |                |       |       |       |      |
| 6th   |       |           |                |       |       |       |      |
| 7th   |       |           |                |       |       |       |      |
| 8th   |       |           |                |       |       |       |      |
| 9th   |       |           |                |       |       |       |      |
| 10th  |       |           |                |       |       |       |      |
| 11th  |       |           |                |       |       |       |      |
| 12th  |       |           |                |       |       |       |      |
| 13th  |       |           |                |       |       |       |      |
| 14th  |       |           |                |       |       |       |      |
| 15th  |       |           |                |       |       |       |      |
| 16th  |       |           |                |       |       |       |      |
| 17th  |       |           |                |       |       |       |      |
| 18th  |       |           |                |       |       |       |      |
| 19th  |       |           |                |       |       |       |      |
| 20th  |       |           |                |       |       |       |      |
| 21st  |       |           |                |       |       |       |      |
| 22nd  |       |           |                |       |       |       |      |
| 23rd  |       |           |                |       |       |       |      |
| 24th  |       |           |                |       |       |       |      |
| 25th  |       |           |                |       |       |       |      |
| 26th  |       |           |                |       |       |       |      |
| 27th  |       |           |                |       |       |       |      |
| 28th  |       |           |                |       |       |       |      |
| 29th  |       |           |                |       |       |       |      |
| 30th  |       |           |                |       |       |       |      |
| 31st  |       |           |                |       |       |       |      |

|        | Guilt | Anxious | Sadness | Shame | Guilt | Worthless |
|--------|-------|---------|---------|-------|-------|-----------|
| 1st    |       |         |         |       |       |           |
| 2nd    |       |         |         |       |       |           |
| 3rd    |       |         |         |       |       |           |
| 4th    |       |         |         |       |       |           |
| 5th    |       |         |         |       |       |           |
| 6th    |       |         |         |       |       |           |
| 7th    |       |         |         |       |       |           |
| 8th    |       |         |         |       |       |           |
| 9th    |       |         |         |       |       |           |
| 10th   |       |         |         |       |       |           |
| 11th   |       |         |         |       |       |           |
| 12th   |       |         |         |       |       |           |
| 13th   |       |         |         |       |       |           |
| 14th   |       |         |         |       |       |           |
| 15th   |       |         |         |       |       |           |
| 16th   |       |         |         |       |       |           |
| 17th   |       |         |         |       |       |           |
| 18th   |       |         |         |       |       |           |
| 19th   |       |         |         |       |       |           |
| 20th   |       |         |         |       |       |           |
| 21st   |       |         |         |       |       |           |
| 22nd   |       |         |         |       |       |           |
| 23rd   |       |         |         |       |       |           |
| 24th   |       |         |         |       |       |           |
| 25th   |       |         |         |       |       |           |
| 26th   |       |         |         |       |       |           |
| 27th   |       |         |         |       |       |           |
| 28th   |       |         |         |       |       |           |
| 29th   |       |         |         |       |       |           |
| 30th   |       |         |         |       |       |           |
| 31st   |       |         |         |       |       |           |

# Food Tracker

| | Healthy food | Junk food | Both | Didn't eat ☹ |
|---|---|---|---|---|
| 1st | | | | |
| 2nd | | | | |
| 3rd | | | | |
| 4th | | | | |
| 5th | | | | |
| 6th | | | | |
| 7th | | | | |
| 8th | | | | |
| 9th | | | | |
| 10th | | | | |
| 11th | | | | |
| 12th | | | | |
| 13th | | | | |
| 14th | | | | |
| 15th | | | | |
| 16th | | | | |
| 17th | | | | |
| 18th | | | | |
| 19th | | | | |
| 20th | | | | |
| 21st | | | | |
| 22nd | | | | |
| 23rd | | | | |
| 24th | | | | |
| 25th | | | | |
| 26th | | | | |
| 27th | | | | |
| 28th | | | | |
| 29th | | | | |
| 30th | | | | |
| 31st | | | | |

# Weight Tracker

**Month:**

| | Kgs/lbs | | Kgs/lbs |
|---|---|---|---|
| 1st | | 16th | |
| 2nd | | 17th | |
| 3rd | | 18th | |
| 4th | | 19th | |
| 5th | | 20th | |
| 6th | | 21st | |
| 7th | | 22nd | |
| 8th | | 23rd | |
| 9th | | 24th | |
| 10th | | 25th | |
| 11th | | 26th | |
| 12th | | 27th | |
| 13th | | 28th | |
| 14th | | 29th | |
| 15th | | 30th | |
| | | 31st | |

# Journal

Good Morning Sunshine!

Lets start the beginning of the month by noting down our details, so this way we can track changes every month

Age:
Weight:
Height:
Date of last menstrual cycle and time frame:

Did you...

- o Get out of bed, woke   - o Brush you teeth   - o Eat breakfast
  up at:                   - o Take a shower     - o Take your meds
- o Smile

Every little task is important sometimes we forget the silliest things so lets make a to-do list to keep track!

To-do list:

Good afternoon!

Did you...

- o Eat lunch   - o Finish your tasks?

Good evening love, how's your day so far?

Did you...

- o Eat snacks       - o Finish all that you had on   - o Eat dinner
- o Have a good day     your to do list                - o Sleep early
- o Have a bad day

Good night and sleep well

Good Morning Sunshine!

Lets start the beginning of the month by noting down our details, so this way we can track changes every month

Age:
Weight:
Height:
Date of last menstrual cycle and time frame:

Did you...

o Get out of bed, woke      o Brush you teeth         o Eat breakfast
  up at:                    o Take a shower           o Take your meds
o Smile

Every little task is important sometimes we forget the silliest things so lets make a to-do list to keep track!

To-do list:

Good afternoon!

Did you...

o Eat lunch                 o Finish your tasks?

Good evening love, how's your day so far?

Did you...

o Eat snacks                o Finish all that you had on   o Eat dinner
o Have a good day             your to do list              o Sleep early
o Have a bad day

Good night and sleep well

Good Morning Sunshine!

Lets start the beginning of the month by noting down our details, so this way we can track changes every month

Age:
Weight:
Height:
Date of last menstrual cycle and time frame:

Did you...

o Get out of bed, woke      o Brush you teeth      o Eat breakfast
  up at:                    o Take a shower        o Take your meds
o Smile

Every little task is important sometimes we forget the silliest things so lets make a to-do list to keep track!

To-do list:

Good afternoon!

Did you...

o Eat lunch                o Finish your tasks?

Good evening love, how's your day so far?

Did you...

o Eat snacks               o Finish all that you had on    o Eat dinner
o Have a good day            your to do list               o Sleep early
o Have a bad day

Good night and sleep well

Good Morning Sunshine!

Lets start the beginning of the month by noting down our details, so this way we can track changes every month

Age:
Weight:
Height:
Date of last menstrual cycle and time frame:

Did you…

o Get out of bed, woke    o Brush you teeth      o Eat breakfast
   up at:                 o Take a shower        o Take your meds
o Smile

Every little task is important sometimes we forget the silliest things so lets make a to-do list to keep track!

To-do list:

Good afternoon!

Did you…

o Eat lunch               o Finish your tasks?

Good evening love, how's your day so far?

Did you…

o Eat snacks              o Finish all that you had on    o Eat dinner
o Have a good day            your to do list             o Sleep early
o Have a bad day

Good night and sleep well

Good Morning Sunshine!

Lets start the beginning of the month by noting down our details, so this way we can track changes every month

Age:
Weight:
Height:
Date of last menstrual cycle and time frame:

Did you…

- o Get out of bed, woke up at:
- o Smile
- o Brush you teeth
- o Take a shower
- o Eat breakfast
- o Take your meds

Every little task is important sometimes we forget the silliest things so lets make a to-do list to keep track!

To-do list:

Good afternoon!

Did you…

- o Eat lunch
- o Finish your tasks?

Good evening love, how's your day so far?

Did you…

- o Eat snacks
- o Have a good day
- o Have a bad day
- o Finish all that you had on your to do list
- o Eat dinner
- o Sleep early

Good night and sleep well

Good Morning Sunshine!

Lets start the beginning of the month by noting down our details, so this way we can track changes every month

Age:
Weight:
Height:
Date of last menstrual cycle and time frame:

Did you…

o Get out of bed, woke    o Brush you teeth    o Eat breakfast
   up at:    o Take a shower    o Take your meds
o Smile

Every little task is important sometimes we forget the silliest things so lets make a to-do list to keep track!

To-do list:

Good afternoon!

Did you…

o Eat lunch    o Finish your tasks?

Good evening love, how's your day so far?

Did you…

o Eat snacks    o Finish all that you had on   o Eat dinner
o Have a good day    your to do list    o Sleep early
o Have a bad day

Good night and sleep well

Good Morning Sunshine!

Lets start the beginning of the month by noting down our details, so this way we can track changes every month

Age:
Weight:
Height:
Date of last menstrual cycle and time frame:

Did you…

o Get out of bed, woke      o Brush you teeth      o Eat breakfast
  up at:                            o Take a shower       o Take your meds
o Smile

Every little task is important sometimes we forget the silliest things so lets make a to-do list to keep track!

To-do list:

Good afternoon!

Did you…

o Eat lunch                  o Finish your tasks?

Good evening love, how's your day so far?

Did you…

o Eat snacks              o Finish all that you had on    o Eat dinner
o Have a good day           your to do list                 o Sleep early
o Have a bad day

Good night and sleep well

dd/mm/yy

Good Morning Sunshine!

Lets start the beginning of the month by noting down our details, so this way we can track changes every month

Age:
Weight:
Height:
Date of last menstrual cycle and time frame:

Did you…

o Get out of bed, woke       o Brush you teeth        o Eat breakfast
   up at:                    o Take a shower          o Take your meds
o Smile

Every little task is important sometimes we forget the silliest things so lets make a to-do list to keep track!

To-do list:

Good afternoon!

Did you…

o Eat lunch                  o Finish your tasks?

Good evening love, how's your day so far?

Did you…

o Eat snacks                 o Finish all that you had on   o Eat dinner
o Have a good day               your to do list            o Sleep early
o Have a bad day

Good night and sleep well

Good Morning Sunshine!

Lets start the beginning of the month by noting down our details, so this way we can track changes every month

Age:
Weight:
Height:
Date of last menstrual cycle and time frame:

Did you…

o Get out of bed, woke     o Brush you teeth          o Eat breakfast
   up at:                  o Take a shower            o Take your meds
o Smile

Every little task is important sometimes we forget the silliest things so lets make a to-do list to keep track!

To-do list:

Good afternoon!

Did you…

o Eat lunch                o Finish your tasks?

Good evening love, how's your day so far?

Did you…

o Eat snacks               o Finish all that you had on   o Eat dinner
o Have a good day             your to do list              o Sleep early
o Have a bad day

Good night and sleep well

Good Morning Sunshine!

Lets start the beginning of the month by noting down our details, so this way we can track changes every month

Age:
Weight:
Height:
Date of last menstrual cycle and time frame:

Did you…

o Get out of bed, woke          o Brush you teeth          o Eat breakfast
   up at:                       o Take a shower            o Take your meds
o Smile

Every little task is important sometimes we forget the silliest things so lets make a to-do list to keep track!

To-do list:

Good afternoon!

Did you…

o Eat lunch                     o Finish your tasks?

Good evening love, how's your day so far?

Did you…

o Eat snacks                    o Finish all that you had on    o Eat dinner
o Have a good day                  your to do list             o Sleep early
o Have a bad day

Good night and sleep well

Good Morning Sunshine!

Lets start the beginning of the month by noting down our details, so this way we can track changes every month

Age:
Weight:
Height:
Date of last menstrual cycle and time frame:

Did you…

o Get out of bed, woke       o Brush you teeth          o Eat breakfast
   up at:                    o Take a shower            o Take your meds
o Smile

Every little task is important sometimes we forget the silliest things so lets make a to-do list to keep track!

To-do list:

Good afternoon!

Did you…

o Eat lunch                  o Finish your tasks?

Good evening love, how's your day so far?

Did you…

o Eat snacks                 o Finish all that you had on   o Eat dinner
o Have a good day               your to do list               o Sleep early
o Have a bad day

Good night and sleep well

dd/mm/yy

Good Morning Sunshine!

Lets start the beginning of the month by noting down our details, so this way we can track changes every month

Age:
Weight:
Height:
Date of last menstrual cycle and time frame:

Did you...

o Get out of bed, woke
   up at:
o Smile

o Brush you teeth
o Take a shower

o Eat breakfast
o Take your meds

Every little task is important sometimes we forget the silliest things so lets make a to-do list to keep track!

To-do list:

Good afternoon!

Did you...

o Eat lunch

o Finish your tasks?

Good evening love, how's your day so far?

Did you...

o Eat snacks
o Have a good day
o Have a bad day

o Finish all that you had on
   your to do list

o Eat dinner
o Sleep early

Good night and sleep well

Good Morning Sunshine!

Lets start the beginning of the month by noting down our details, so this way we can track changes every month

Age:
Weight:
Height:
Date of last menstrual cycle and time frame:

Did you…

o Get out of bed, woke    o Brush you teeth       o Eat breakfast
  up at:                  o Take a shower         o Take your meds
o Smile

Every little task is important sometimes we forget the silliest things so lets make a to-do list to keep track!

To-do list:

Good afternoon!

Did you…

o Eat lunch                o Finish your tasks?

Good evening love, how's your day so far?

Did you…

o Eat snacks               o Finish all that you had on    o Eat dinner
o Have a good day            your to do list              o Sleep early
o Have a bad day

Good night and sleep well

Good Morning Sunshine!

Lets start the beginning of the month by noting down our details, so this way we can track changes every month

Age:
Weight:
Height:
Date of last menstrual cycle and time frame:

Did you…

o Get out of bed, woke       o Brush you teeth        o Eat breakfast
   up at:                    o Take a shower          o Take your meds
o Smile

Every little task is important sometimes we forget the silliest things so lets make a to-do list to keep track!

To-do list:

Good afternoon!

Did you…

o Eat lunch                  o Finish your tasks?

Good evening love, how's your day so far?

Did you…

o Eat snacks                 o Finish all that you had on   o Eat dinner
o Have a good day               your to do list            o Sleep early
o Have a bad day

Good night and sleep well

Good Morning Sunshine!

Lets start the beginning of the month by noting down our details, so this way we can track changes every month

Age:
Weight:
Height:
Date of last menstrual cycle and time frame:

Did you...

o Get out of bed, woke      o Brush you teeth       o Eat breakfast
  up at:                    o Take a shower         o Take your meds
o Smile

Every little task is important sometimes we forget the silliest things so lets make a to-do list to keep track!

To-do list:

Good afternoon!

Did you...

o Eat lunch                o Finish your tasks?

Good evening love, how's your day so far?

Did you...

o Eat snacks               o Finish all that you had on   o Eat dinner
o Have a good day            your to do list              o Sleep early
o Have a bad day

Good night and sleep well

dd/mm/yy

Good Morning Sunshine!

Lets start the beginning of the month by noting down our details, so this way we can track changes every month

Age:
Weight:
Height:
Date of last menstrual cycle and time frame:

Did you...

o Get out of bed, woke      o Brush you teeth        o Eat breakfast
   up at:                   o Take a shower          o Take your meds
o Smile

Every little task is important sometimes we forget the silliest things so lets make a to-do list to keep track!

To-do list:

Good afternoon!

Did you...

o Eat lunch                 o Finish your tasks?

Good evening love, how's your day so far?

Did you...

o Eat snacks                o Finish all that you had on    o Eat dinner
o Have a good day              your to do list              o Sleep early
o Have a bad day

Good night and sleep well

Good Morning Sunshine!

Lets start the beginning of the month by noting down our details, so this way we can track changes every month

Age:
Weight:
Height:
Date of last menstrual cycle and time frame:

Did you…

o Get out of bed, woke          o Brush you teeth          o Eat breakfast
   up at:                       o Take a shower             o Take your meds
o Smile

Every little task is important sometimes we forget the silliest things so lets make a to-do list to keep track!

To-do list:

Good afternoon!

Did you…

o Eat lunch                    o Finish your tasks?

Good evening love, how's your day so far?

Did you…

o Eat snacks                   o Finish all that you had on    o Eat dinner
o Have a good day                 your to do list              o Sleep early
o Have a bad day

Good night and sleep well

Good Morning Sunshine!

Lets start the beginning of the month by noting down our details, so this way we can track changes every month

Age:
Weight:
Height:
Date of last menstrual cycle and time frame:

Did you…

| | | |
|---|---|---|
| o Get out of bed, woke up at: | o Brush you teeth | o Eat breakfast |
| o Smile | o Take a shower | o Take your meds |

Every little task is important sometimes we forget the silliest things so lets make a to-do list to keep track!

To-do list:

Good afternoon!

Did you…

o Eat lunch          o Finish your tasks?

Good evening love, how's your day so far?

Did you…

| | | |
|---|---|---|
| o Eat snacks | o Finish all that you had on your to do list | o Eat dinner |
| o Have a good day | | o Sleep early |
| o Have a bad day | | |

Good night and sleep well

Good Morning Sunshine!

Lets start the beginning of the month by noting down our details, so this way we can track changes every month

Age:
Weight:
Height:
Date of last menstrual cycle and time frame:

Did you…

- o Get out of bed, woke        - o Brush you teeth        - o Eat breakfast
  up at:                        - o Take a shower          - o Take your meds
- o Smile

Every little task is important sometimes we forget the silliest things so lets make a to-do list to keep track!

To-do list:

Good afternoon!

Did you…

- o Eat lunch                  - o Finish your tasks?

Good evening love, how's your day so far?

Did you…

- o Eat snacks        - o Finish all that you had on    - o Eat dinner
- o Have a good day       your to do list               - o Sleep early
- o Have a bad day

Good night and sleep well

Good Morning Sunshine!

Lets start the beginning of the month by noting down our details, so this way we can track changes every month

Age:
Weight:
Height:
Date of last menstrual cycle and time frame:

Did you...

o Get out of bed, woke        o Brush you teeth          o Eat breakfast
   up at:                     o Take a shower            o Take your meds
o Smile

Every little task is important sometimes we forget the silliest things so lets make a to-do list to keep track!

To-do list:

Good afternoon!

Did you...

o Eat lunch                   o Finish your tasks?

Good evening love, how's your day so far?

Did you...

o Eat snacks                  o Finish all that you had on    o Eat dinner
o Have a good day                your to do list               o Sleep early
o Have a bad day

Good night and sleep well

Good Morning Sunshine!

Lets start the beginning of the month by noting down our details, so this way we can track changes every month

Age:
Weight:
Height:
Date of last menstrual cycle and time frame:

Did you…

- o Get out of bed, woke up at:
- o Smile
- o Brush you teeth
- o Take a shower
- o Eat breakfast
- o Take your meds

Every little task is important sometimes we forget the silliest things so lets make a to-do list to keep track!

To-do list:

Good afternoon!

Did you…

- o Eat lunch
- o Finish your tasks?

Good evening love, how's your day so far?

Did you…

- o Eat snacks
- o Have a good day
- o Have a bad day
- o Finish all that you had on your to do list
- o Eat dinner
- o Sleep early

Good night and sleep well

Good Morning Sunshine!

Lets start the beginning of the month by noting down our details, so this way we can track changes every month

Age:
Weight:
Height:
Date of last menstrual cycle and time frame:

Did you…

o Get out of bed, woke      o Brush you teeth         o Eat breakfast
   up at:                   o Take a shower           o Take your meds
o Smile

Every little task is important sometimes we forget the silliest things so lets make a to-do list to keep track!

To-do list:

Good afternoon!

Did you…

o Eat lunch                 o Finish your tasks?

Good evening love, how's your day so far?

Did you…

o Eat snacks               o Finish all that you had on   o Eat dinner
o Have a good day             your to do list             o Sleep early
o Have a bad day

Good night and sleep well

Good Morning Sunshine!

Lets start the beginning of the month by noting down our details, so this way we can track changes every month

Age:
Weight:
Height:
Date of last menstrual cycle and time frame:

Did you...

o Get out of bed, woke    o Brush you teeth    o Eat breakfast
  up at:                   o Take a shower     o Take your meds
o Smile

Every little task is important sometimes we forget the silliest things so lets make a to-do list to keep track!

To-do list:

Good afternoon!

Did you...

o Eat lunch            o Finish your tasks?

Good evening love, how's your day so far?

Did you...

o Eat snacks          o Finish all that you had on   o Eat dinner
o Have a good day       your to do list              o Sleep early
o Have a bad day

Good night and sleep well

Good Morning Sunshine!

Lets start the beginning of the month by noting down our details, so this way we can track changes every month

Age:
Weight:
Height:
Date of last menstrual cycle and time frame:

Did you…

o Get out of bed, woke   o Brush you teeth      o Eat breakfast
   up at:                o Take a shower        o Take your meds
o Smile

Every little task is important sometimes we forget the silliest things so lets make a to-do list to keep track!

To-do list:

Good afternoon!

Did you…

o Eat lunch              o Finish your tasks?

Good evening love, how's your day so far?

Did you…

o Eat snacks             o Finish all that you had on   o Eat dinner
o Have a good day          your to do list             o Sleep early
o Have a bad day

Good night and sleep well

Good Morning Sunshine!

Lets start the beginning of the month by noting down our details, so this way we can track changes every month

Age:
Weight:
Height:
Date of last menstrual cycle and time frame:

Did you...

o Get out of bed, woke      o Brush you teeth        o Eat breakfast
   up at:                    o Take a shower          o Take your meds
o Smile

Every little task is important sometimes we forget the silliest things so lets make a to-do list to keep track!

To-do list:

Good afternoon!

Did you...

o Eat lunch              o Finish your tasks?

Good evening love, how's your day so far?

Did you...

o Eat snacks             o Finish all that you had on   o Eat dinner
o Have a good day           your to do list             o Sleep early
o Have a bad day

Good night and sleep well

Good Morning Sunshine!

Lets start the beginning of the month by noting down our details, so this way we can track changes every month

Age:
Weight:
Height:
Date of last menstrual cycle and time frame:

Did you...

| | | |
|---|---|---|
| o Get out of bed, woke up at: | o Brush you teeth | o Eat breakfast |
| | o Take a shower | o Take your meds |
| o Smile | | |

Every little task is important sometimes we forget the silliest things so lets make a to-do list to keep track!

To-do list:

Good afternoon!

Did you...

o Eat lunch          o Finish your tasks?

Good evening love, how's your day so far?

Did you...

| | | |
|---|---|---|
| o Eat snacks | o Finish all that you had on | o Eat dinner |
| o Have a good day | your to do list | o Sleep early |
| o Have a bad day | | |

Good night and sleep well

Good Morning Sunshine!

Lets start the beginning of the month by noting down our details, so this way we can track changes every month

Age:
Weight:
Height:
Date of last menstrual cycle and time frame:

Did you...

o Get out of bed, woke      o Brush you teeth      o Eat breakfast
   up at:                   o Take a shower        o Take your meds
o Smile

Every little task is important sometimes we forget the silliest things so lets make a to-do list to keep track!

To-do list:

Good afternoon!

Did you...

o Eat lunch                 o Finish your tasks?

Good evening love, how's your day so far?

Did you...

o Eat snacks                o Finish all that you had on    o Eat dinner
o Have a good day              your to do list              o Sleep early
o Have a bad day

Good night and sleep well

dd/mm/yy

Good Morning Sunshine!

Lets start the beginning of the month by noting down our details, so this way we can track changes every month

Age:
Weight:
Height:
Date of last menstrual cycle and time frame:

Did you…

o Get out of bed, woke     o Brush you teeth       o Eat breakfast
   up at:                  o Take a shower         o Take your meds
o Smile

Every little task is important sometimes we forget the silliest things so lets make a to-do list to keep track!

To-do list:

Good afternoon!

Did you…

o Eat lunch              o Finish your tasks?

Good evening love, how's your day so far?

Did you…

o Eat snacks             o Finish all that you had on    o Eat dinner
o Have a good day           your to do list              o Sleep early
o Have a bad day

Good night and sleep well

Good Morning Sunshine!

Lets start the beginning of the month by noting down our details, so this way we can track changes every month

Age:
Weight:
Height:
Date of last menstrual cycle and time frame:

Did you…

o Get out of bed, woke        o Brush you teeth          o Eat breakfast
   up at:                     o Take a shower            o Take your meds
o Smile

Every little task is important sometimes we forget the silliest things so lets make a to-do list to keep track!

To-do list:

Good afternoon!

Did you…

o Eat lunch                   o Finish your tasks?

Good evening love, how's your day so far?

Did you…

o Eat snacks                  o Finish all that you had on    o Eat dinner
o Have a good day                your to do list              o Sleep early
o Have a bad day

Good night and sleep well

Good Morning Sunshine!

Lets start the beginning of the month by noting down our details, so this way we can track changes every month

Age:
Weight:
Height:
Date of last menstrual cycle and time frame:

Did you...

o Get out of bed, woke        o Brush you teeth          o Eat breakfast
   up at:                     o Take a shower           o Take your meds
o Smile

Every little task is important sometimes we forget the silliest things so lets make a to-do list to keep track!

To-do list:

Good afternoon!

Did you...

o Eat lunch                   o Finish your tasks?

Good evening love, how's your day so far?

Did you...

o Eat snacks                  o Finish all that you had on   o Eat dinner
o Have a good day                your to do list             o Sleep early
o Have a bad day

Good night and sleep well

Good Morning Sunshine!

Lets start the beginning of the month by noting down our details, so this way we can track changes every month

Age:
Weight:
Height:
Date of last menstrual cycle and time frame:

Did you...

o Get out of bed, woke      o Brush you teeth       o Eat breakfast
   up at:                   o Take a shower         o Take your meds
o Smile

Every little task is important sometimes we forget the silliest things so lets make a to-do list to keep track!

To-do list:

Good afternoon!

Did you...

o Eat lunch              o Finish your tasks?

Good evening love, how's your day so far?

Did you...

o Eat snacks             o Finish all that you had on    o Eat dinner
o Have a good day           your to do list             o Sleep early
o Have a bad day

Good night and sleep well

# This Month...

o I tried something new by...

o I helped somebody by...

o I become a better person by...

o I lost ____ kgs by...

o I gained ____kgs by...

o

o

o

# Habit Tracker

**Month:**

| | 1st | 2nd | 3rd | 4th | 5th | |
|---|---|---|---|---|---|---|
| Sleep | | | | | | |
| Caffeine | | | | | | |
| Alcohol | | | | | | |
| Cigarettes | | | | | | |
| Exercise | | | | | | |
| | 6th | 7th | 8th | 9th | 10th | |
| Sleep | | | | | | |
| Caffeine | | | | | | |
| Alcohol | | | | | | |
| Cigarettes | | | | | | |
| Exercise | | | | | | |
| | 11th | 12th | 13th | 14th | 15th | |
| Sleep | | | | | | |
| Caffeine | | | | | | |
| Alcohol | | | | | | |
| Cigarettes | | | | | | |
| Exercise | | | | | | |
| | 16th | 17th | 18th | 19th | 20th | |
| Sleep | | | | | | |
| Caffeine | | | | | | |
| Alcohol | | | | | | |
| Cigarettes | | | | | | |
| Exercise | | | | | | |
| | 21th | 22th | 23th | 24th | 25th | |
| Sleep | | | | | | |
| Caffeine | | | | | | |
| Alcohol | | | | | | |
| Cigarettes | | | | | | |
| Exercise | | | | | | |
| | 26th | 27th | 28th | 29th | 30th | 31st |
| Sleep | | | | | | |
| Caffeine | | | | | | |
| Alcohol | | | | | | |
| Cigarettes | | | | | | |
| Exercise | | | | | | |

# Emotion tracker

*How are you felling today? It is important to be in touch with yourself and your emotions.*

| | Anger | Hurt/Pain | Disappointment | Upset | Happy | Blah! | Lazy |
|---|---|---|---|---|---|---|---|
| 1st | | | | | | | |
| 2nd | | | | | | | |
| 3rd | | | | | | | |
| 4th | | | | | | | |
| 5th | | | | | | | |
| 6th | | | | | | | |
| 7th | | | | | | | |
| 8th | | | | | | | |
| 9th | | | | | | | |
| 10th | | | | | | | |
| 11th | | | | | | | |
| 12th | | | | | | | |
| 13th | | | | | | | |
| 14th | | | | | | | |
| 15th | | | | | | | |
| 16th | | | | | | | |
| 17th | | | | | | | |
| 18th | | | | | | | |
| 19th | | | | | | | |
| 20th | | | | | | | |
| 21st | | | | | | | |
| 22nd | | | | | | | |
| 23rd | | | | | | | |
| 24th | | | | | | | |
| 25th | | | | | | | |
| 26th | | | | | | | |
| 27th | | | | | | | |
| 28th | | | | | | | |
| 29th | | | | | | | |
| 30th | | | | | | | |
| 31st | | | | | | | |

|        | Guilt | Anxious | Sadness | Shame | Guilt | Worthless |
|--------|-------|---------|---------|-------|-------|-----------|
| 1st    |       |         |         |       |       |           |
| 2nd    |       |         |         |       |       |           |
| 3rd    |       |         |         |       |       |           |
| 4th    |       |         |         |       |       |           |
| 5th    |       |         |         |       |       |           |
| 6th    |       |         |         |       |       |           |
| 7th    |       |         |         |       |       |           |
| 8th    |       |         |         |       |       |           |
| 9th    |       |         |         |       |       |           |
| 10th   |       |         |         |       |       |           |
| 11th   |       |         |         |       |       |           |
| 12th   |       |         |         |       |       |           |
| 13th   |       |         |         |       |       |           |
| 14th   |       |         |         |       |       |           |
| 15th   |       |         |         |       |       |           |
| 16th   |       |         |         |       |       |           |
| 17th   |       |         |         |       |       |           |
| 18th   |       |         |         |       |       |           |
| 19th   |       |         |         |       |       |           |
| 20th   |       |         |         |       |       |           |
| 21st   |       |         |         |       |       |           |
| 22nd   |       |         |         |       |       |           |
| 23rd   |       |         |         |       |       |           |
| 24th   |       |         |         |       |       |           |
| 25th   |       |         |         |       |       |           |
| 26th   |       |         |         |       |       |           |
| 27th   |       |         |         |       |       |           |
| 28th   |       |         |         |       |       |           |
| 29th   |       |         |         |       |       |           |
| 30th   |       |         |         |       |       |           |
| 31st   |       |         |         |       |       |           |

# Food Tracker

| | Healthy food | Junk food | Both | Didn't eat ☹ |
|---|---|---|---|---|
| 1st | | | | |
| 2nd | | | | |
| 3rd | | | | |
| 4th | | | | |
| 5th | | | | |
| 6th | | | | |
| 7th | | | | |
| 8th | | | | |
| 9th | | | | |
| 10th | | | | |
| 11th | | | | |
| 12th | | | | |
| 13th | | | | |
| 14th | | | | |
| 15th | | | | |
| 16th | | | | |
| 17th | | | | |
| 18th | | | | |
| 19th | | | | |
| 20th | | | | |
| 21st | | | | |
| 22nd | | | | |
| 23rd | | | | |
| 24th | | | | |
| 25th | | | | |
| 26th | | | | |
| 27th | | | | |
| 28th | | | | |
| 29th | | | | |
| 30th | | | | |
| 31st | | | | |

# Weight Tracker

**Month:**

| | Kgs/lbs | | Kgs/lbs |
|---|---|---|---|
| 1st | | 16th | |
| 2nd | | 17th | |
| 3rd | | 18th | |
| 4th | | 19th | |
| 5th | | 20th | |
| 6th | | 21st | |
| 7th | | 22nd | |
| 8th | | 23rd | |
| 9th | | 24th | |
| 10th | | 25th | |
| 11th | | 26th | |
| 12th | | 27th | |
| 13th | | 28th | |
| 14th | | 29th | |
| 15th | | 30th | |
| | | 31st | |

# Journal

Good Morning Sunshine!

Lets start the beginning of the month by noting down our details, so this way we can track changes every month

Age:
Weight:
Height:
Date of last menstrual cycle and time frame:

Did you…

- o Get out of bed, woke up at:
- o Smile
- o Brush you teeth
- o Take a shower
- o Eat breakfast
- o Take your meds

Every little task is important sometimes we forget the silliest things so lets make a to-do list to keep track!

To-do list:

Good afternoon!

Did you…

- o Eat lunch
- o Finish your tasks?

Good evening love, how's your day so far?

Did you…

- o Eat snacks
- o Have a good day
- o Have a bad day
- o Finish all that you had on your to do list
- o Eat dinner
- o Sleep early

Good night and sleep well

dd/mm/yy

Good Morning Sunshine!

Lets start the beginning of the month by noting down our details, so this way we can track changes every month

Age:
Weight:
Height:
Date of last menstrual cycle and time frame:

Did you...

o Get out of bed, woke    o Brush you teeth       o Eat breakfast
  up at:               o Take a shower         o Take your meds
o Smile

Every little task is important sometimes we forget the silliest things so lets make a to-do list to keep track!

To-do list:

Good afternoon!

Did you...

o Eat lunch               o Finish your tasks?

Good evening love, how's your day so far?

Did you...

o Eat snacks              o Finish all that you had on    o Eat dinner
o Have a good day            your to do list              o Sleep early
o Have a bad day

Good night and sleep well

dd/mm/yy

Good Morning Sunshine!

Lets start the beginning of the month by noting down our details, so this way we can track changes every month

Age:
Weight:
Height:
Date of last menstrual cycle and time frame:

Did you…

- o Get out of bed, woke up at:
- o Smile
- o Brush you teeth
- o Take a shower
- o Eat breakfast
- o Take your meds

Every little task is important sometimes we forget the silliest things so lets make a to-do list to keep track!

To-do list:

Good afternoon!

Did you…

- o Eat lunch
- o Finish your tasks?

Good evening love, how's your day so far?

Did you…

- o Eat snacks
- o Have a good day
- o Have a bad day
- o Finish all that you had on your to do list
- o Eat dinner
- o Sleep early

Good night and sleep well

Good Morning Sunshine!

Lets start the beginning of the month by noting down our details, so this way we can track changes every month

Age:
Weight:
Height:
Date of last menstrual cycle and time frame:

Did you...

o Get out of bed, woke        o Brush you teeth        o Eat breakfast
   up at:        o Take a shower        o Take your meds
o Smile

Every little task is important sometimes we forget the silliest things so lets make a to-do list to keep track!

To-do list:

Good afternoon!

Did you...

o Eat lunch        o Finish your tasks?

Good evening love, how's your day so far?

Did you...

o Eat snacks        o Finish all that you had on        o Eat dinner
o Have a good day           your to do list        o Sleep early
o Have a bad day

Good night and sleep well

Good Morning Sunshine!

Lets start the beginning of the month by noting down our details, so this way we can track changes every month

Age:
Weight:
Height:
Date of last menstrual cycle and time frame:

Did you…

o Get out of bed, woke     o Brush you teeth      o Eat breakfast
  up at:                   o Take a shower        o Take your meds
o Smile

Every little task is important sometimes we forget the silliest things so lets make a to-do list to keep track!

To-do list:

Good afternoon!

Did you…

o Eat lunch               o Finish your tasks?

Good evening love, how's your day so far?

Did you…

o Eat snacks              o Finish all that you had on   o Eat dinner
o Have a good day           your to do list              o Sleep early
o Have a bad day

Good night and sleep well

dd/mm/yy

Good Morning Sunshine!

Lets start the beginning of the month by noting down our details, so this way we can track changes every month

Age:
Weight:
Height:
Date of last menstrual cycle and time frame:

Did you…

- o Get out of bed, woke up at:
- o Smile
- o Brush you teeth
- o Take a shower
- o Eat breakfast
- o Take your meds

Every little task is important sometimes we forget the silliest things so lets make a to-do list to keep track!

To-do list:

Good afternoon!

Did you…

- o Eat lunch
- o Finish your tasks?

Good evening love, how's your day so far?

Did you…

- o Eat snacks
- o Have a good day
- o Have a bad day
- o Finish all that you had on your to do list
- o Eat dinner
- o Sleep early

Good night and sleep well

dd/mm/yy

Good Morning Sunshine!

Lets start the beginning of the month by noting down our details, so this way we can track changes every month

Age:
Weight:
Height:
Date of last menstrual cycle and time frame:

Did you…

- o Get out of bed, woke up at:
- o Smile
- o Brush you teeth
- o Take a shower
- o Eat breakfast
- o Take your meds

Every little task is important sometimes we forget the silliest things so lets make a to-do list to keep track!

To-do list:

Good afternoon!

Did you…

- o Eat lunch
- o Finish your tasks?

Good evening love, how's your day so far?

Did you…

- o Eat snacks
- o Have a good day
- o Have a bad day
- o Finish all that you had on your to do list
- o Eat dinner
- o Sleep early

Good night and sleep well

Good Morning Sunshine!

Lets start the beginning of the month by noting down our details, so this way we can track changes every month

Age:
Weight:
Height:
Date of last menstrual cycle and time frame:

Did you…

o Get out of bed, woke    o Brush you teeth        o Eat breakfast
  up at:                 o Take a shower          o Take your meds
o Smile

Every little task is important sometimes we forget the silliest things so lets make a to-do list to keep track!

To-do list:

Good afternoon!

Did you…

o Eat lunch               o Finish your tasks?

Good evening love, how's your day so far?

Did you…

o Eat snacks              o Finish all that you had on   o Eat dinner
o Have a good day            your to do list            o Sleep early
o Have a bad day

Good night and sleep well

Good Morning Sunshine!

Lets start the beginning of the month by noting down our details, so this way we can track changes every month

Age:
Weight:
Height:
Date of last menstrual cycle and time frame:

Did you…

- o Get out of bed, woke
  up at:
- o Smile

- o Brush you teeth
- o Take a shower

- o Eat breakfast
- o Take your meds

Every little task is important sometimes we forget the silliest things so lets make a to-do list to keep track!

To-do list:

Good afternoon!

Did you…

- o Eat lunch

- o Finish your tasks?

Good evening love, how's your day so far?

Did you…

- o Eat snacks
- o Have a good day
- o Have a bad day

- o Finish all that you had on
  your to do list

- o Eat dinner
- o Sleep early

Good night and sleep well

dd/mm/yy

Good Morning Sunshine!

Lets start the beginning of the month by noting down our details, so this way we can track changes every month

Age:
Weight:
Height:
Date of last menstrual cycle and time frame:

Did you...

o Get out of bed, woke    o Brush you teeth    o Eat breakfast
    up at:              o Take a shower     o Take your meds
o Smile

Every little task is important sometimes we forget the silliest things so lets make a to-do list to keep track!

To-do list:

Good afternoon!

Did you...

o Eat lunch            o Finish your tasks?

Good evening love, how's your day so far?

Did you...

o Eat snacks       o Finish all that you had on   o Eat dinner
o Have a good day     your to do list           o Sleep early
o Have a bad day

Good night and sleep well

Good Morning Sunshine!

Lets start the beginning of the month by noting down our details, so this way we can track changes every month

Age:
Weight:
Height:
Date of last menstrual cycle and time frame:

Did you...

o Get out of bed, woke      o Brush you teeth          o Eat breakfast
  up at:                    o Take a shower            o Take your meds
o Smile

Every little task is important sometimes we forget the silliest things so lets make a to-do list to keep track!

To-do list:

Good afternoon!

Did you...

o Eat lunch                 o Finish your tasks?

Good evening love, how's your day so far?

Did you...

o Eat snacks                o Finish all that you had on    o Eat dinner
o Have a good day             your to do list               o Sleep early
o Have a bad day

Good night and sleep well

Good Morning Sunshine!

Lets start the beginning of the month by noting down our details, so this way we can track changes every month

Age:
Weight:
Height:
Date of last menstrual cycle and time frame:

Did you…

o Get out of bed, woke          o Brush you teeth          o Eat breakfast
   up at:                          o Take a shower            o Take your meds
o Smile

Every little task is important sometimes we forget the silliest things so lets make a to-do list to keep track!

To-do list:

Good afternoon!

Did you…

o Eat lunch                    o Finish your tasks?

Good evening love, how's your day so far?

Did you…

o Eat snacks              o Finish all that you had on    o Eat dinner
o Have a good day            your to do list                o Sleep early
o Have a bad day

Good night and sleep well

Good Morning Sunshine!

Lets start the beginning of the month by noting down our details, so this way we can track changes every month

Age:
Weight:
Height:
Date of last menstrual cycle and time frame:

Did you...

o Get out of bed, woke        o Brush you teeth        o Eat breakfast
   up at:                            o Take a shower        o Take your meds
o Smile

Every little task is important sometimes we forget the silliest things so lets make a to-do list to keep track!

To-do list:

Good afternoon!

Did you...

o Eat lunch                    o Finish your tasks?

Good evening love, how's your day so far?

Did you...

o Eat snacks          o Finish all that you had on    o Eat dinner
o Have a good day        your to do list              o Sleep early
o Have a bad day

Good night and sleep well

dd/mm/yy

Good Morning Sunshine!

Lets start the beginning of the month by noting down our details, so this way we can track changes every month

Age:
Weight:
Height:
Date of last menstrual cycle and time frame:

Did you…

o Get out of bed, woke        o Brush you teeth          o Eat breakfast
   up at:                     o Take a shower            o Take your meds
o Smile

Every little task is important sometimes we forget the silliest things so lets make a to-do list to keep track!

To-do list:

Good afternoon!

Did you…

o Eat lunch              o Finish your tasks?

Good evening love, how's your day so far?

Did you…

o Eat snacks             o Finish all that you had on   o Eat dinner
o Have a good day           your to do list             o Sleep early
o Have a bad day

Good night and sleep well

dd/mm/yy

Good Morning Sunshine!

Lets start the beginning of the month by noting down our details, so this way we can track changes every month

Age:
Weight:
Height:
Date of last menstrual cycle and time frame:

Did you…

- o Get out of bed, woke up at:
- o Smile
- o Brush you teeth
- o Take a shower
- o Eat breakfast
- o Take your meds

Every little task is important sometimes we forget the silliest things so lets make a to-do list to keep track!

To-do list:

Good afternoon!

Did you…

- o Eat lunch
- o Finish your tasks?

Good evening love, how's your day so far?

Did you…

- o Eat snacks
- o Have a good day
- o Have a bad day
- o Finish all that you had on your to do list
- o Eat dinner
- o Sleep early

Good night and sleep well

Good Morning Sunshine!

Lets start the beginning of the month by noting down our details, so this way we can track changes every month

Age:
Weight:
Height:
Date of last menstrual cycle and time frame:

Did you…

- o Get out of bed, woke up at:
- o Smile
- o Brush you teeth
- o Take a shower
- o Eat breakfast
- o Take your meds

Every little task is important sometimes we forget the silliest things so lets make a to-do list to keep track!

To-do list:

Good afternoon!

Did you…

- o Eat lunch
- o Finish your tasks?

Good evening love, how's your day so far?

Did you…

- o Eat snacks
- o Have a good day
- o Have a bad day
- o Finish all that you had on your to do list
- o Eat dinner
- o Sleep early

Good night and sleep well

Good Morning Sunshine!

Lets start the beginning of the month by noting down our details, so this way we can track changes every month

Age:
Weight:
Height:
Date of last menstrual cycle and time frame:

Did you…

o Get out of bed, woke    o Brush you teeth       o Eat breakfast
   up at:                 o Take a shower         o Take your meds
o Smile

Every little task is important sometimes we forget the silliest things so lets make a to-do list to keep track!

To-do list:

Good afternoon!

Did you…

o Eat lunch               o Finish your tasks?

Good evening love, how's your day so far?

Did you…

o Eat snacks              o Finish all that you had on   o Eat dinner
o Have a good day            your to do list            o Sleep early
o Have a bad day

Good night and sleep well

Good Morning Sunshine!

Lets start the beginning of the month by noting down our details, so this way we can track changes every month

Age:
Weight:
Height:
Date of last menstrual cycle and time frame:

Did you...

o Get out of bed, woke     o Brush you teeth        o Eat breakfast
   up at:                  o Take a shower          o Take your meds
o Smile

Every little task is important sometimes we forget the silliest things so lets make a to-do list to keep track!

To-do list:

Good afternoon!

Did you...

o Eat lunch              o Finish your tasks?

Good evening love, how's your day so far?

Did you...

o Eat snacks             o Finish all that you had on    o Eat dinner
o Have a good day           your to do list             o Sleep early
o Have a bad day

Good night and sleep well

Good Morning Sunshine!

Lets start the beginning of the month by noting down our details, so this way we can track changes every month

Age:
Weight:
Height:
Date of last menstrual cycle and time frame:

Did you...

o Get out of bed, woke      o Brush you teeth        o Eat breakfast
  up at:                    o Take a shower          o Take your meds
o Smile

Every little task is important sometimes we forget the silliest things so lets make a to-do list to keep track!

To-do list:

Good afternoon!

Did you...

o Eat lunch                 o Finish your tasks?

Good evening love, how's your day so far?

Did you...

o Eat snacks                o Finish all that you had on   o Eat dinner
o Have a good day             your to do list             o Sleep early
o Have a bad day

Good night and sleep well

Good Morning Sunshine!

Lets start the beginning of the month by noting down our details, so this way we can track changes every month

Age:
Weight:
Height:
Date of last menstrual cycle and time frame:

Did you…

- Get out of bed, woke
  up at:
- Smile
- Brush you teeth
- Take a shower
- Eat breakfast
- Take your meds

Every little task is important sometimes we forget the silliest things so lets make a to-do list to keep track!

To-do list:

Good afternoon!

Did you…

- Eat lunch
- Finish your tasks?

Good evening love, how's your day so far?

Did you…

- Eat snacks
- Have a good day
- Have a bad day
- Finish all that you had on
  your to do list
- Eat dinner
- Sleep early

Good night and sleep well

Good Morning Sunshine!

Lets start the beginning of the month by noting down our details, so this way we can track changes every month

Age:
Weight:
Height:
Date of last menstrual cycle and time frame:

Did you…

o Get out of bed, woke    o Brush you teeth    o Eat breakfast
  up at:                  o Take a shower      o Take your meds
o Smile

Every little task is important sometimes we forget the silliest things so lets make a to-do list to keep track!

To-do list:

Good afternoon!

Did you…

o Eat lunch            o Finish your tasks?

Good evening love, how's your day so far?

Did you…

o Eat snacks            o Finish all that you had on   o Eat dinner
o Have a good day         your to do list             o Sleep early
o Have a bad day

Good night and sleep well

Good Morning Sunshine!

Lets start the beginning of the month by noting down our details, so this way we can track changes every month

Age:
Weight:
Height:
Date of last menstrual cycle and time frame:

Did you...

o Get out of bed, woke    o Brush you teeth       o Eat breakfast
  up at:                  o Take a shower         o Take your meds
o Smile

Every little task is important sometimes we forget the silliest things so lets make a to-do list to keep track!

To-do list:

Good afternoon!

Did you...

o Eat lunch              o Finish your tasks?

Good evening love, how's your day so far?

Did you...

o Eat snacks             o Finish all that you had on   o Eat dinner
o Have a good day          your to do list              o Sleep early
o Have a bad day

Good night and sleep well

Good Morning Sunshine!

Lets start the beginning of the month by noting down our details, so this way we can track changes every month

Age:
Weight:
Height:
Date of last menstrual cycle and time frame:

Did you…

o Get out of bed, woke        o Brush you teeth        o Eat breakfast
  up at:                          o Take a shower          o Take your meds
o Smile

Every little task is important sometimes we forget the silliest things so lets make a to-do list to keep track!

To-do list:

Good afternoon!

Did you…

o Eat lunch                    o Finish your tasks?

Good evening love, how's your day so far?

Did you…

o Eat snacks              o Finish all that you had on    o Eat dinner
o Have a good day            your to do list              o Sleep early
o Have a bad day

Good night and sleep well

Good Morning Sunshine!

Lets start the beginning of the month by noting down our details, so this way we can track changes every month

Age:
Weight:
Height:
Date of last menstrual cycle and time frame:

Did you...

o Get out of bed, woke      o Brush you teeth        o Eat breakfast
   up at:                   o Take a shower          o Take your meds
o Smile

Every little task is important sometimes we forget the silliest things so lets make a to-do list to keep track!

To-do list:

Good afternoon!

Did you...

o Eat lunch                 o Finish your tasks?

Good evening love, how's your day so far?

Did you...

o Eat snacks                o Finish all that you had on   o Eat dinner
o Have a good day              your to do list              o Sleep early
o Have a bad day

Good night and sleep well

Good Morning Sunshine!

Lets start the beginning of the month by noting down our details, so this way we can track changes every month

Age:
Weight:
Height:
Date of last menstrual cycle and time frame:

Did you...

o Get out of bed, woke        o Brush you teeth          o Eat breakfast
   up at:                     o Take a shower            o Take your meds
o Smile

Every little task is important sometimes we forget the silliest things so lets make a to-do list to keep track!

To-do list:

Good afternoon!

Did you...

o Eat lunch                o Finish your tasks?

Good evening love, how's your day so far?

Did you...

o Eat snacks               o Finish all that you had on   o Eat dinner
o Have a good day             your to do list              o Sleep early
o Have a bad day

Good night and sleep well

Good Morning Sunshine!

Lets start the beginning of the month by noting down our details, so this way we can track changes every month

Age:
Weight:
Height:
Date of last menstrual cycle and time frame:

Did you…

o Get out of bed, woke    o Brush you teeth    o Eat breakfast
   up at:    o Take a shower    o Take your meds
o Smile

Every little task is important sometimes we forget the silliest things so lets make a to-do list to keep track!

To-do list:

Good afternoon!

Did you…

o Eat lunch    o Finish your tasks?

Good evening love, how's your day so far?

Did you…

o Eat snacks    o Finish all that you had on    o Eat dinner
o Have a good day      your to do list    o Sleep early
o Have a bad day

Good night and sleep well

Good Morning Sunshine!

Lets start the beginning of the month by noting down our details, so this way we can track changes every month

Age:
Weight:
Height:
Date of last menstrual cycle and time frame:

Did you…

o Get out of bed, woke        o Brush you teeth        o Eat breakfast
  up at:                      o Take a shower          o Take your meds
o Smile

Every little task is important sometimes we forget the silliest things so lets make a to-do list to keep track!

To-do list:

Good afternoon!

Did you…

o Eat lunch            o Finish your tasks?

Good evening love, how's your day so far?

Did you…

o Eat snacks           o Finish all that you had on    o Eat dinner
o Have a good day        your to do list               o Sleep early
o Have a bad day

Good night and sleep well

Good Morning Sunshine!

Lets start the beginning of the month by noting down our details, so this way we can track changes every month

Age:
Weight:
Height:
Date of last menstrual cycle and time frame:

Did you…

o Get out of bed, woke      o Brush you teeth        o Eat breakfast
   up at:                   o Take a shower          o Take your meds
o Smile

Every little task is important sometimes we forget the silliest things so lets make a to-do list to keep track!

To-do list:

Good afternoon!

Did you…

o Eat lunch                o Finish your tasks?

Good evening love, how's your day so far?

Did you…

o Eat snacks               o Finish all that you had on    o Eat dinner
o Have a good day             your to do list              o Sleep early
o Have a bad day

Good night and sleep well

Good Morning Sunshine!

Lets start the beginning of the month by noting down our details, so this way we can track changes every month

Age:
Weight:
Height:
Date of last menstrual cycle and time frame:

Did you…

- o Get out of bed, woke up at:
- o Smile
- o Brush you teeth
- o Take a shower
- o Eat breakfast
- o Take your meds

Every little task is important sometimes we forget the silliest things so lets make a to-do list to keep track!

To-do list:

Good afternoon!

Did you…

- o Eat lunch
- o Finish your tasks?

Good evening love, how's your day so far?

Did you…

- o Eat snacks
- o Have a good day
- o Have a bad day
- o Finish all that you had on your to do list
- o Eat dinner
- o Sleep early

Good night and sleep well

Good Morning Sunshine!

Lets start the beginning of the month by noting down our details, so this way we can track changes every month

Age:
Weight:
Height:
Date of last menstrual cycle and time frame:

Did you…

o Get out of bed, woke    o Brush you teeth       o Eat breakfast
  up at:                  o Take a shower         o Take your meds
o Smile

Every little task is important sometimes we forget the silliest things so lets make a to-do list to keep track!

To-do list:

Good afternoon!

Did you…

o Eat lunch               o Finish your tasks?

Good evening love, how's your day so far?

Did you…

o Eat snacks              o Finish all that you had on   o Eat dinner
o Have a good day           your to do list              o Sleep early
o Have a bad day

Good night and sleep well

dd/mm/yy

Good Morning Sunshine!

Lets start the beginning of the month by noting down our details, so this way we can track changes every month

Age:
Weight:
Height:
Date of last menstrual cycle and time frame:

Did you…

- o Get out of bed, woke up at:
- o Smile

- o Brush you teeth
- o Take a shower

- o Eat breakfast
- o Take your meds

Every little task is important sometimes we forget the silliest things so lets make a to-do list to keep track!

To-do list:

Good afternoon!

Did you…

- o Eat lunch

- o Finish your tasks?

Good evening love, how's your day so far?

Did you…

- o Eat snacks
- o Have a good day
- o Have a bad day

- o Finish all that you had on your to do list

- o Eat dinner
- o Sleep early

Good night and sleep well

# This Month...

o I tried something new by…

o I helped somebody by…

o I become a better person by…

o I lost ____ kgs by…

o I gained ____kgs by…

o

o

o

# Habit Tracker

**Month:**

| | 1st | 2nd | 3rd | 4th | 5th | |
|---|---|---|---|---|---|---|
| Sleep | | | | | | |
| Caffeine | | | | | | |
| Alcohol | | | | | | |
| Cigarettes | | | | | | |
| Exercise | | | | | | |
| | 6th | 7th | 8th | 9th | 10th | |
| Sleep | | | | | | |
| Caffeine | | | | | | |
| Alcohol | | | | | | |
| Cigarettes | | | | | | |
| Exercise | | | | | | |
| | 11th | 12th | 13th | 14th | 15th | |
| Sleep | | | | | | |
| Caffeine | | | | | | |
| Alcohol | | | | | | |
| Cigarettes | | | | | | |
| Exercise | | | | | | |
| | 16th | 17th | 18th | 19th | 20th | |
| Sleep | | | | | | |
| Caffeine | | | | | | |
| Alcohol | | | | | | |
| Cigarettes | | | | | | |
| Exercise | | | | | | |
| | 21th | 22th | 23th | 24th | 25th | |
| Sleep | | | | | | |
| Caffeine | | | | | | |
| Alcohol | | | | | | |
| Cigarettes | | | | | | |
| Exercise | | | | | | |
| | 26th | 27th | 28th | 29th | 30th | 31st |
| Sleep | | | | | | |
| Caffeine | | | | | | |
| Alcohol | | | | | | |
| Cigarettes | | | | | | |
| Exercise | | | | | | |

# Emotion tracker

*How are you felling today? It is important to be in touch with yourself and your emotions.*

|  | Anger | Hurt/Pain | Disappointment | Upset | Happy | Blah! | Lazy |
|---|---|---|---|---|---|---|---|
| 1st |  |  |  |  |  |  |  |
| 2nd |  |  |  |  |  |  |  |
| 3rd |  |  |  |  |  |  |  |
| 4th |  |  |  |  |  |  |  |
| 5th |  |  |  |  |  |  |  |
| 6th |  |  |  |  |  |  |  |
| 7th |  |  |  |  |  |  |  |
| 8th |  |  |  |  |  |  |  |
| 9th |  |  |  |  |  |  |  |
| 10th |  |  |  |  |  |  |  |
| 11th |  |  |  |  |  |  |  |
| 12th |  |  |  |  |  |  |  |
| 13th |  |  |  |  |  |  |  |
| 14th |  |  |  |  |  |  |  |
| 15th |  |  |  |  |  |  |  |
| 16th |  |  |  |  |  |  |  |
| 17th |  |  |  |  |  |  |  |
| 18th |  |  |  |  |  |  |  |
| 19th |  |  |  |  |  |  |  |
| 20th |  |  |  |  |  |  |  |
| 21st |  |  |  |  |  |  |  |
| 22nd |  |  |  |  |  |  |  |
| 23rd |  |  |  |  |  |  |  |
| 24th |  |  |  |  |  |  |  |
| 25th |  |  |  |  |  |  |  |
| 26th |  |  |  |  |  |  |  |
| 27th |  |  |  |  |  |  |  |
| 28th |  |  |  |  |  |  |  |
| 29th |  |  |  |  |  |  |  |
| 30th |  |  |  |  |  |  |  |
| 31st |  |  |  |  |  |  |  |

|  | Guilt | Anxious | Sadness | Shame | Guilt | Worthless |
|---|---|---|---|---|---|---|
| 1st |  |  |  |  |  |  |
| 2nd |  |  |  |  |  |  |
| 3rd |  |  |  |  |  |  |
| 4th |  |  |  |  |  |  |
| 5th |  |  |  |  |  |  |
| 6th |  |  |  |  |  |  |
| 7th |  |  |  |  |  |  |
| 8th |  |  |  |  |  |  |
| 9th |  |  |  |  |  |  |
| 10th |  |  |  |  |  |  |
| 11th |  |  |  |  |  |  |
| 12th |  |  |  |  |  |  |
| 13th |  |  |  |  |  |  |
| 14th |  |  |  |  |  |  |
| 15th |  |  |  |  |  |  |
| 16th |  |  |  |  |  |  |
| 17th |  |  |  |  |  |  |
| 18th |  |  |  |  |  |  |
| 19th |  |  |  |  |  |  |
| 20th |  |  |  |  |  |  |
| 21st |  |  |  |  |  |  |
| 22nd |  |  |  |  |  |  |
| 23rd |  |  |  |  |  |  |
| 24th |  |  |  |  |  |  |
| 25th |  |  |  |  |  |  |
| 26th |  |  |  |  |  |  |
| 27th |  |  |  |  |  |  |
| 28th |  |  |  |  |  |  |
| 29th |  |  |  |  |  |  |
| 30th |  |  |  |  |  |  |
| 31st |  |  |  |  |  |  |

# Food Tracker

| | Healthy food | Junk food | Both | Didn't eat ☹ |
|---|---|---|---|---|
| 1st | | | | |
| 2nd | | | | |
| 3rd | | | | |
| 4th | | | | |
| 5th | | | | |
| 6th | | | | |
| 7th | | | | |
| 8th | | | | |
| 9th | | | | |
| 10th | | | | |
| 11th | | | | |
| 12th | | | | |
| 13th | | | | |
| 14th | | | | |
| 15th | | | | |
| 16th | | | | |
| 17th | | | | |
| 18th | | | | |
| 19th | | | | |
| 20th | | | | |
| 21st | | | | |
| 22nd | | | | |
| 23rd | | | | |
| 24th | | | | |
| 25th | | | | |
| 26th | | | | |
| 27th | | | | |
| 28th | | | | |
| 29th | | | | |
| 30th | | | | |
| 31st | | | | |

# Weight Tracker

**Month:**

| | Kgs/lbs | | Kgs/lbs |
|---|---|---|---|
| 1st | | 16th | |
| 2nd | | 17th | |
| 3rd | | 18th | |
| 4th | | 19th | |
| 5th | | 20th | |
| 6th | | 21st | |
| 7th | | 22nd | |
| 8th | | 23rd | |
| 9th | | 24th | |
| 10th | | 25th | |
| 11th | | 26th | |
| 12th | | 27th | |
| 13th | | 28th | |
| 14th | | 29th | |
| 15th | | 30th | |
| | | 31st | |

# Journal

Good Morning Sunshine!

Lets start the beginning of the month by noting down our details, so this way we can track changes every month

Age:
Weight:
Height:
Date of last menstrual cycle and time frame:

Did you…

- o Get out of bed, woke up at:
- o Smile

- o Brush you teeth
- o Take a shower

- o Eat breakfast
- o Take your meds

Every little task is important sometimes we forget the silliest things so lets make a to-do list to keep track!

To-do list:

Good afternoon!

Did you…

- o Eat lunch

- o Finish your tasks?

Good evening love, how's your day so far?

Did you…

- o Eat snacks
- o Have a good day
- o Have a bad day

- o Finish all that you had on your to do list

- o Eat dinner
- o Sleep early

Good night and sleep well

Good Morning Sunshine!

Lets start the beginning of the month by noting down our details, so this way we can track changes every month

Age:
Weight:
Height:
Date of last menstrual cycle and time frame:

Did you…

o Get out of bed, woke        o Brush you teeth        o Eat breakfast
  up at:                      o Take a shower          o Take your meds
o Smile

Every little task is important sometimes we forget the silliest things so lets make a to-do list to keep track!

To-do list:

Good afternoon!

Did you…

o Eat lunch              o Finish your tasks?

Good evening love, how's your day so far?

Did you…

o Eat snacks             o Finish all that you had on    o Eat dinner
o Have a good day          your to do list               o Sleep early
o Have a bad day

Good night and sleep well

Good Morning Sunshine!

Lets start the beginning of the month by noting down our details, so this way we can track changes every month

Age:
Weight:
Height:
Date of last menstrual cycle and time frame:

Did you...

o Get out of bed, woke      o Brush you teeth       o Eat breakfast
  up at:                     o Take a shower         o Take your meds
o Smile

Every little task is important sometimes we forget the silliest things so lets make a to-do list to keep track!

To-do list:

Good afternoon!

Did you...

o Eat lunch                 o Finish your tasks?

Good evening love, how's your day so far?

Did you...

o Eat snacks                o Finish all that you had on    o Eat dinner
o Have a good day             your to do list                o Sleep early
o Have a bad day

Good night and sleep well

Good Morning Sunshine!

Lets start the beginning of the month by noting down our details, so this way we can track changes every month

Age:
Weight:
Height:
Date of last menstrual cycle and time frame:

Did you...

| | | |
|---|---|---|
| o Get out of bed, woke up at: | o Brush you teeth | o Eat breakfast |
| | o Take a shower | o Take your meds |
| o Smile | | |

Every little task is important sometimes we forget the silliest things so lets make a to-do list to keep track!

To-do list:

Good afternoon!

Did you...

o Eat lunch          o Finish your tasks?

Good evening love, how's your day so far?

Did you...

| | | |
|---|---|---|
| o Eat snacks | o Finish all that you had on your to do list | o Eat dinner |
| o Have a good day | | o Sleep early |
| o Have a bad day | | |

Good night and sleep well

Good Morning Sunshine!

Lets start the beginning of the month by noting down our details, so this way we can track changes every month

Age:
Weight:
Height:
Date of last menstrual cycle and time frame:

Did you…

- o Get out of bed, woke up at:
- o Smile
- o Brush you teeth
- o Take a shower
- o Eat breakfast
- o Take your meds

Every little task is important sometimes we forget the silliest things so lets make a to-do list to keep track!

To-do list:

Good afternoon!

Did you…

- o Eat lunch
- o Finish your tasks?

Good evening love, how's your day so far?

Did you…

- o Eat snacks
- o Have a good day
- o Have a bad day
- o Finish all that you had on your to do list
- o Eat dinner
- o Sleep early

Good night and sleep well

dd/mm/yy

Good Morning Sunshine!

Lets start the beginning of the month by noting down our details, so this way we can track changes every month

Age:
Weight:
Height:
Date of last menstrual cycle and time frame:

Did you…

o Get out of bed, woke      o Brush you teeth        o Eat breakfast
   up at:                   o Take a shower          o Take your meds
o Smile

Every little task is important sometimes we forget the silliest things so lets make a to-do list to keep track!

To-do list:

Good afternoon!

Did you…

o Eat lunch              o Finish your tasks?

Good evening love, how's your day so far?

Did you…

o Eat snacks             o Finish all that you had on   o Eat dinner
o Have a good day           your to do list            o Sleep early
o Have a bad day

Good night and sleep well

Good Morning Sunshine!

Lets start the beginning of the month by noting down our details, so this way we can track changes every month

Age:
Weight:
Height:
Date of last menstrual cycle and time frame:

Did you…

- o Get out of bed, woke up at:
- o Smile

- o Brush you teeth
- o Take a shower

- o Eat breakfast
- o Take your meds

Every little task is important sometimes we forget the silliest things so lets make a to-do list to keep track!

To-do list:

Good afternoon!

Did you…

- o Eat lunch

- o Finish your tasks?

Good evening love, how's your day so far?

Did you…

- o Eat snacks
- o Have a good day
- o Have a bad day

- o Finish all that you had on your to do list

- o Eat dinner
- o Sleep early

Good night and sleep well

Good Morning Sunshine!

Lets start the beginning of the month by noting down our details, so this way we can track changes every month

Age:
Weight:
Height:
Date of last menstrual cycle and time frame:

Did you…

o Get out of bed, woke        o Brush you teeth        o Eat breakfast
   up at:                              o Take a shower         o Take your meds
o Smile

Every little task is important sometimes we forget the silliest things so lets make a to-do list to keep track!

To-do list:

Good afternoon!

Did you…

o Eat lunch                    o Finish your tasks?

Good evening love, how's your day so far?

Did you…

o Eat snacks                  o Finish all that you had on    o Eat dinner
o Have a good day            your to do list                 o Sleep early
o Have a bad day

Good night and sleep well

Good Morning Sunshine!

Lets start the beginning of the month by noting down our details, so this way we can track changes every month

Age:
Weight:
Height:
Date of last menstrual cycle and time frame:

Did you...

o Get out of bed, woke      o Brush you teeth        o Eat breakfast
   up at:                   o Take a shower          o Take your meds
o Smile

Every little task is important sometimes we forget the silliest things so lets make a to-do list to keep track!

To-do list:

Good afternoon!

Did you...

o Eat lunch              o Finish your tasks?

Good evening love, how's your day so far?

Did you...

o Eat snacks            o Finish all that you had on   o Eat dinner
o Have a good day          your to do list            o Sleep early
o Have a bad day

Good night and sleep well

Good Morning Sunshine!

Lets start the beginning of the month by noting down our details, so this way we can track changes every month

Age:
Weight:
Height:
Date of last menstrual cycle and time frame:

Did you…

o Get out of bed, woke     o Brush you teeth          o Eat breakfast
  up at:                 o Take a shower            o Take your meds
o Smile

Every little task is important sometimes we forget the silliest things so lets make a to-do list to keep track!

To-do list:



Good afternoon!

Did you…

o Eat lunch                o Finish your tasks?

Good evening love, how's your day so far?

Did you…

o Eat snacks               o Finish all that you had on   o Eat dinner
o Have a good day            your to do list            o Sleep early
o Have a bad day

Good night and sleep well

Good Morning Sunshine!

Lets start the beginning of the month by noting down our details, so this way we can track changes every month

Age:
Weight:
Height:
Date of last menstrual cycle and time frame:

Did you…

o Get out of bed, woke    o Brush you teeth    o Eat breakfast
  up at:    o Take a shower    o Take your meds
o Smile

Every little task is important sometimes we forget the silliest things so lets make a to-do list to keep track!

To-do list:

Good afternoon!

Did you…

o Eat lunch    o Finish your tasks?

Good evening love, how's your day so far?

Did you…

o Eat snacks    o Finish all that you had on    o Eat dinner
o Have a good day      your to do list    o Sleep early
o Have a bad day

Good night and sleep well

Good Morning Sunshine!

Lets start the beginning of the month by noting down our details, so this way we can track changes every month

Age:
Weight:
Height:
Date of last menstrual cycle and time frame:

Did you...

o Get out of bed, woke       o Brush you teeth        o Eat breakfast
  up at:                     o Take a shower          o Take your meds
o Smile

Every little task is important sometimes we forget the silliest things so lets make a to-do list to keep track!

To-do list:

Good afternoon!

Did you...

o Eat lunch                  o Finish your tasks?

Good evening love, how's your day so far?

Did you...

o Eat snacks                 o Finish all that you had on   o Eat dinner
o Have a good day              your to do list              o Sleep early
o Have a bad day

Good night and sleep well

Good Morning Sunshine!

Lets start the beginning of the month by noting down our details, so this way we can track changes every month

Age:
Weight:
Height:
Date of last menstrual cycle and time frame:

Did you...

o Get out of bed, woke      o Brush you teeth       o Eat breakfast
   up at:                   o Take a shower         o Take your meds
o Smile

Every little task is important sometimes we forget the silliest things so lets make a to-do list to keep track!

To-do list:

Good afternoon!

Did you...

o Eat lunch                 o Finish your tasks?

Good evening love, how's your day so far?

Did you...

o Eat snacks                o Finish all that you had on   o Eat dinner
o Have a good day              your to do list            o Sleep early
o Have a bad day

Good night and sleep well

Good Morning Sunshine!

Lets start the beginning of the month by noting down our details, so this way we can track changes every month

Age:
Weight:
Height:
Date of last menstrual cycle and time frame:

Did you…

o Get out of bed, woke        o Brush you teeth        o Eat breakfast
   up at:                     o Take a shower          o Take your meds
o Smile

Every little task is important sometimes we forget the silliest things so lets make a to-do list to keep track!

To-do list:

Good afternoon!

Did you…

o Eat lunch                   o Finish your tasks?

Good evening love, how's your day so far?

Did you…

o Eat snacks                  o Finish all that you had on    o Eat dinner
o Have a good day                your to do list             o Sleep early
o Have a bad day

Good night and sleep well

Good Morning Sunshine!

Lets start the beginning of the month by noting down our details, so this way we can track changes every month

Age:
Weight:
Height:
Date of last menstrual cycle and time frame:

Did you…

o Get out of bed, woke    o Brush you teeth    o Eat breakfast
    up at:                o Take a shower    o Take your meds
o Smile

Every little task is important sometimes we forget the silliest things so lets make a to-do list to keep track!

To-do list:

Good afternoon!

Did you…

o Eat lunch               o Finish your tasks?

Good evening love, how's your day so far?

Did you…

o Eat snacks        o Finish all that you had on    o Eat dinner
o Have a good day        your to do list           o Sleep early
o Have a bad day

Good night and sleep well

Good Morning Sunshine!

Lets start the beginning of the month by noting down our details, so this way we can track changes every month

Age:
Weight:
Height:
Date of last menstrual cycle and time frame:

Did you…

- o Get out of bed, woke up at:
- o Smile
- o Brush you teeth
- o Take a shower
- o Eat breakfast
- o Take your meds

Every little task is important sometimes we forget the silliest things so lets make a to-do list to keep track!

To-do list:

Good afternoon!

Did you…

- o Eat lunch
- o Finish your tasks?

Good evening love, how's your day so far?

Did you…

- o Eat snacks
- o Have a good day
- o Have a bad day
- o Finish all that you had on your to do list
- o Eat dinner
- o Sleep early

Good night and sleep well

Good Morning Sunshine!

Lets start the beginning of the month by noting down our details, so this way we can track changes every month

Age:
Weight:
Height:
Date of last menstrual cycle and time frame:

Did you...

o Get out of bed, woke    o Brush you teeth      o Eat breakfast
   up at:                o Take a shower        o Take your meds
o Smile

Every little task is important sometimes we forget the silliest things so lets make a to-do list to keep track!

To-do list:

Good afternoon!

Did you...

o Eat lunch                o Finish your tasks?

Good evening love, how's your day so far?

Did you...

o Eat snacks               o Finish all that you had on    o Eat dinner
o Have a good day            your to do list          o Sleep early
o Have a bad day

Good night and sleep well

dd/mm/yy

Good Morning Sunshine!

Lets start the beginning of the month by noting down our details, so this way we can track changes every month

Age:
Weight:
Height:
Date of last menstrual cycle and time frame:

Did you…

- o Get out of bed, woke up at:
- o Smile
- o Brush you teeth
- o Take a shower
- o Eat breakfast
- o Take your meds

Every little task is important sometimes we forget the silliest things so lets make a to-do list to keep track!

To-do list:

Good afternoon!

Did you…

- o Eat lunch
- o Finish your tasks?

Good evening love, how's your day so far?

Did you…

- o Eat snacks
- o Have a good day
- o Have a bad day
- o Finish all that you had on your to do list
- o Eat dinner
- o Sleep early

Good night and sleep well

dd/mm/yy

Good Morning Sunshine!

Lets start the beginning of the month by noting down our details, so this way we can track changes every month

Age:
Weight:
Height:
Date of last menstrual cycle and time frame:

Did you...

o Get out of bed, woke    o Brush you teeth    o Eat breakfast
   up at:    o Take a shower    o Take your meds
o Smile

Every little task is important sometimes we forget the silliest things so lets make a to-do list to keep track!

To-do list:

Good afternoon!

Did you...

o Eat lunch      o Finish your tasks?

Good evening love, how's your day so far?

Did you...

o Eat snacks    o Finish all that you had on   o Eat dinner
o Have a good day     your to do list    o Sleep early
o Have a bad day

Good night and sleep well

Good Morning Sunshine!

Lets start the beginning of the month by noting down our details, so this way we can track changes every month

Age:
Weight:
Height:
Date of last menstrual cycle and time frame:

Did you...

o Get out of bed, woke      o Brush you teeth       o Eat breakfast
   up at:                    o Take a shower         o Take your meds
o Smile

Every little task is important sometimes we forget the silliest things so lets make a to-do list to keep track!

To-do list:

Good afternoon!

Did you...

o Eat lunch                  o Finish your tasks?

Good evening love, how's your day so far?

Did you...

o Eat snacks                 o Finish all that you had on    o Eat dinner
o Have a good day               your to do list               o Sleep early
o Have a bad day

Good night and sleep well

Good Morning Sunshine!

Lets start the beginning of the month by noting down our details, so this way we can track changes every month

Age:
Weight:
Height:
Date of last menstrual cycle and time frame:

Did you...

o Get out of bed, woke    o Brush you teeth    o Eat breakfast
   up at:    o Take a shower    o Take your meds
o Smile

Every little task is important sometimes we forget the silliest things so lets make a to-do list to keep track!

To-do list:

Good afternoon!

Did you...

o Eat lunch    o Finish your tasks?

Good evening love, how's your day so far?

Did you...

o Eat snacks    o Finish all that you had on    o Eat dinner
o Have a good day       your to do list    o Sleep early
o Have a bad day

Good night and sleep well

Good Morning Sunshine!

Lets start the beginning of the month by noting down our details, so this way we can track changes every month

Age:
Weight:
Height:
Date of last menstrual cycle and time frame:

Did you…

o Get out of bed, woke    o Brush you teeth       o Eat breakfast
   up at:                 o Take a shower         o Take your meds
o Smile

Every little task is important sometimes we forget the silliest things so lets make a to-do list to keep track!

To-do list:

Good afternoon!

Did you…

o Eat lunch              o Finish your tasks?

Good evening love, how's your day so far?

Did you…

o Eat snacks             o Finish all that you had on    o Eat dinner
o Have a good day           your to do list               o Sleep early
o Have a bad day

Good night and sleep well

Good Morning Sunshine!

Lets start the beginning of the month by noting down our details, so this way we can track changes every month

Age:
Weight:
Height:
Date of last menstrual cycle and time frame:

Did you...

- o Get out of bed, woke   up at:
- o Smile
- o Brush you teeth
- o Take a shower
- o Eat breakfast
- o Take your meds

Every little task is important sometimes we forget the silliest things so lets make a to-do list to keep track!

To-do list:

Good afternoon!

Did you...

- o Eat lunch
- o Finish your tasks?

Good evening love, how's your day so far?

Did you...

- o Eat snacks
- o Have a good day
- o Have a bad day
- o Finish all that you had on   your to do list
- o Eat dinner
- o Sleep early

Good night and sleep well

Good Morning Sunshine!

Lets start the beginning of the month by noting down our details, so this way we can track changes every month

Age:
Weight:
Height:
Date of last menstrual cycle and time frame:

Did you…

o Get out of bed, woke    o Brush you teeth       o Eat breakfast
   up at:                 o Take a shower         o Take your meds
o Smile

Every little task is important sometimes we forget the silliest things so lets make a to-do list to keep track!

To-do list:

Good afternoon!

Did you…

o Eat lunch              o Finish your tasks?

Good evening love, how's your day so far?

Did you…

o Eat snacks             o Finish all that you had on   o Eat dinner
o Have a good day           your to do list             o Sleep early
o Have a bad day

Good night and sleep well

Good Morning Sunshine!

Lets start the beginning of the month by noting down our details, so this way we can track changes every month

Age:
Weight:
Height:
Date of last menstrual cycle and time frame:

Did you…

- o Get out of bed, woke up at:
- o Smile
- o Brush you teeth
- o Take a shower
- o Eat breakfast
- o Take your meds

Every little task is important sometimes we forget the silliest things so lets make a to-do list to keep track!

To-do list:

Good afternoon!

Did you…

- o Eat lunch
- o Finish your tasks?

Good evening love, how's your day so far?

Did you…

- o Eat snacks
- o Have a good day
- o Have a bad day
- o Finish all that you had on your to do list
- o Eat dinner
- o Sleep early

Good night and sleep well

Good Morning Sunshine!

Lets start the beginning of the month by noting down our details, so this way we can track changes every month

Age:
Weight:
Height:
Date of last menstrual cycle and time frame:

Did you…

o Get out of bed, woke      o Brush you teeth          o Eat breakfast
   up at:                   o Take a shower            o Take your meds
o Smile

Every little task is important sometimes we forget the silliest things so lets make a to-do list to keep track!

To-do list:

Good afternoon!

Did you…

o Eat lunch                 o Finish your tasks?

Good evening love, how's your day so far?

Did you…

o Eat snacks                o Finish all that you had on   o Eat dinner
o Have a good day              your to do list            o Sleep early
o Have a bad day

Good night and sleep well

Good Morning Sunshine!

Lets start the beginning of the month by noting down our details, so this way we can track changes every month

Age:
Weight:
Height:
Date of last menstrual cycle and time frame:

Did you…

- o Get out of bed, woke up at:
- o Smile

- o Brush you teeth
- o Take a shower

- o Eat breakfast
- o Take your meds

Every little task is important sometimes we forget the silliest things so lets make a to-do list to keep track!

To-do list:

Good afternoon!

Did you…

- o Eat lunch

- o Finish your tasks?

Good evening love, how's your day so far?

Did you…

- o Eat snacks
- o Have a good day
- o Have a bad day

- o Finish all that you had on your to do list

- o Eat dinner
- o Sleep early

Good night and sleep well

Good Morning Sunshine!

Lets start the beginning of the month by noting down our details, so this way we can track changes every month

Age:
Weight:
Height:
Date of last menstrual cycle and time frame:

Did you…

o Get out of bed, woke
   up at:
o Smile

o Brush you teeth
o Take a shower

o Eat breakfast
o Take your meds

Every little task is important sometimes we forget the silliest things so lets make a to-do list to keep track!

To-do list:

Good afternoon!

Did you…

o Eat lunch

o Finish your tasks?

Good evening love, how's your day so far?

Did you…

o Eat snacks
o Have a good day
o Have a bad day

o Finish all that you had on
   your to do list

o Eat dinner
o Sleep early

Good night and sleep well

Good Morning Sunshine!

Lets start the beginning of the month by noting down our details, so this way we can track changes every month

Age:
Weight:
Height:
Date of last menstrual cycle and time frame:

Did you...

| | | |
|---|---|---|
| o Get out of bed, woke up at: | o Brush you teeth | o Eat breakfast |
| o Smile | o Take a shower | o Take your meds |

Every little task is important sometimes we forget the silliest things so lets make a to-do list to keep track!

To-do list:

Good afternoon!

Did you...

o Eat lunch          o Finish your tasks?

Good evening love, how's your day so far?

Did you...

| | | |
|---|---|---|
| o Eat snacks | o Finish all that you had on your to do list | o Eat dinner |
| o Have a good day | | o Sleep early |
| o Have a bad day | | |

Good night and sleep well

Good Morning Sunshine!

Lets start the beginning of the month by noting down our details, so this way we can track changes every month

Age:
Weight:
Height:
Date of last menstrual cycle and time frame:

Did you...

o Get out of bed, woke          o Brush you teeth          o Eat breakfast
   up at:          o Take a shower          o Take your meds
o Smile

Every little task is important sometimes we forget the silliest things so lets make a to-do list to keep track!

To-do list:

Good afternoon!

Did you...

o Eat lunch          o Finish your tasks?

Good evening love, how's your day so far?

Did you...

o Eat snacks          o Finish all that you had on          o Eat dinner
o Have a good day             your to do list          o Sleep early
o Have a bad day

Good night and sleep well

dd/mm/yy

Good Morning Sunshine!

Lets start the beginning of the month by noting down our details, so this way we can track changes every month

Age:
Weight:
Height:
Date of last menstrual cycle and time frame:

Did you…

- o Get out of bed, woke up at:
- o Smile
- o Brush you teeth
- o Take a shower
- o Eat breakfast
- o Take your meds

Every little task is important sometimes we forget the silliest things so lets make a to-do list to keep track!

To-do list:

Good afternoon!

Did you…

- o Eat lunch
- o Finish your tasks?

Good evening love, how's your day so far?

Did you…

- o Eat snacks
- o Have a good day
- o Have a bad day
- o Finish all that you had on your to do list
- o Eat dinner
- o Sleep early

Good night and sleep well

# This Month...

o I tried something new by…


o I helped somebody by…


o I become a better person by…


o I lost ___ kgs by…


o I gained ___kgs by…

o

o

o

# Habit Tracker

**Month:**

|            | 1st | 2nd | 3rd | 4th | 5th |     |
|------------|-----|-----|-----|-----|-----|-----|
| Sleep      |     |     |     |     |     |     |
| Caffeine   |     |     |     |     |     |     |
| Alcohol    |     |     |     |     |     |     |
| Cigarettes |     |     |     |     |     |     |
| Exercise   |     |     |     |     |     |     |
|            | 6th | 7th | 8th | 9th | 10th |    |
| Sleep      |     |     |     |     |     |     |
| Caffeine   |     |     |     |     |     |     |
| Alcohol    |     |     |     |     |     |     |
| Cigarettes |     |     |     |     |     |     |
| Exercise   |     |     |     |     |     |     |
|            | 11th | 12th | 13th | 14th | 15th |  |
| Sleep      |     |     |     |     |     |     |
| Caffeine   |     |     |     |     |     |     |
| Alcohol    |     |     |     |     |     |     |
| Cigarettes |     |     |     |     |     |     |
| Exercise   |     |     |     |     |     |     |
|            | 16th | 17th | 18th | 19th | 20th |  |
| Sleep      |     |     |     |     |     |     |
| Caffeine   |     |     |     |     |     |     |
| Alcohol    |     |     |     |     |     |     |
| Cigarettes |     |     |     |     |     |     |
| Exercise   |     |     |     |     |     |     |
|            | 21th | 22th | 23th | 24th | 25th |  |
| Sleep      |     |     |     |     |     |     |
| Caffeine   |     |     |     |     |     |     |
| Alcohol    |     |     |     |     |     |     |
| Cigarettes |     |     |     |     |     |     |
| Exercise   |     |     |     |     |     |     |
|            | 26th | 27th | 28th | 29th | 30th | 31st |
| Sleep      |     |     |     |     |     |     |
| Caffeine   |     |     |     |     |     |     |
| Alcohol    |     |     |     |     |     |     |
| Cigarettes |     |     |     |     |     |     |
| Exercise   |     |     |     |     |     |     |

# Emotion tracker

*How are you felling today? It is important to be in touch with yourself and your emotions.*

| | Anger | Hurt/Pain | Disappointment | Upset | Happy | Blah! | Lazy |
|---|---|---|---|---|---|---|---|
| 1st | | | | | | | |
| 2nd | | | | | | | |
| 3rd | | | | | | | |
| 4th | | | | | | | |
| 5th | | | | | | | |
| 6th | | | | | | | |
| 7th | | | | | | | |
| 8th | | | | | | | |
| 9th | | | | | | | |
| 10th | | | | | | | |
| 11th | | | | | | | |
| 12th | | | | | | | |
| 13th | | | | | | | |
| 14th | | | | | | | |
| 15th | | | | | | | |
| 16th | | | | | | | |
| 17th | | | | | | | |
| 18th | | | | | | | |
| 19th | | | | | | | |
| 20th | | | | | | | |
| 21st | | | | | | | |
| 22nd | | | | | | | |
| 23rd | | | | | | | |
| 24th | | | | | | | |
| 25th | | | | | | | |
| 26th | | | | | | | |
| 27th | | | | | | | |
| 28th | | | | | | | |
| 29th | | | | | | | |
| 30th | | | | | | | |
| 31st | | | | | | | |

|        | Guilt | Anxious | Sadness | Shame | Guilt | Worthless |
|--------|-------|---------|---------|-------|-------|-----------|
| 1st    |       |         |         |       |       |           |
| 2nd    |       |         |         |       |       |           |
| 3rd    |       |         |         |       |       |           |
| 4th    |       |         |         |       |       |           |
| 5th    |       |         |         |       |       |           |
| 6th    |       |         |         |       |       |           |
| 7th    |       |         |         |       |       |           |
| 8th    |       |         |         |       |       |           |
| 9th    |       |         |         |       |       |           |
| 10th   |       |         |         |       |       |           |
| 11th   |       |         |         |       |       |           |
| 12th   |       |         |         |       |       |           |
| 13th   |       |         |         |       |       |           |
| 14th   |       |         |         |       |       |           |
| 15th   |       |         |         |       |       |           |
| 16th   |       |         |         |       |       |           |
| 17th   |       |         |         |       |       |           |
| 18th   |       |         |         |       |       |           |
| 19th   |       |         |         |       |       |           |
| 20th   |       |         |         |       |       |           |
| 21st   |       |         |         |       |       |           |
| 22nd   |       |         |         |       |       |           |
| 23rd   |       |         |         |       |       |           |
| 24th   |       |         |         |       |       |           |
| 25th   |       |         |         |       |       |           |
| 26th   |       |         |         |       |       |           |
| 27th   |       |         |         |       |       |           |
| 28th   |       |         |         |       |       |           |
| 29th   |       |         |         |       |       |           |
| 30th   |       |         |         |       |       |           |
| 31st   |       |         |         |       |       |           |

# Food Tracker

| | Healthy food | Junk food | Both | Didn't eat ☹ |
|---|---|---|---|---|
| 1st | | | | |
| 2nd | | | | |
| 3rd | | | | |
| 4th | | | | |
| 5th | | | | |
| 6th | | | | |
| 7th | | | | |
| 8th | | | | |
| 9th | | | | |
| 10th | | | | |
| 11th | | | | |
| 12th | | | | |
| 13th | | | | |
| 14th | | | | |
| 15th | | | | |
| 16th | | | | |
| 17th | | | | |
| 18th | | | | |
| 19th | | | | |
| 20th | | | | |
| 21st | | | | |
| 22nd | | | | |
| 23rd | | | | |
| 24th | | | | |
| 25th | | | | |
| 26th | | | | |
| 27th | | | | |
| 28th | | | | |
| 29th | | | | |
| 30th | | | | |
| 31st | | | | |

# Weight Tracker

**Month:**

| | Kgs/lbs | | Kgs/lbs |
|---|---|---|---|
| 1st | | 16th | |
| 2nd | | 17th | |
| 3rd | | 18th | |
| 4th | | 19th | |
| 5th | | 20th | |
| 6th | | 21st | |
| 7th | | 22nd | |
| 8th | | 23rd | |
| 9th | | 24th | |
| 10th | | 25th | |
| 11th | | 26th | |
| 12th | | 27th | |
| 13th | | 28th | |
| 14th | | 29th | |
| 15th | | 30th | |
| | | 31st | |

# Journal

dd/mm/yy

Good Morning Sunshine!

Lets start the beginning of the month by noting down our details, so this way we can track changes every month

Age:
Weight:
Height:
Date of last menstrual cycle and time frame:

Did you…

o Get out of bed, woke      o Brush you teeth        o Eat breakfast
   up at:                   o Take a shower          o Take your meds
o Smile

Every little task is important sometimes we forget the silliest things so lets make a to-do list to keep track!

To-do list:

Good afternoon!

Did you…

o Eat lunch                 o Finish your tasks?

Good evening love, how's your day so far?

Did you…

o Eat snacks                o Finish all that you had on   o Eat dinner
o Have a good day              your to do list             o Sleep early
o Have a bad day

Good night and sleep well

Good Morning Sunshine!

Lets start the beginning of the month by noting down our details, so this way we can track changes every month

Age:
Weight:
Height:
Date of last menstrual cycle and time frame:

Did you...

o Get out of bed, woke    o Brush you teeth      o Eat breakfast
   up at:                 o Take a shower        o Take your meds
o Smile

Every little task is important sometimes we forget the silliest things so lets make a to-do list to keep track!

To-do list:

Good afternoon!

Did you...

o Eat lunch              o Finish your tasks?

Good evening love, how's your day so far?

Did you...

o Eat snacks             o Finish all that you had on    o Eat dinner
o Have a good day           your to do list              o Sleep early
o Have a bad day

Good night and sleep well

Good Morning Sunshine!

Lets start the beginning of the month by noting down our details, so this way we can track changes every month

Age:
Weight:
Height:
Date of last menstrual cycle and time frame:

Did you…

o Get out of bed, woke     o Brush you teeth     o Eat breakfast
   up at:                 o Take a shower     o Take your meds
o Smile

Every little task is important sometimes we forget the silliest things so lets make a to-do list to keep track!

To-do list:

Good afternoon!

Did you…

o Eat lunch            o Finish your tasks?

Good evening love, how's your day so far?

Did you…

o Eat snacks        o Finish all that you had on   o Eat dinner
o Have a good day       your to do list          o Sleep early
o Have a bad day

Good night and sleep well

Good Morning Sunshine!

Lets start the beginning of the month by noting down our details, so this way we can track changes every month

Age:
Weight:
Height:
Date of last menstrual cycle and time frame:

Did you...

o Get out of bed, woke     o Brush you teeth        o Eat breakfast
  up at:                   o Take a shower          o Take your meds
o Smile

Every little task is important sometimes we forget the silliest things so lets make a to-do list to keep track!

To-do list:

Good afternoon!

Did you...

o Eat lunch                o Finish your tasks?

Good evening love, how's your day so far?

Did you...

o Eat snacks               o Finish all that you had on    o Eat dinner
o Have a good day            your to do list               o Sleep early
o Have a bad day

Good night and sleep well

Good Morning Sunshine!

Lets start the beginning of the month by noting down our details, so this way we can track changes every month

Age:
Weight:
Height:
Date of last menstrual cycle and time frame:

Did you...

o Get out of bed, woke     o Brush you teeth          o Eat breakfast
  up at:                   o Take a shower            o Take your meds
o Smile

Every little task is important sometimes we forget the silliest things so lets make a to-do list to keep track!

To-do list:

Good afternoon!

Did you...

o Eat lunch                o Finish your tasks?

Good evening love, how's your day so far?

Did you...

o Eat snacks               o Finish all that you had on   o Eat dinner
o Have a good day            your to do list               o Sleep early
o Have a bad day

Good night and sleep well

Good Morning Sunshine!

Lets start the beginning of the month by noting down our details, so this way we can track changes every month

Age:
Weight:
Height:
Date of last menstrual cycle and time frame:

Did you...

o Get out of bed, woke      o Brush you teeth          o Eat breakfast
   up at:                   o Take a shower            o Take your meds
o Smile

Every little task is important sometimes we forget the silliest things so lets make a to-do list to keep track!

To-do list:

Good afternoon!

Did you...

o Eat lunch                 o Finish your tasks?

Good evening love, how's your day so far?

Did you...

o Eat snacks                o Finish all that you had on   o Eat dinner
o Have a good day              your to do list              o Sleep early
o Have a bad day

Good night and sleep well

Good Morning Sunshine!

Lets start the beginning of the month by noting down our details, so this way we can track changes every month

Age:
Weight:
Height:
Date of last menstrual cycle and time frame:

Did you…

o Get out of bed, woke        o Brush you teeth        o Eat breakfast
  up at:                      o Take a shower          o Take your meds
o Smile

Every little task is important sometimes we forget the silliest things so lets make a to-do list to keep track!

To-do list:

Good afternoon!

Did you…

o Eat lunch                   o Finish your tasks?

Good evening love, how's your day so far?

Did you…

o Eat snacks                  o Finish all that you had on    o Eat dinner
o Have a good day               your to do list               o Sleep early
o Have a bad day

Good night and sleep well

Good Morning Sunshine!

Lets start the beginning of the month by noting down our details, so this way we can track changes every month

Age:
Weight:
Height:
Date of last menstrual cycle and time frame:

Did you...

o Get out of bed, woke    o Brush you teeth    o Eat breakfast
   up at:                 o Take a shower      o Take your meds
o Smile

Every little task is important sometimes we forget the silliest things so lets make a to-do list to keep track!

To-do list:

Good afternoon!

Did you...

o Eat lunch              o Finish your tasks?

Good evening love, how's your day so far?

Did you...

o Eat snacks             o Finish all that you had on    o Eat dinner
o Have a good day           your to do list             o Sleep early
o Have a bad day

Good night and sleep well

dd/mm/yy

Good Morning Sunshine!

Lets start the beginning of the month by noting down our details, so this way we can track changes every month

Age:
Weight:
Height:
Date of last menstrual cycle and time frame:

Did you…

- o Get out of bed, woke
  up at:
- o Smile
- o Brush you teeth
- o Take a shower
- o Eat breakfast
- o Take your meds

Every little task is important sometimes we forget the silliest things so lets make a to-do list to keep track!

To-do list:

Good afternoon!

Did you…

- o Eat lunch
- o Finish your tasks?

Good evening love, how's your day so far?

Did you…

- o Eat snacks
- o Have a good day
- o Have a bad day
- o Finish all that you had on
  your to do list
- o Eat dinner
- o Sleep early

Good night and sleep well

Good Morning Sunshine!

Lets start the beginning of the month by noting down our details, so this way we can track changes every month

Age:
Weight:
Height:
Date of last menstrual cycle and time frame:

Did you…

- o Get out of bed, woke up at:
- o Smile
- o Brush you teeth
- o Take a shower
- o Eat breakfast
- o Take your meds

Every little task is important sometimes we forget the silliest things so lets make a to-do list to keep track!

To-do list:

Good afternoon!

Did you…

- o Eat lunch
- o Finish your tasks?

Good evening love, how's your day so far?

Did you…

- o Eat snacks
- o Have a good day
- o Have a bad day
- o Finish all that you had on your to do list
- o Eat dinner
- o Sleep early

Good night and sleep well

Good Morning Sunshine!

Lets start the beginning of the month by noting down our details, so this way we can track changes every month

Age:
Weight:
Height:
Date of last menstrual cycle and time frame:

Did you…

o Get out of bed, woke   o Brush you teeth        o Eat breakfast
   up at:                 o Take a shower          o Take your meds
o Smile

Every little task is important sometimes we forget the silliest things so lets make a to-do list to keep track!

To-do list:

Good afternoon!

Did you…

o Eat lunch              o Finish your tasks?

Good evening love, how's your day so far?

Did you…

o Eat snacks             o Finish all that you had on   o Eat dinner
o Have a good day           your to do list              o Sleep early
o Have a bad day

Good night and sleep well

Good Morning Sunshine!

Lets start the beginning of the month by noting down our details, so this way we can track changes every month

Age:
Weight:
Height:
Date of last menstrual cycle and time frame:

Did you…

o Get out of bed, woke   o Brush you teeth        o Eat breakfast
   up at:                o Take a shower          o Take your meds
o Smile

Every little task is important sometimes we forget the silliest things so lets make a to-do list to keep track!

To-do list:

Good afternoon!

Did you…

o Eat lunch              o Finish your tasks?

Good evening love, how's your day so far?

Did you…

o Eat snacks             o Finish all that you had on   o Eat dinner
o Have a good day           your to do list              o Sleep early
o Have a bad day

Good night and sleep well

Good Morning Sunshine!

Lets start the beginning of the month by noting down our details, so this way we can track changes every month

Age:
Weight:
Height:
Date of last menstrual cycle and time frame:

Did you…

o Get out of bed, woke    o Brush you teeth       o Eat breakfast
  up at:                  o Take a shower         o Take your meds
o Smile

Every little task is important sometimes we forget the silliest things so lets make a to-do list to keep track!

To-do list:


Good afternoon!

Did you…

o Eat lunch              o Finish your tasks?

Good evening love, how's your day so far?

Did you…

o Eat snacks             o Finish all that you had on    o Eat dinner
o Have a good day          your to do list               o Sleep early
o Have a bad day

Good night and sleep well

Good Morning Sunshine!

Lets start the beginning of the month by noting down our details, so this way we can track changes every month

Age:
Weight:
Height:
Date of last menstrual cycle and time frame:

Did you…

o Get out of bed, woke    o Brush you teeth      o Eat breakfast
   up at:                 o Take a shower        o Take your meds
o Smile

Every little task is important sometimes we forget the silliest things so lets make a to-do list to keep track!

To-do list:

Good afternoon!

Did you…

o Eat lunch               o Finish your tasks?

Good evening love, how's your day so far?

Did you…

o Eat snacks              o Finish all that you had on   o Eat dinner
o Have a good day            your to do list            o Sleep early
o Have a bad day

Good night and sleep well

Good Morning Sunshine!

Lets start the beginning of the month by noting down our details, so this way we can track changes every month

Age:
Weight:
Height:
Date of last menstrual cycle and time frame:

Did you...

o Get out of bed, woke    o Brush you teeth       o Eat breakfast
  up at:                  o Take a shower         o Take your meds
o Smile

Every little task is important sometimes we forget the silliest things so lets make a to-do list to keep track!

To-do list:

Good afternoon!

Did you...

o Eat lunch                o Finish your tasks?

Good evening love, how's your day so far?

Did you...

o Eat snacks               o Finish all that you had on   o Eat dinner
o Have a good day            your to do list             o Sleep early
o Have a bad day

Good night and sleep well

dd/mm/yy

Good Morning Sunshine!

Lets start the beginning of the month by noting down our details, so this way we can track changes every month

Age:
Weight:
Height:
Date of last menstrual cycle and time frame:

Did you…

o Get out of bed, woke up at:
o Smile

o Brush you teeth
o Take a shower

o Eat breakfast
o Take your meds

Every little task is important sometimes we forget the silliest things so lets make a to-do list to keep track!

To-do list:

Good afternoon!

Did you…

o Eat lunch

o Finish your tasks?

Good evening love, how's your day so far?

Did you…

o Eat snacks
o Have a good day
o Have a bad day

o Finish all that you had on your to do list

o Eat dinner
o Sleep early

Good night and sleep well

Good Morning Sunshine!

Lets start the beginning of the month by noting down our details, so this way we can track changes every month

Age:
Weight:
Height:
Date of last menstrual cycle and time frame:

Did you…

- o Get out of bed, woke up at:
- o Smile
- o Brush you teeth
- o Take a shower
- o Eat breakfast
- o Take your meds

Every little task is important sometimes we forget the silliest things so lets make a to-do list to keep track!

To-do list:

Good afternoon!

Did you…

- o Eat lunch
- o Finish your tasks?

Good evening love, how's your day so far?

Did you…

- o Eat snacks
- o Have a good day
- o Have a bad day
- o Finish all that you had on your to do list
- o Eat dinner
- o Sleep early

Good night and sleep well

Good Morning Sunshine!

Lets start the beginning of the month by noting down our details, so this way we can track changes every month

Age:
Weight:
Height:
Date of last menstrual cycle and time frame:

Did you…

o Get out of bed, woke        o Brush you teeth          o Eat breakfast
  up at:                        o Take a shower            o Take your meds
o Smile

Every little task is important sometimes we forget the silliest things so lets make a to-do list to keep track!

To-do list:

Good afternoon!

Did you…

o Eat lunch                   o Finish your tasks?

Good evening love, how's your day so far?

Did you…

o Eat snacks                  o Finish all that you had on    o Eat dinner
o Have a good day                your to do list             o Sleep early
o Have a bad day

Good night and sleep well

Good Morning Sunshine!

Lets start the beginning of the month by noting down our details, so this way we can track changes every month

Age:
Weight:
Height:
Date of last menstrual cycle and time frame:

Did you...

- o Get out of bed, woke up at:
- o Smile
- o Brush you teeth
- o Take a shower
- o Eat breakfast
- o Take your meds

Every little task is important sometimes we forget the silliest things so lets make a to-do list to keep track!

To-do list:

Good afternoon!

Did you...

- o Eat lunch
- o Finish your tasks?

Good evening love, how's your day so far?

Did you...

- o Eat snacks
- o Have a good day
- o Have a bad day
- o Finish all that you had on your to do list
- o Eat dinner
- o Sleep early

Good night and sleep well

Good Morning Sunshine!

Lets start the beginning of the month by noting down our details, so this way we can track changes every month

Age:
Weight:
Height:
Date of last menstrual cycle and time frame:

Did you...

o Get out of bed, woke      o Brush you teeth       o Eat breakfast
   up at:                    o Take a shower         o Take your meds
o Smile

Every little task is important sometimes we forget the silliest things so lets make a to-do list to keep track!

To-do list:

Good afternoon!

Did you...

o Eat lunch                 o Finish your tasks?

Good evening love, how's your day so far?

Did you...

o Eat snacks                o Finish all that you had on    o Eat dinner
o Have a good day              your to do list                o Sleep early
o Have a bad day

Good night and sleep well

Good Morning Sunshine!

Lets start the beginning of the month by noting down our details, so this way we can track changes every month

Age:
Weight:
Height:
Date of last menstrual cycle and time frame:

Did you…

o Get out of bed, woke       o Brush you teeth        o Eat breakfast
   up at:                    o Take a shower          o Take your meds
o Smile

Every little task is important sometimes we forget the silliest things so lets make a to-do list to keep track!

To-do list:

Good afternoon!

Did you…

o Eat lunch                  o Finish your tasks?

Good evening love, how's your day so far?

Did you…

o Eat snacks                 o Finish all that you had on   o Eat dinner
o Have a good day               your to do list             o Sleep early
o Have a bad day

Good night and sleep well

Good Morning Sunshine!

Lets start the beginning of the month by noting down our details, so this way we can track changes every month

Age:
Weight:
Height:
Date of last menstrual cycle and time frame:

Did you...

o Get out of bed, woke     o Brush you teeth        o Eat breakfast
   up at:                  o Take a shower          o Take your meds
o Smile

Every little task is important sometimes we forget the silliest things so lets make a to-do list to keep track!

To-do list:

Good afternoon!

Did you...

o Eat lunch                o Finish your tasks?

Good evening love, how's your day so far?

Did you...

o Eat snacks              o Finish all that you had on    o Eat dinner
o Have a good day            your to do list              o Sleep early
o Have a bad day

Good night and sleep well

Good Morning Sunshine!

Lets start the beginning of the month by noting down our details, so this way we can track changes every month

Age:
Weight:
Height:
Date of last menstrual cycle and time frame:

Did you...

o Get out of bed, woke    o Brush you teeth    o Eat breakfast
  up at:                  o Take a shower      o Take your meds
o Smile

Every little task is important sometimes we forget the silliest things so lets make a to-do list to keep track!

To-do list:

Good afternoon!

Did you...

o Eat lunch              o Finish your tasks?

Good evening love, how's your day so far?

Did you...

o Eat snacks             o Finish all that you had on    o Eat dinner
o Have a good day          your to do list               o Sleep early
o Have a bad day

Good night and sleep well

Good Morning Sunshine!

Lets start the beginning of the month by noting down our details, so this way we can track changes every month

Age:
Weight:
Height:
Date of last menstrual cycle and time frame:

Did you…

o Get out of bed, woke      o Brush you teeth       o Eat breakfast
   up at:                   o Take a shower         o Take your meds
o Smile

Every little task is important sometimes we forget the silliest things so lets make a to-do list to keep track!

To-do list:

Good afternoon!

Did you…

o Eat lunch                 o Finish your tasks?

Good evening love, how's your day so far?

Did you…

o Eat snacks                o Finish all that you had on    o Eat dinner
o Have a good day              your to do list             o Sleep early
o Have a bad day

Good night and sleep well

Good Morning Sunshine!

Lets start the beginning of the month by noting down our details, so this way we can track changes every month

Age:
Weight:
Height:
Date of last menstrual cycle and time frame:

Did you...

o Get out of bed, woke      o Brush you teeth        o Eat breakfast
   up at:                   o Take a shower          o Take your meds
o Smile

Every little task is important sometimes we forget the silliest things so lets make a to-do list to keep track!

To-do list:

Good afternoon!

Did you...

o Eat lunch                 o Finish your tasks?

Good evening love, how's your day so far?

Did you...

o Eat snacks                o Finish all that you had on     o Eat dinner
o Have a good day              your to do list                o Sleep early
o Have a bad day

Good night and sleep well

Good Morning Sunshine!

Lets start the beginning of the month by noting down our details, so this way we can track changes every month

Age:
Weight:
Height:
Date of last menstrual cycle and time frame:

Did you…

o Get out of bed, woke       o Brush you teeth        o Eat breakfast
   up at:                        o Take a shower          o Take your meds
o Smile

Every little task is important sometimes we forget the silliest things so lets make a to-do list to keep track!

To-do list:

Good afternoon!

Did you…

o Eat lunch                      o Finish your tasks?

Good evening love, how's your day so far?

Did you…

o Eat snacks                     o Finish all that you had on   o Eat dinner
o Have a good day                   your to do list               o Sleep early
o Have a bad day

Good night and sleep well

Good Morning Sunshine!

Lets start the beginning of the month by noting down our details, so this way we can track changes every month

Age:
Weight:
Height:
Date of last menstrual cycle and time frame:

Did you…

o Get out of bed, woke        o Brush you teeth        o Eat breakfast
   up at:                     o Take a shower          o Take your meds
o Smile

Every little task is important sometimes we forget the silliest things so lets make a to-do list to keep track!

To-do list:

Good afternoon!

Did you…

o Eat lunch                   o Finish your tasks?

Good evening love, how's your day so far?

Did you…

o Eat snacks                  o Finish all that you had on    o Eat dinner
o Have a good day                your to do list              o Sleep early
o Have a bad day

Good night and sleep well

dd/mm/yy

Good Morning Sunshine!

Lets start the beginning of the month by noting down our details, so this way we can track changes every month

Age:
Weight:
Height:
Date of last menstrual cycle and time frame:

Did you...

o Get out of bed, woke
  up at:
o Smile

o Brush you teeth
o Take a shower

o Eat breakfast
o Take your meds

Every little task is important sometimes we forget the silliest things so lets make a to-do list to keep track!

To-do list:

Good afternoon!

Did you...

o Eat lunch

o Finish your tasks?

Good evening love, how's your day so far?

Did you...

o Eat snacks
o Have a good day
o Have a bad day

o Finish all that you had on
  your to do list

o Eat dinner
o Sleep early

Good night and sleep well

Good Morning Sunshine!

Lets start the beginning of the month by noting down our details, so this way we can track changes every month

Age:
Weight:
Height:
Date of last menstrual cycle and time frame:

Did you…

o Get out of bed, woke       o Brush you teeth        o Eat breakfast
   up at:                    o Take a shower          o Take your meds
o Smile

Every little task is important sometimes we forget the silliest things so lets make a to-do list to keep track!

To-do list:

Good afternoon!

Did you…

o Eat lunch                 o Finish your tasks?

Good evening love, how's your day so far?

Did you…

o Eat snacks                o Finish all that you had on   o Eat dinner
o Have a good day              your to do list             o Sleep early
o Have a bad day

Good night and sleep well

Good Morning Sunshine!

Lets start the beginning of the month by noting down our details, so this way we can track changes every month

Age:
Weight:
Height:
Date of last menstrual cycle and time frame:

Did you...

- o Get out of bed, woke up at:
- o Smile
- o Brush you teeth
- o Take a shower
- o Eat breakfast
- o Take your meds

Every little task is important sometimes we forget the silliest things so lets make a to-do list to keep track!

To-do list:

Good afternoon!

Did you...

- o Eat lunch
- o Finish your tasks?

Good evening love, how's your day so far?

Did you...

- o Eat snacks
- o Have a good day
- o Have a bad day
- o Finish all that you had on your to do list
- o Eat dinner
- o Sleep early

Good night and sleep well

Good Morning Sunshine!

Lets start the beginning of the month by noting down our details, so this way we can track changes every month

Age:
Weight:
Height:
Date of last menstrual cycle and time frame:

Did you...

o Get out of bed, woke    o Brush you teeth     o Eat breakfast
   up at:                 o Take a shower       o Take your meds
o Smile

Every little task is important sometimes we forget the silliest things so lets make a to-do list to keep track!

To-do list:

Good afternoon!

Did you...

o Eat lunch                o Finish your tasks?

Good evening love, how's your day so far?

Did you...

o Eat snacks               o Finish all that you had on    o Eat dinner
o Have a good day             your to do list              o Sleep early
o Have a bad day

Good night and sleep well

# This Month...

o I tried something new by...

o I helped somebody by...

o I become a better person by...

o I lost ___ kgs by...

o I gained ___kgs by...

o

o

o

# Habit Tracker

**Month:**

|  | 1st | 2nd | 3rd | 4th | 5th |  |
|---|---|---|---|---|---|---|
| Sleep |  |  |  |  |  |  |
| Caffeine |  |  |  |  |  |  |
| Alcohol |  |  |  |  |  |  |
| Cigarettes |  |  |  |  |  |  |
| Exercise |  |  |  |  |  |  |
|  | 6th | 7th | 8th | 9th | 10th |  |
| Sleep |  |  |  |  |  |  |
| Caffeine |  |  |  |  |  |  |
| Alcohol |  |  |  |  |  |  |
| Cigarettes |  |  |  |  |  |  |
| Exercise |  |  |  |  |  |  |
|  | 11th | 12th | 13th | 14th | 15th |  |
| Sleep |  |  |  |  |  |  |
| Caffeine |  |  |  |  |  |  |
| Alcohol |  |  |  |  |  |  |
| Cigarettes |  |  |  |  |  |  |
| Exercise |  |  |  |  |  |  |
|  | 16th | 17th | 18th | 19th | 20th |  |
| Sleep |  |  |  |  |  |  |
| Caffeine |  |  |  |  |  |  |
| Alcohol |  |  |  |  |  |  |
| Cigarettes |  |  |  |  |  |  |
| Exercise |  |  |  |  |  |  |
|  | 21th | 22th | 23th | 24th | 25th |  |
| Sleep |  |  |  |  |  |  |
| Caffeine |  |  |  |  |  |  |
| Alcohol |  |  |  |  |  |  |
| Cigarettes |  |  |  |  |  |  |
| Exercise |  |  |  |  |  |  |
|  | 26th | 27th | 28th | 29th | 30th | 31st |
| Sleep |  |  |  |  |  |  |
| Caffeine |  |  |  |  |  |  |
| Alcohol |  |  |  |  |  |  |
| Cigarettes |  |  |  |  |  |  |
| Exercise |  |  |  |  |  |  |

# Emotion tracker

*How are you felling today? It is important to be in touch with yourself and your emotions.*

|  | Anger | Hurt/Pain | Disappointment | Upset | Happy | Blah! | Lazy |
|---|---|---|---|---|---|---|---|
| 1st | | | | | | | |
| 2nd | | | | | | | |
| 3rd | | | | | | | |
| 4th | | | | | | | |
| 5th | | | | | | | |
| 6th | | | | | | | |
| 7th | | | | | | | |
| 8th | | | | | | | |
| 9th | | | | | | | |
| 10th | | | | | | | |
| 11th | | | | | | | |
| 12th | | | | | | | |
| 13th | | | | | | | |
| 14th | | | | | | | |
| 15th | | | | | | | |
| 16th | | | | | | | |
| 17th | | | | | | | |
| 18th | | | | | | | |
| 19th | | | | | | | |
| 20th | | | | | | | |
| 21st | | | | | | | |
| 22nd | | | | | | | |
| 23rd | | | | | | | |
| 24th | | | | | | | |
| 25th | | | | | | | |
| 26th | | | | | | | |
| 27th | | | | | | | |
| 28th | | | | | | | |
| 29th | | | | | | | |
| 30th | | | | | | | |
| 31st | | | | | | | |

| | Guilt | Anxious | Sadness | Shame | Guilt | Worthless |
|---|---|---|---|---|---|---|
| 1st | | | | | | |
| 2nd | | | | | | |
| 3rd | | | | | | |
| 4th | | | | | | |
| 5th | | | | | | |
| 6th | | | | | | |
| 7th | | | | | | |
| 8th | | | | | | |
| 9th | | | | | | |
| 10th | | | | | | |
| 11th | | | | | | |
| 12th | | | | | | |
| 13th | | | | | | |
| 14th | | | | | | |
| 15th | | | | | | |
| 16th | | | | | | |
| 17th | | | | | | |
| 18th | | | | | | |
| 19th | | | | | | |
| 20th | | | | | | |
| 21st | | | | | | |
| 22nd | | | | | | |
| 23rd | | | | | | |
| 24th | | | | | | |
| 25th | | | | | | |
| 26th | | | | | | |
| 27th | | | | | | |
| 28th | | | | | | |
| 29th | | | | | | |
| 30th | | | | | | |
| 31st | | | | | | |

# Food Tracker

| | Healthy food | Junk food | Both | Didn't eat ☹ |
|---|---|---|---|---|
| 1st | | | | |
| 2nd | | | | |
| 3rd | | | | |
| 4th | | | | |
| 5th | | | | |
| 6th | | | | |
| 7th | | | | |
| 8th | | | | |
| 9th | | | | |
| 10th | | | | |
| 11th | | | | |
| 12th | | | | |
| 13th | | | | |
| 14th | | | | |
| 15th | | | | |
| 16th | | | | |
| 17th | | | | |
| 18th | | | | |
| 19th | | | | |
| 20th | | | | |
| 21st | | | | |
| 22nd | | | | |
| 23rd | | | | |
| 24th | | | | |
| 25th | | | | |
| 26th | | | | |
| 27th | | | | |
| 28th | | | | |
| 29th | | | | |
| 30th | | | | |
| 31st | | | | |

# Weight Tracker

**Month:**

| | Kgs/lbs | | Kgs/lbs |
|---|---|---|---|
| 1st | | 16th | |
| 2nd | | 17th | |
| 3rd | | 18th | |
| 4th | | 19th | |
| 5th | | 20th | |
| 6th | | 21st | |
| 7th | | 22nd | |
| 8th | | 23rd | |
| 9th | | 24th | |
| 10th | | 25th | |
| 11th | | 26th | |
| 12th | | 27th | |
| 13th | | 28th | |
| 14th | | 29th | |
| 15th | | 30th | |
| | | 31st | |

# Journal

Good Morning Sunshine!

Lets start the beginning of the month by noting down our details, so this way we can track changes every month

Age:
Weight:
Height:
Date of last menstrual cycle and time frame:

Did you…

- o Get out of bed, woke up at:
- o Smile

- o Brush you teeth
- o Take a shower

- o Eat breakfast
- o Take your meds

Every little task is important sometimes we forget the silliest things so lets make a to-do list to keep track!

To-do list:

Good afternoon!

Did you…

- o Eat lunch

- o Finish your tasks?

Good evening love, how's your day so far?

Did you…

- o Eat snacks
- o Have a good day
- o Have a bad day

- o Finish all that you had on your to do list

- o Eat dinner
- o Sleep early

Good night and sleep well

Good Morning Sunshine!

Lets start the beginning of the month by noting down our details, so this way we can track changes every month

Age:
Weight:
Height:
Date of last menstrual cycle and time frame:

Did you...

o Get out of bed, woke      o Brush you teeth          o Eat breakfast
   up at:                   o Take a shower            o Take your meds
o Smile

Every little task is important sometimes we forget the silliest things so lets make a to-do list to keep track!

To-do list:

Good afternoon!

Did you...

o Eat lunch                 o Finish your tasks?

Good evening love, how's your day so far?

Did you...

o Eat snacks                o Finish all that you had on   o Eat dinner
o Have a good day              your to do list              o Sleep early
o Have a bad day

Good night and sleep well

Good Morning Sunshine!

Lets start the beginning of the month by noting down our details, so this way we can track changes every month

Age:
Weight:
Height:
Date of last menstrual cycle and time frame:

Did you…

- o Get out of bed, woke up at:
- o Smile
- o Brush you teeth
- o Take a shower
- o Eat breakfast
- o Take your meds

Every little task is important sometimes we forget the silliest things so lets make a to-do list to keep track!

To-do list:

Good afternoon!

Did you…

- o Eat lunch
- o Finish your tasks?

Good evening love, how's your day so far?

Did you…

- o Eat snacks
- o Have a good day
- o Have a bad day
- o Finish all that you had on your to do list
- o Eat dinner
- o Sleep early

Good night and sleep well

Good Morning Sunshine!

Lets start the beginning of the month by noting down our details, so this way we can track changes every month

Age:
Weight:
Height:
Date of last menstrual cycle and time frame:

Did you…

o Get out of bed, woke    o Brush you teeth       o Eat breakfast
   up at:                 o Take a shower          o Take your meds
o Smile

Every little task is important sometimes we forget the silliest things so lets make a to-do list to keep track!

To-do list:

Good afternoon!

Did you…

o Eat lunch              o Finish your tasks?

Good evening love, how's your day so far?

Did you…

o Eat snacks             o Finish all that you had on    o Eat dinner
o Have a good day           your to do list              o Sleep early
o Have a bad day

Good night and sleep well

Good Morning Sunshine!

Lets start the beginning of the month by noting down our details, so this way we can track changes every month

Age:
Weight:
Height:
Date of last menstrual cycle and time frame:

Did you…

o Get out of bed, woke        o Brush you teeth        o Eat breakfast
  up at:                        o Take a shower         o Take your meds
o Smile

Every little task is important sometimes we forget the silliest things so lets make a to-do list to keep track!

To-do list:

Good afternoon!

Did you…

o Eat lunch                    o Finish your tasks?

Good evening love, how's your day so far?

Did you…

o Eat snacks          o Finish all that you had on    o Eat dinner
o Have a good day       your to do list            o Sleep early
o Have a bad day

Good night and sleep well

Good Morning Sunshine!

Lets start the beginning of the month by noting down our details, so this way we can track changes every month

Age:
Weight:
Height:
Date of last menstrual cycle and time frame:

Did you…

o Get out of bed, woke      o Brush you teeth          o Eat breakfast
   up at:                   o Take a shower            o Take your meds
o Smile

Every little task is important sometimes we forget the silliest things so lets make a to-do list to keep track!

To-do list:

Good afternoon!

Did you…

o Eat lunch                 o Finish your tasks?

Good evening love, how's your day so far?

Did you…

o Eat snacks                o Finish all that you had on   o Eat dinner
o Have a good day              your to do list              o Sleep early
o Have a bad day

Good night and sleep well

Good Morning Sunshine!

Lets start the beginning of the month by noting down our details, so this way we can track changes every month

Age:
Weight:
Height:
Date of last menstrual cycle and time frame:

Did you…

o Get out of bed, woke      o Brush you teeth        o Eat breakfast
   up at:                   o Take a shower          o Take your meds
o Smile

Every little task is important sometimes we forget the silliest things so lets make a to-do list to keep track!

To-do list:

Good afternoon!

Did you…

o Eat lunch                 o Finish your tasks?

Good evening love, how's your day so far?

Did you…

o Eat snacks                o Finish all that you had on   o Eat dinner
o Have a good day              your to do list              o Sleep early
o Have a bad day

Good night and sleep well

Good Morning Sunshine!

Lets start the beginning of the month by noting down our details, so this way we can track changes every month

Age:
Weight:
Height:
Date of last menstrual cycle and time frame:

Did you…

- o Get out of bed, woke     o Brush you teeth          o Eat breakfast
  up at:                     o Take a shower            o Take your meds
- o Smile

Every little task is important sometimes we forget the silliest things so lets make a to-do list to keep track!

To-do list:

Good afternoon!

Did you…

- o Eat lunch                o Finish your tasks?

Good evening love, how's your day so far?

Did you…

- o Eat snacks               o Finish all that you had on   o Eat dinner
- o Have a good day            your to do list               o Sleep early
- o Have a bad day

Good night and sleep well

dd/mm/yy

Good Morning Sunshine!

Lets start the beginning of the month by noting down our details, so this way we can track changes every month

Age:
Weight:
Height:
Date of last menstrual cycle and time frame:

Did you…

- o Get out of bed, woke up at:
- o Smile
- o Brush you teeth
- o Take a shower
- o Eat breakfast
- o Take your meds

Every little task is important sometimes we forget the silliest things so lets make a to-do list to keep track!

To-do list:

Good afternoon!

Did you…

- o Eat lunch
- o Finish your tasks?

Good evening love, how's your day so far?

Did you…

- o Eat snacks
- o Have a good day
- o Have a bad day
- o Finish all that you had on your to do list
- o Eat dinner
- o Sleep early

Good night and sleep well

Good Morning Sunshine!

Lets start the beginning of the month by noting down our details, so this way we can track changes every month

Age:
Weight:
Height:
Date of last menstrual cycle and time frame:

Did you...

o Get out of bed, woke        o Brush you teeth          o Eat breakfast
   up at:                     o Take a shower            o Take your meds
o Smile

Every little task is important sometimes we forget the silliest things so lets make a to-do list to keep track!

To-do list:

Good afternoon!

Did you...

o Eat lunch                   o Finish your tasks?

Good evening love, how's your day so far?

Did you...

o Eat snacks                  o Finish all that you had on    o Eat dinner
o Have a good day                your to do list              o Sleep early
o Have a bad day

Good night and sleep well

Good Morning Sunshine!

Lets start the beginning of the month by noting down our details, so this way we can track changes every month

Age:
Weight:
Height:
Date of last menstrual cycle and time frame:

Did you…

o Get out of bed, woke    o Brush you teeth    o Eat breakfast
   up at:                o Take a shower    o Take your meds
o Smile

Every little task is important sometimes we forget the silliest things so lets make a to-do list to keep track!

To-do list:

Good afternoon!

Did you…

o Eat lunch              o Finish your tasks?

Good evening love, how's your day so far?

Did you…

o Eat snacks        o Finish all that you had on    o Eat dinner
o Have a good day      your to do list            o Sleep early
o Have a bad day

Good night and sleep well

Good Morning Sunshine!

Lets start the beginning of the month by noting down our details, so this way we can track changes every month

Age:
Weight:
Height:
Date of last menstrual cycle and time frame:

Did you...

o Get out of bed, woke          o Brush you teeth          o Eat breakfast
   up at:                       o Take a shower             o Take your meds
o Smile

Every little task is important sometimes we forget the silliest things so lets make a to-do list to keep track!

To-do list:

Good afternoon!

Did you...

o Eat lunch                  o Finish your tasks?

Good evening love, how's your day so far?

Did you...

o Eat snacks               o Finish all that you had on    o Eat dinner
o Have a good day             your to do list              o Sleep early
o Have a bad day

Good night and sleep well

Good Morning Sunshine!

Lets start the beginning of the month by noting down our details, so this way we can track changes every month

Age:
Weight:
Height:
Date of last menstrual cycle and time frame:

Did you…

o Get out of bed, woke         o Brush you teeth          o Eat breakfast
   up at:                      o Take a shower            o Take your meds
o Smile

Every little task is important sometimes we forget the silliest things so lets make a to-do list to keep track!

To-do list:

Good afternoon!

Did you…

o Eat lunch                    o Finish your tasks?

Good evening love, how's your day so far?

Did you…

o Eat snacks                   o Finish all that you had on    o Eat dinner
o Have a good day                 your to do list              o Sleep early
o Have a bad day

Good night and sleep well

dd/mm/yy

Good Morning Sunshine!

Lets start the beginning of the month by noting down our details, so this way we can track changes every month

Age:
Weight:
Height:
Date of last menstrual cycle and time frame:

Did you…

- o Get out of bed, woke up at:
- o Smile
- o Brush you teeth
- o Take a shower
- o Eat breakfast
- o Take your meds

Every little task is important sometimes we forget the silliest things so lets make a to-do list to keep track!

To-do list:

Good afternoon!

Did you…

- o Eat lunch
- o Finish your tasks?

Good evening love, how's your day so far?

Did you…

- o Eat snacks
- o Have a good day
- o Have a bad day
- o Finish all that you had on your to do list
- o Eat dinner
- o Sleep early

Good night and sleep well

dd/mm/yy

Good Morning Sunshine!

Lets start the beginning of the month by noting down our details, so this way we can track changes every month

Age:
Weight:
Height:
Date of last menstrual cycle and time frame:

Did you…

- o Get out of bed, woke up at:
- o Smile
- o Brush you teeth
- o Take a shower
- o Eat breakfast
- o Take your meds

Every little task is important sometimes we forget the silliest things so lets make a to-do list to keep track!

To-do list:

Good afternoon!

Did you…

- o Eat lunch
- o Finish your tasks?

Good evening love, how's your day so far?

Did you…

- o Eat snacks
- o Have a good day
- o Have a bad day
- o Finish all that you had on your to do list
- o Eat dinner
- o Sleep early

Good night and sleep well

Good Morning Sunshine!

Lets start the beginning of the month by noting down our details, so this way we can track changes every month

Age:
Weight:
Height:
Date of last menstrual cycle and time frame:

Did you...

o Get out of bed, woke    o Brush you teeth      o Eat breakfast
  up at:              o Take a shower        o Take your meds
o Smile

Every little task is important sometimes we forget the silliest things so lets make a to-do list to keep track!

To-do list:

Good afternoon!

Did you...

o Eat lunch              o Finish your tasks?

Good evening love, how's your day so far?

Did you...

o Eat snacks             o Finish all that you had on   o Eat dinner
o Have a good day          your to do list          o Sleep early
o Have a bad day

Good night and sleep well

Good Morning Sunshine!

Lets start the beginning of the month by noting down our details, so this way we can track changes every month

Age:
Weight:
Height:
Date of last menstrual cycle and time frame:

Did you...

o Get out of bed, woke       o Brush you teeth        o Eat breakfast
  up at:                     o Take a shower          o Take your meds
o Smile

Every little task is important sometimes we forget the silliest things so lets make a to-do list to keep track!

To-do list:

Good afternoon!

Did you...

o Eat lunch                  o Finish your tasks?

Good evening love, how's your day so far?

Did you...

o Eat snacks                 o Finish all that you had on   o Eat dinner
o Have a good day              your to do list              o Sleep early
o Have a bad day

Good night and sleep well

Good Morning Sunshine!

Lets start the beginning of the month by noting down our details, so this way we can track changes every month

Age:
Weight:
Height:
Date of last menstrual cycle and time frame:

Did you…

o Get out of bed, woke       o Brush you teeth          o Eat breakfast
   up at:                    o Take a shower            o Take your meds
o Smile

Every little task is important sometimes we forget the silliest things so lets make a to-do list to keep track!

To-do list:

Good afternoon!

Did you…

o Eat lunch                  o Finish your tasks?

Good evening love, how's your day so far?

Did you…

o Eat snacks                 o Finish all that you had on   o Eat dinner
o Have a good day               your to do list              o Sleep early
o Have a bad day

Good night and sleep well

dd/mm/yy

Good Morning Sunshine!

Lets start the beginning of the month by noting down our details, so this way we can track changes every month

Age:
Weight:
Height:
Date of last menstrual cycle and time frame:

Did you...

o Get out of bed, woke      o Brush you teeth       o Eat breakfast
  up at:                    o Take a shower         o Take your meds
o Smile

Every little task is important sometimes we forget the silliest things so lets make a to-do list to keep track!

To-do list:

Good afternoon!

Did you...

o Eat lunch               o Finish your tasks?

Good evening love, how's your day so far?

Did you...

o Eat snacks              o Finish all that you had on   o Eat dinner
o Have a good day           your to do list             o Sleep early
o Have a bad day

Good night and sleep well

Good Morning Sunshine!

Lets start the beginning of the month by noting down our details, so this way we can track changes every month

Age:
Weight:
Height:
Date of last menstrual cycle and time frame:

Did you…

- o Get out of bed, woke up at:
- o Smile
- o Brush you teeth
- o Take a shower
- o Eat breakfast
- o Take your meds

Every little task is important sometimes we forget the silliest things so lets make a to-do list to keep track!

To-do list:

Good afternoon!

Did you…

- o Eat lunch
- o Finish your tasks?

Good evening love, how's your day so far?

Did you…

- o Eat snacks
- o Have a good day
- o Have a bad day
- o Finish all that you had on your to do list
- o Eat dinner
- o Sleep early

Good night and sleep well

Good Morning Sunshine!

Lets start the beginning of the month by noting down our details, so this way we can track changes every month

Age:
Weight:
Height:
Date of last menstrual cycle and time frame:

Did you…

- Get out of bed, woke
  up at:
- Smile

- Brush you teeth
- Take a shower

- Eat breakfast
- Take your meds

Every little task is important sometimes we forget the silliest things so lets make a to-do list to keep track!

To-do list:

Good afternoon!

Did you…

- Eat lunch

- Finish your tasks?

Good evening love, how's your day so far?

Did you…

- Eat snacks
- Have a good day
- Have a bad day

- Finish all that you had on
  your to do list

- Eat dinner
- Sleep early

Good night and sleep well

Good Morning Sunshine!

Lets start the beginning of the month by noting down our details, so this way we can track changes every month

Age:
Weight:
Height:
Date of last menstrual cycle and time frame:

Did you…

o Get out of bed, woke       o Brush you teeth        o Eat breakfast
   up at:                    o Take a shower          o Take your meds
o Smile

Every little task is important sometimes we forget the silliest things so lets make a to-do list to keep track!

To-do list:

Good afternoon!

Did you…

o Eat lunch                  o Finish your tasks?

Good evening love, how's your day so far?

Did you…

o Eat snacks                 o Finish all that you had on   o Eat dinner
o Have a good day               your to do list             o Sleep early
o Have a bad day

Good night and sleep well

Good Morning Sunshine!

Lets start the beginning of the month by noting down our details, so this way we can track changes every month

Age:
Weight:
Height:
Date of last menstrual cycle and time frame:

Did you...

- o Get out of bed, woke    o Brush you teeth    o Eat breakfast
     up at:    o Take a shower    o Take your meds
- o Smile

Every little task is important sometimes we forget the silliest things so lets make a to-do list to keep track!

To-do list:

Good afternoon!

Did you...

- o Eat lunch    o Finish your tasks?

Good evening love, how's your day so far?

Did you...

- o Eat snacks    o Finish all that you had on    o Eat dinner
- o Have a good day    your to do list    o Sleep early
- o Have a bad day

Good night and sleep well

Good Morning Sunshine!

Lets start the beginning of the month by noting down our details, so this way we can track changes every month

Age:
Weight:
Height:
Date of last menstrual cycle and time frame:

Did you…

o Get out of bed, woke       o Brush you teeth          o Eat breakfast
   up at:                    o Take a shower            o Take your meds
o Smile

Every little task is important sometimes we forget the silliest things so lets make a to-do list to keep track!

To-do list:

Good afternoon!

Did you…

o Eat lunch                  o Finish your tasks?

Good evening love, how's your day so far?

Did you…

o Eat snacks                 o Finish all that you had on   o Eat dinner
o Have a good day               your to do list              o Sleep early
o Have a bad day

Good night and sleep well

Good Morning Sunshine!

Lets start the beginning of the month by noting down our details, so this way we can track changes every month

Age:
Weight:
Height:
Date of last menstrual cycle and time frame:

Did you...

o Get out of bed, woke    o Brush you teeth       o Eat breakfast
   up at:                 o Take a shower         o Take your meds
o Smile

Every little task is important sometimes we forget the silliest things so lets make a to-do list to keep track!

To-do list:

Good afternoon!

Did you...

o Eat lunch              o Finish your tasks?

Good evening love, how's your day so far?

Did you...

o Eat snacks             o Finish all that you had on   o Eat dinner
o Have a good day           your to do list             o Sleep early
o Have a bad day

Good night and sleep well

Good Morning Sunshine!

Lets start the beginning of the month by noting down our details, so this way we can track changes every month

Age:
Weight:
Height:
Date of last menstrual cycle and time frame:

Did you…

- o Get out of bed, woke    o Brush you teeth    o Eat breakfast
  up at:                   o Take a shower      o Take your meds
- o Smile

Every little task is important sometimes we forget the silliest things so lets make a to-do list to keep track!

To-do list:

Good afternoon!

Did you…

- o Eat lunch              o Finish your tasks?

Good evening love, how's your day so far?

Did you…

- o Eat snacks             o Finish all that you had on    o Eat dinner
- o Have a good day           your to do list              o Sleep early
- o Have a bad day

Good night and sleep well

Good Morning Sunshine!

Lets start the beginning of the month by noting down our details, so this way we can track changes every month

Age:
Weight:
Height:
Date of last menstrual cycle and time frame:

Did you…

o Get out of bed, woke          o Brush you teeth          o Eat breakfast
   up at:          o Take a shower          o Take your meds
o Smile

Every little task is important sometimes we forget the silliest things so lets make a to-do list to keep track!

To-do list:

Good afternoon!

Did you…

o Eat lunch          o Finish your tasks?

Good evening love, how's your day so far?

Did you…

o Eat snacks          o Finish all that you had on          o Eat dinner
o Have a good day             your to do list          o Sleep early
o Have a bad day

Good night and sleep well

Good Morning Sunshine!

Lets start the beginning of the month by noting down our details, so this way we can track changes every month

Age:
Weight:
Height:
Date of last menstrual cycle and time frame:

Did you…

- o Get out of bed, woke up at:
- o Smile
- o Brush you teeth
- o Take a shower
- o Eat breakfast
- o Take your meds

Every little task is important sometimes we forget the silliest things so lets make a to-do list to keep track!

To-do list:

Good afternoon!

Did you…

- o Eat lunch
- o Finish your tasks?

Good evening love, how's your day so far?

Did you…

- o Eat snacks
- o Have a good day
- o Have a bad day
- o Finish all that you had on your to do list
- o Eat dinner
- o Sleep early

Good night and sleep well

Good Morning Sunshine!

Lets start the beginning of the month by noting down our details, so this way we can track changes every month

Age:
Weight:
Height:
Date of last menstrual cycle and time frame:

Did you...

o Get out of bed, woke    o Brush you teeth       o Eat breakfast
   up at:                 o Take a shower         o Take your meds
o Smile

Every little task is important sometimes we forget the silliest things so lets make a to-do list to keep track!

To-do list:

Good afternoon!

Did you...

o Eat lunch              o Finish your tasks?

Good evening love, how's your day so far?

Did you...

o Eat snacks             o Finish all that you had on   o Eat dinner
o Have a good day           your to do list               o Sleep early
o Have a bad day

Good night and sleep well

Good Morning Sunshine!

Lets start the beginning of the month by noting down our details, so this way we can track changes every month

Age:
Weight:
Height:
Date of last menstrual cycle and time frame:

Did you...

o Get out of bed, woke      o Brush you teeth       o Eat breakfast
  up at:                        o Take a shower         o Take your meds
o Smile

Every little task is important sometimes we forget the silliest things so lets make a to-do list to keep track!

To-do list:

Good afternoon!

Did you...

o Eat lunch                 o Finish your tasks?

Good evening love, how's your day so far?

Did you...

o Eat snacks                o Finish all that you had on    o Eat dinner
o Have a good day             your to do list               o Sleep early
o Have a bad day

Good night and sleep well

Good Morning Sunshine!

Lets start the beginning of the month by noting down our details, so this way we can track changes every month

Age:
Weight:
Height:
Date of last menstrual cycle and time frame:

Did you...

o Get out of bed, woke      o Brush you teeth      o Eat breakfast
   up at:                   o Take a shower        o Take your meds
o Smile

Every little task is important sometimes we forget the silliest things so lets make a to-do list to keep track!

To-do list:

Good afternoon!

Did you...

o Eat lunch              o Finish your tasks?

Good evening love, how's your day so far?

Did you...

o Eat snacks            o Finish all that you had on    o Eat dinner
o Have a good day          your to do list             o Sleep early
o Have a bad day

Good night and sleep well

# This Month...

o I tried something new by...

o I helped somebody by...

o I become a better person by...

o I lost ___ kgs by...

o I gained ___kgs by...

o

o

o

# Habit Tracker

**Month:**

|  | 1st | 2nd | 3rd | 4th | 5th | |
|---|---|---|---|---|---|---|
| Sleep | | | | | | |
| Caffeine | | | | | | |
| Alcohol | | | | | | |
| Cigarettes | | | | | | |
| Exercise | | | | | | |
|  | 6th | 7th | 8th | 9th | 10th | |
| Sleep | | | | | | |
| Caffeine | | | | | | |
| Alcohol | | | | | | |
| Cigarettes | | | | | | |
| Exercise | | | | | | |
|  | 11th | 12th | 13th | 14th | 15th | |
| Sleep | | | | | | |
| Caffeine | | | | | | |
| Alcohol | | | | | | |
| Cigarettes | | | | | | |
| Exercise | | | | | | |
|  | 16th | 17th | 18th | 19th | 20th | |
| Sleep | | | | | | |
| Caffeine | | | | | | |
| Alcohol | | | | | | |
| Cigarettes | | | | | | |
| Exercise | | | | | | |
|  | 21th | 22th | 23th | 24th | 25th | |
| Sleep | | | | | | |
| Caffeine | | | | | | |
| Alcohol | | | | | | |
| Cigarettes | | | | | | |
| Exercise | | | | | | |
|  | 26th | 27th | 28th | 29th | 30th | 31st |
| Sleep | | | | | | |
| Caffeine | | | | | | |
| Alcohol | | | | | | |
| Cigarettes | | | | | | |
| Exercise | | | | | | |

# Emotion tracker

*How are you felling today? It is important to be in touch with yourself and your emotions.*

|      | Anger | Hurt/Pain | Disappointment | Upset | Happy | Blah! | Lazy |
|------|-------|-----------|----------------|-------|-------|-------|------|
| 1st  |       |           |                |       |       |       |      |
| 2nd  |       |           |                |       |       |       |      |
| 3rd  |       |           |                |       |       |       |      |
| 4th  |       |           |                |       |       |       |      |
| 5th  |       |           |                |       |       |       |      |
| 6th  |       |           |                |       |       |       |      |
| 7th  |       |           |                |       |       |       |      |
| 8th  |       |           |                |       |       |       |      |
| 9th  |       |           |                |       |       |       |      |
| 10th |       |           |                |       |       |       |      |
| 11th |       |           |                |       |       |       |      |
| 12th |       |           |                |       |       |       |      |
| 13th |       |           |                |       |       |       |      |
| 14th |       |           |                |       |       |       |      |
| 15th |       |           |                |       |       |       |      |
| 16th |       |           |                |       |       |       |      |
| 17th |       |           |                |       |       |       |      |
| 18th |       |           |                |       |       |       |      |
| 19th |       |           |                |       |       |       |      |
| 20th |       |           |                |       |       |       |      |
| 21st |       |           |                |       |       |       |      |
| 22nd |       |           |                |       |       |       |      |
| 23rd |       |           |                |       |       |       |      |
| 24th |       |           |                |       |       |       |      |
| 25th |       |           |                |       |       |       |      |
| 26th |       |           |                |       |       |       |      |
| 27th |       |           |                |       |       |       |      |
| 28th |       |           |                |       |       |       |      |
| 29th |       |           |                |       |       |       |      |
| 30th |       |           |                |       |       |       |      |
| 31st |       |           |                |       |       |       |      |

|  | Guilt | Anxious | Sadness | Shame | Guilt | Worthless |
|---|---|---|---|---|---|---|
| 1st |  |  |  |  |  |  |
| 2nd |  |  |  |  |  |  |
| 3rd |  |  |  |  |  |  |
| 4th |  |  |  |  |  |  |
| 5th |  |  |  |  |  |  |
| 6th |  |  |  |  |  |  |
| 7th |  |  |  |  |  |  |
| 8th |  |  |  |  |  |  |
| 9th |  |  |  |  |  |  |
| 10th |  |  |  |  |  |  |
| 11th |  |  |  |  |  |  |
| 12th |  |  |  |  |  |  |
| 13th |  |  |  |  |  |  |
| 14th |  |  |  |  |  |  |
| 15th |  |  |  |  |  |  |
| 16th |  |  |  |  |  |  |
| 17th |  |  |  |  |  |  |
| 18th |  |  |  |  |  |  |
| 19th |  |  |  |  |  |  |
| 20th |  |  |  |  |  |  |
| 21st |  |  |  |  |  |  |
| 22nd |  |  |  |  |  |  |
| 23rd |  |  |  |  |  |  |
| 24th |  |  |  |  |  |  |
| 25th |  |  |  |  |  |  |
| 26th |  |  |  |  |  |  |
| 27th |  |  |  |  |  |  |
| 28th |  |  |  |  |  |  |
| 29th |  |  |  |  |  |  |
| 30th |  |  |  |  |  |  |
| 31st |  |  |  |  |  |  |

# Food Tracker

| | Healthy food | Junk food | Both | Didn't eat ☹ |
|---|---|---|---|---|
| 1st | | | | |
| 2nd | | | | |
| 3rd | | | | |
| 4th | | | | |
| 5th | | | | |
| 6th | | | | |
| 7th | | | | |
| 8th | | | | |
| 9th | | | | |
| 10th | | | | |
| 11th | | | | |
| 12th | | | | |
| 13th | | | | |
| 14th | | | | |
| 15th | | | | |
| 16th | | | | |
| 17th | | | | |
| 18th | | | | |
| 19th | | | | |
| 20th | | | | |
| 21st | | | | |
| 22nd | | | | |
| 23rd | | | | |
| 24th | | | | |
| 25th | | | | |
| 26th | | | | |
| 27th | | | | |
| 28th | | | | |
| 29th | | | | |
| 30th | | | | |
| 31st | | | | |

# Weight Tracker

**Month:**

| | Kgs/lbs | | Kgs/lbs |
|---|---|---|---|
| 1st | | 16th | |
| 2nd | | 17th | |
| 3rd | | 18th | |
| 4th | | 19th | |
| 5th | | 20th | |
| 6th | | 21st | |
| 7th | | 22nd | |
| 8th | | 23rd | |
| 9th | | 24th | |
| 10th | | 25th | |
| 11th | | 26th | |
| 12th | | 27th | |
| 13th | | 28th | |
| 14th | | 29th | |
| 15th | | 30th | |
| | | 31st | |

# Journal

Good Morning Sunshine!

Lets start the beginning of the month by noting down our details, so this way we can track changes every month

Age:
Weight:
Height:
Date of last menstrual cycle and time frame:

Did you...

- o Get out of bed, woke
    up at:
- o Smile

- o Brush you teeth
- o Take a shower

- o Eat breakfast
- o Take your meds

Every little task is important sometimes we forget the silliest things so lets make a to-do list to keep track!

To-do list:

Good afternoon!

Did you...

- o Eat lunch

- o Finish your tasks?

Good evening love, how's your day so far?

Did you...

- o Eat snacks
- o Have a good day
- o Have a bad day

- o Finish all that you had on
    your to do list

- o Eat dinner
- o Sleep early

Good night and sleep well

Good Morning Sunshine!

Lets start the beginning of the month by noting down our details, so this way we can track changes every month

Age:
Weight:
Height:
Date of last menstrual cycle and time frame:

Did you…

o Get out of bed, woke        o Brush you teeth          o Eat breakfast
   up at:                     o Take a shower            o Take your meds
o Smile

Every little task is important sometimes we forget the silliest things so lets make a to-do list to keep track!

To-do list:

Good afternoon!

Did you…

o Eat lunch                   o Finish your tasks?

Good evening love, how's your day so far?

Did you…

o Eat snacks                  o Finish all that you had on    o Eat dinner
o Have a good day                your to do list               o Sleep early
o Have a bad day

Good night and sleep well

Good Morning Sunshine!

Lets start the beginning of the month by noting down our details, so this way we can track changes every month

Age:
Weight:
Height:
Date of last menstrual cycle and time frame:

Did you...

o Get out of bed, woke       o Brush you teeth       o Eat breakfast
   up at:                     o Take a shower         o Take your meds
o Smile

Every little task is important sometimes we forget the silliest things so lets make a to-do list to keep track!

To-do list:

Good afternoon!

Did you...

o Eat lunch                  o Finish your tasks?

Good evening love, how's your day so far?

Did you...

o Eat snacks                 o Finish all that you had on    o Eat dinner
o Have a good day               your to do list               o Sleep early
o Have a bad day

Good night and sleep well

Good Morning Sunshine!

Lets start the beginning of the month by noting down our details, so this way we can track changes every month

Age:
Weight:
Height:
Date of last menstrual cycle and time frame:

Did you...

o Get out of bed, woke          o Brush you teeth          o Eat breakfast
   up at:                        o Take a shower            o Take your meds
o Smile

Every little task is important sometimes we forget the silliest things so lets make a to-do list to keep track!

To-do list:

Good afternoon!

Did you...

o Eat lunch                    o Finish your tasks?

Good evening love, how's your day so far?

Did you...

o Eat snacks                   o Finish all that you had on   o Eat dinner
o Have a good day                 your to do list            o Sleep early
o Have a bad day

Good night and sleep well

Good Morning Sunshine!

Lets start the beginning of the month by noting down our details, so this way we can track changes every month

Age:
Weight:
Height:
Date of last menstrual cycle and time frame:

Did you…

- o Get out of bed, woke up at:
- o Smile
- o Brush you teeth
- o Take a shower
- o Eat breakfast
- o Take your meds

Every little task is important sometimes we forget the silliest things so lets make a to-do list to keep track!

To-do list:

Good afternoon!

Did you…

- o Eat lunch
- o Finish your tasks?

Good evening love, how's your day so far?

Did you…

- o Eat snacks
- o Have a good day
- o Have a bad day
- o Finish all that you had on your to do list
- o Eat dinner
- o Sleep early

Good night and sleep well

Good Morning Sunshine!

Lets start the beginning of the month by noting down our details, so this way we can track changes every month

Age:
Weight:
Height:
Date of last menstrual cycle and time frame:

Did you…

o Get out of bed, woke       o Brush you teeth          o Eat breakfast
   up at:                    o Take a shower            o Take your meds
o Smile

Every little task is important sometimes we forget the silliest things so lets make a to-do list to keep track!

To-do list:

Good afternoon!

Did you…

o Eat lunch                  o Finish your tasks?

Good evening love, how's your day so far?

Did you…

o Eat snacks                 o Finish all that you had on   o Eat dinner
o Have a good day               your to do list              o Sleep early
o Have a bad day

Good night and sleep well

Good Morning Sunshine!

Lets start the beginning of the month by noting down our details, so this way we can track changes every month

Age:
Weight:
Height:
Date of last menstrual cycle and time frame:

Did you…

- o Get out of bed, woke up at:
- o Smile
- o Brush you teeth
- o Take a shower
- o Eat breakfast
- o Take your meds

Every little task is important sometimes we forget the silliest things so lets make a to-do list to keep track!

To-do list:

Good afternoon!

Did you…

- o Eat lunch
- o Finish your tasks?

Good evening love, how's your day so far?

Did you…

- o Eat snacks
- o Have a good day
- o Have a bad day
- o Finish all that you had on your to do list
- o Eat dinner
- o Sleep early

Good night and sleep well

Good Morning Sunshine!

Lets start the beginning of the month by noting down our details, so this way we can track changes every month

Age:
Weight:
Height:
Date of last menstrual cycle and time frame:

Did you…

o Get out of bed, woke      o Brush you teeth        o Eat breakfast
    up at:                  o Take a shower          o Take your meds
o Smile

Every little task is important sometimes we forget the silliest things so lets make a to-do list to keep track!

To-do list:

Good afternoon!

Did you…

o Eat lunch                o Finish your tasks?

Good evening love, how's your day so far?

Did you…

o Eat snacks               o Finish all that you had on   o Eat dinner
o Have a good day              your to do list            o Sleep early
o Have a bad day

Good night and sleep well

Good Morning Sunshine!

Lets start the beginning of the month by noting down our details, so this way we can track changes every month

Age:
Weight:
Height:
Date of last menstrual cycle and time frame:

Did you...

- o Get out of bed, woke up at:
- o Smile

- o Brush you teeth
- o Take a shower

- o Eat breakfast
- o Take your meds

Every little task is important sometimes we forget the silliest things so lets make a to-do list to keep track!

To-do list:

Good afternoon!

Did you...

- o Eat lunch

- o Finish your tasks?

Good evening love, how's your day so far?

Did you...

- o Eat snacks
- o Have a good day
- o Have a bad day

- o Finish all that you had on your to do list

- o Eat dinner
- o Sleep early

Good night and sleep well

Good Morning Sunshine!

Lets start the beginning of the month by noting down our details, so this way we can track changes every month

Age:
Weight:
Height:
Date of last menstrual cycle and time frame:

Did you…

| | | |
|---|---|---|
| o Get out of bed, woke up at: | o Brush you teeth | o Eat breakfast |
| o Smile | o Take a shower | o Take your meds |

Every little task is important sometimes we forget the silliest things so lets make a to-do list to keep track!

To-do list:

Good afternoon!

Did you…

o Eat lunch          o Finish your tasks?

Good evening love, how's your day so far?

Did you…

| | | |
|---|---|---|
| o Eat snacks | o Finish all that you had on your to do list | o Eat dinner |
| o Have a good day | | o Sleep early |
| o Have a bad day | | |

Good night and sleep well

Good Morning Sunshine!

Lets start the beginning of the month by noting down our details, so this way we can track changes every month

Age:
Weight:
Height:
Date of last menstrual cycle and time frame:

Did you…

o Get out of bed, woke      o Brush you teeth       o Eat breakfast
  up at:                        o Take a shower        o Take your meds
o Smile

Every little task is important sometimes we forget the silliest things so lets make a to-do list to keep track!

To-do list:

Good afternoon!

Did you…

o Eat lunch                        o Finish your tasks?

Good evening love, how's your day so far?

Did you…

o Eat snacks               o Finish all that you had on    o Eat dinner
o Have a good day             your to do list                o Sleep early
o Have a bad day

Good night and sleep well

Good Morning Sunshine!

Lets start the beginning of the month by noting down our details, so this way we can track changes every month

Age:
Weight:
Height:
Date of last menstrual cycle and time frame:

Did you…

o Get out of bed, woke     o Brush you teeth     o Eat breakfast
   up at:                  o Take a shower       o Take your meds
o Smile

Every little task is important sometimes we forget the silliest things so lets make a to-do list to keep track!

To-do list:

Good afternoon!

Did you…

o Eat lunch     o Finish your tasks?

Good evening love, how's your day so far?

Did you…

o Eat snacks        o Finish all that you had on    o Eat dinner
o Have a good day      your to do list             o Sleep early
o Have a bad day

Good night and sleep well

Good Morning Sunshine!

Lets start the beginning of the month by noting down our details, so this way we can track changes every month

Age:
Weight:
Height:
Date of last menstrual cycle and time frame:

Did you…

o Get out of bed, woke    o Brush you teeth    o Eat breakfast
   up at:                 o Take a shower      o Take your meds
o Smile

Every little task is important sometimes we forget the silliest things so lets make a to-do list to keep track!

To-do list:

Good afternoon!

Did you…

o Eat lunch              o Finish your tasks?

Good evening love, how's your day so far?

Did you…

o Eat snacks             o Finish all that you had on    o Eat dinner
o Have a good day           your to do list              o Sleep early
o Have a bad day

Good night and sleep well

dd/mm/yy

Good Morning Sunshine!

Lets start the beginning of the month by noting down our details, so this way we can track changes every month

Age:
Weight:
Height:
Date of last menstrual cycle and time frame:

Did you...

- o Get out of bed, woke up at:
- o Smile
- o Brush you teeth
- o Take a shower
- o Eat breakfast
- o Take your meds

Every little task is important sometimes we forget the silliest things so lets make a to-do list to keep track!

To-do list:

Good afternoon!

Did you...

- o Eat lunch
- o Finish your tasks?

Good evening love, how's your day so far?

Did you...

- o Eat snacks
- o Have a good day
- o Have a bad day
- o Finish all that you had on your to do list
- o Eat dinner
- o Sleep early

Good night and sleep well

dd/mm/yy

Good Morning Sunshine!

Lets start the beginning of the month by noting down our details, so this way we can track changes every month

Age:
Weight:
Height:
Date of last menstrual cycle and time frame:

Did you…

- o Get out of bed, woke up at:
- o Smile
- o Brush you teeth
- o Take a shower
- o Eat breakfast
- o Take your meds

Every little task is important sometimes we forget the silliest things so lets make a to-do list to keep track!

To-do list:

Good afternoon!

Did you…

- o Eat lunch
- o Finish your tasks?

Good evening love, how's your day so far?

Did you…

- o Eat snacks
- o Have a good day
- o Have a bad day
- o Finish all that you had on your to do list
- o Eat dinner
- o Sleep early

Good night and sleep well

Good Morning Sunshine!

Lets start the beginning of the month by noting down our details, so this way we can track changes every month

Age:
Weight:
Height:
Date of last menstrual cycle and time frame:

Did you...

- o Get out of bed, woke up at:
- o Smile

- o Brush you teeth
- o Take a shower

- o Eat breakfast
- o Take your meds

Every little task is important sometimes we forget the silliest things so lets make a to-do list to keep track!

To-do list:

Good afternoon!

Did you...

- o Eat lunch

- o Finish your tasks?

Good evening love, how's your day so far?

Did you...

- o Eat snacks
- o Have a good day
- o Have a bad day

- o Finish all that you had on your to do list

- o Eat dinner
- o Sleep early

Good night and sleep well

Good Morning Sunshine!

Lets start the beginning of the month by noting down our details, so this way we can track changes every month

Age:
Weight:
Height:
Date of last menstrual cycle and time frame:

Did you…

o Get out of bed, woke      o Brush you teeth       o Eat breakfast
  up at:                    o Take a shower         o Take your meds
o Smile

Every little task is important sometimes we forget the silliest things so lets make a to-do list to keep track!

To-do list:

Good afternoon!

Did you…

o Eat lunch                 o Finish your tasks?

Good evening love, how's your day so far?

Did you…

o Eat snacks                o Finish all that you had on    o Eat dinner
o Have a good day             your to do list               o Sleep early
o Have a bad day

Good night and sleep well

Good Morning Sunshine!

Lets start the beginning of the month by noting down our details, so this way we can track changes every month

Age:
Weight:
Height:
Date of last menstrual cycle and time frame:

Did you...

o Get out of bed, woke        o Brush you teeth          o Eat breakfast
   up at:                     o Take a shower            o Take your meds
o Smile

Every little task is important sometimes we forget the silliest things so lets make a to-do list to keep track!

To-do list:

Good afternoon!

Did you...

o Eat lunch                   o Finish your tasks?

Good evening love, how's your day so far?

Did you...

o Eat snacks                  o Finish all that you had on    o Eat dinner
o Have a good day                your to do list              o Sleep early
o Have a bad day

Good night and sleep well

Good Morning Sunshine!

Lets start the beginning of the month by noting down our details, so this way we can track changes every month

Age:
Weight:
Height:
Date of last menstrual cycle and time frame:

Did you…

o Get out of bed, woke          o Brush you teeth          o Eat breakfast
   up at:                       o Take a shower            o Take your meds
o Smile

Every little task is important sometimes we forget the silliest things so lets make a to-do list to keep track!

To-do list:

Good afternoon!

Did you…

o Eat lunch                o Finish your tasks?

Good evening love, how's your day so far?

Did you…

o Eat snacks               o Finish all that you had on   o Eat dinner
o Have a good day             your to do list             o Sleep early
o Have a bad day

Good night and sleep well

Good Morning Sunshine!

Lets start the beginning of the month by noting down our details, so this way we can track changes every month

Age:
Weight:
Height:
Date of last menstrual cycle and time frame:

Did you...

- o Get out of bed, woke up at:
- o Smile
- o Brush you teeth
- o Take a shower
- o Eat breakfast
- o Take your meds

Every little task is important sometimes we forget the silliest things so lets make a to-do list to keep track!

To-do list:

Good afternoon!

Did you...

- o Eat lunch
- o Finish your tasks?

Good evening love, how's your day so far?

Did you...

- o Eat snacks
- o Have a good day
- o Have a bad day
- o Finish all that you had on your to do list
- o Eat dinner
- o Sleep early

Good night and sleep well

Good Morning Sunshine!

Lets start the beginning of the month by noting down our details, so this way we can track changes every month

Age:
Weight:
Height:
Date of last menstrual cycle and time frame:

Did you…

o Get out of bed, woke          o Brush you teeth          o Eat breakfast
    up at:                        o Take a shower            o Take your meds
o Smile

Every little task is important sometimes we forget the silliest things so lets make a to-do list to keep track!

To-do list:

Good afternoon!

Did you…

o Eat lunch                    o Finish your tasks?

Good evening love, how's your day so far?

Did you…

o Eat snacks                   o Finish all that you had on   o Eat dinner
o Have a good day                 your to do list              o Sleep early
o Have a bad day

Good night and sleep well

Good Morning Sunshine!

Lets start the beginning of the month by noting down our details, so this way we can track changes every month

Age:
Weight:
Height:
Date of last menstrual cycle and time frame:

Did you...

o Get out of bed, woke    o Brush you teeth    o Eat breakfast
   up at:               o Take a shower    o Take your meds
o Smile

Every little task is important sometimes we forget the silliest things so lets make a to-do list to keep track!

To-do list:

Good afternoon!

Did you...

o Eat lunch            o Finish your tasks?

Good evening love, how's your day so far?

Did you...

o Eat snacks        o Finish all that you had on    o Eat dinner
o Have a good day      your to do list           o Sleep early
o Have a bad day

Good night and sleep well

Good Morning Sunshine!

Lets start the beginning of the month by noting down our details, so this way we can track changes every month

Age:
Weight:
Height:
Date of last menstrual cycle and time frame:

Did you…

- o Get out of bed, woke up at:
- o Smile
- o Brush you teeth
- o Take a shower
- o Eat breakfast
- o Take your meds

Every little task is important sometimes we forget the silliest things so lets make a to-do list to keep track!

To-do list:

Good afternoon!

Did you…

- o Eat lunch
- o Finish your tasks?

Good evening love, how's your day so far?

Did you…

- o Eat snacks
- o Have a good day
- o Have a bad day
- o Finish all that you had on your to do list
- o Eat dinner
- o Sleep early

Good night and sleep well

Good Morning Sunshine!

Lets start the beginning of the month by noting down our details, so this way we can track changes every month

Age:
Weight:
Height:
Date of last menstrual cycle and time frame:

Did you...

| | | |
|---|---|---|
| o Get out of bed, woke up at: | o Brush you teeth | o Eat breakfast |
| | o Take a shower | o Take your meds |
| o Smile | | |

Every little task is important sometimes we forget the silliest things so lets make a to-do list to keep track!

To-do list:

Good afternoon!

Did you...

o Eat lunch                    o Finish your tasks?

Good evening love, how's your day so far?

Did you...

| | | |
|---|---|---|
| o Eat snacks | o Finish all that you had on | o Eat dinner |
| o Have a good day | your to do list | o Sleep early |
| o Have a bad day | | |

Good night and sleep well

Good Morning Sunshine!

Lets start the beginning of the month by noting down our details, so this way we can track changes every month

Age:
Weight:
Height:
Date of last menstrual cycle and time frame:

Did you…

o Get out of bed, woke    o Brush you teeth    o Eat breakfast
  up at:                  o Take a shower      o Take your meds
o Smile

Every little task is important sometimes we forget the silliest things so lets make a to-do list to keep track!

To-do list:

Good afternoon!

Did you…

o Eat lunch                o Finish your tasks?

Good evening love, how's your day so far?

Did you…

o Eat snacks          o Finish all that you had on    o Eat dinner
o Have a good day       your to do list              o Sleep early
o Have a bad day

Good night and sleep well

Good Morning Sunshine!

Lets start the beginning of the month by noting down our details, so this way we can track changes every month

Age:
Weight:
Height:
Date of last menstrual cycle and time frame:

Did you…

o Get out of bed, woke    o Brush you teeth      o Eat breakfast
   up at:                 o Take a shower        o Take your meds
o Smile

Every little task is important sometimes we forget the silliest things so lets make a to-do list to keep track!

To-do list:

Good afternoon!

Did you…

o Eat lunch              o Finish your tasks?

Good evening love, how's your day so far?

Did you…

o Eat snacks             o Finish all that you had on   o Eat dinner
o Have a good day           your to do list            o Sleep early
o Have a bad day

Good night and sleep well

Good Morning Sunshine!

Lets start the beginning of the month by noting down our details, so this way we can track changes every month

Age:
Weight:
Height:
Date of last menstrual cycle and time frame:

Did you...

- o Get out of bed, woke up at:
- o Smile
- o Brush you teeth
- o Take a shower
- o Eat breakfast
- o Take your meds

Every little task is important sometimes we forget the silliest things so lets make a to-do list to keep track!

To-do list:

Good afternoon!

Did you...

- o Eat lunch
- o Finish your tasks?

Good evening love, how's your day so far?

Did you...

- o Eat snacks
- o Have a good day
- o Have a bad day
- o Finish all that you had on your to do list
- o Eat dinner
- o Sleep early

Good night and sleep well

Good Morning Sunshine!

Lets start the beginning of the month by noting down our details, so this way we can track changes every month

Age:
Weight:
Height:
Date of last menstrual cycle and time frame:

Did you…

o Get out of bed, woke     o Brush you teeth        o Eat breakfast
   up at:                  o Take a shower          o Take your meds
o Smile

Every little task is important sometimes we forget the silliest things so lets make a to-do list to keep track!

To-do list:

Good afternoon!

Did you…

o Eat lunch              o Finish your tasks?

Good evening love, how's your day so far?

Did you…

o Eat snacks             o Finish all that you had on    o Eat dinner
o Have a good day           your to do list             o Sleep early
o Have a bad day

Good night and sleep well

Good Morning Sunshine!

Lets start the beginning of the month by noting down our details, so this way we can track changes every month

Age:
Weight:
Height:
Date of last menstrual cycle and time frame:

Did you…

- o Get out of bed, woke up at:
- o Smile
- o Brush you teeth
- o Take a shower
- o Eat breakfast
- o Take your meds

Every little task is important sometimes we forget the silliest things so lets make a to-do list to keep track!

To-do list:

Good afternoon!

Did you…

- o Eat lunch
- o Finish your tasks?

Good evening love, how's your day so far?

Did you…

- o Eat snacks
- o Have a good day
- o Have a bad day
- o Finish all that you had on your to do list
- o Eat dinner
- o Sleep early

Good night and sleep well

Good Morning Sunshine!

Lets start the beginning of the month by noting down our details, so this way we can track changes every month

Age:
Weight:
Height:
Date of last menstrual cycle and time frame:

Did you…

o Get out of bed, woke     o Brush you teeth        o Eat breakfast
  up at:                   o Take a shower          o Take your meds
o Smile

Every little task is important sometimes we forget the silliest things so lets make a to-do list to keep track!

To-do list:

Good afternoon!

Did you…

o Eat lunch               o Finish your tasks?

Good evening love, how's your day so far?

Did you…

o Eat snacks              o Finish all that you had on    o Eat dinner
o Have a good day           your to do list              o Sleep early
o Have a bad day

Good night and sleep well

Good Morning Sunshine!

Lets start the beginning of the month by noting down our details, so this way we can track changes every month

Age:
Weight:
Height:
Date of last menstrual cycle and time frame:

Did you...

- o Get out of bed, woke up at:
- o Smile
- o Brush you teeth
- o Take a shower
- o Eat breakfast
- o Take your meds

Every little task is important sometimes we forget the silliest things so lets make a to-do list to keep track!

To-do list:

Good afternoon!

Did you...

- o Eat lunch
- o Finish your tasks?

Good evening love, how's your day so far?

Did you...

- o Eat snacks
- o Have a good day
- o Have a bad day
- o Finish all that you had on your to do list
- o Eat dinner
- o Sleep early

Good night and sleep well

# This Month...

o I tried something new by...

o I helped somebody by...

o I become a better person by...

o I lost ___ kgs by...

o I gained ___kgs by...

o

o

o

# Habit Tracker

**Month:**

|           | 1st | 2nd | 3rd | 4th | 5th | |
|-----------|-----|-----|-----|-----|-----|---|
| Sleep     |     |     |     |     |     | |
| Caffeine  |     |     |     |     |     | |
| Alcohol   |     |     |     |     |     | |
| Cigarettes|     |     |     |     |     | |
| Exercise  |     |     |     |     |     | |
|           | 6th | 7th | 8th | 9th | 10th | |
| Sleep     |     |     |     |     |     | |
| Caffeine  |     |     |     |     |     | |
| Alcohol   |     |     |     |     |     | |
| Cigarettes|     |     |     |     |     | |
| Exercise  |     |     |     |     |     | |
|           | 11th | 12th | 13th | 14th | 15th | |
| Sleep     |     |     |     |     |     | |
| Caffeine  |     |     |     |     |     | |
| Alcohol   |     |     |     |     |     | |
| Cigarettes|     |     |     |     |     | |
| Exercise  |     |     |     |     |     | |
|           | 16th | 17th | 18th | 19th | 20th | |
| Sleep     |     |     |     |     |     | |
| Caffeine  |     |     |     |     |     | |
| Alcohol   |     |     |     |     |     | |
| Cigarettes|     |     |     |     |     | |
| Exercise  |     |     |     |     |     | |
|           | 21th | 22th | 23th | 24th | 25th | |
| Sleep     |     |     |     |     |     | |
| Caffeine  |     |     |     |     |     | |
| Alcohol   |     |     |     |     |     | |
| Cigarettes|     |     |     |     |     | |
| Exercise  |     |     |     |     |     | |
|           | 26th | 27th | 28th | 29th | 30th | 31st |
| Sleep     |     |     |     |     |     | |
| Caffeine  |     |     |     |     |     | |
| Alcohol   |     |     |     |     |     | |
| Cigarettes|     |     |     |     |     | |
| Exercise  |     |     |     |     |     | |

# Emotion tracker

*How are you felling today? It is important to be in touch with yourself and your emotions.*

|  | Anger | Hurt/Pain | Disappointment | Upset | Happy | Blah! | Lazy |
|---|---|---|---|---|---|---|---|
| 1st |  |  |  |  |  |  |  |
| 2nd |  |  |  |  |  |  |  |
| 3rd |  |  |  |  |  |  |  |
| 4th |  |  |  |  |  |  |  |
| 5th |  |  |  |  |  |  |  |
| 6th |  |  |  |  |  |  |  |
| 7th |  |  |  |  |  |  |  |
| 8th |  |  |  |  |  |  |  |
| 9th |  |  |  |  |  |  |  |
| 10th |  |  |  |  |  |  |  |
| 11th |  |  |  |  |  |  |  |
| 12th |  |  |  |  |  |  |  |
| 13th |  |  |  |  |  |  |  |
| 14th |  |  |  |  |  |  |  |
| 15th |  |  |  |  |  |  |  |
| 16th |  |  |  |  |  |  |  |
| 17th |  |  |  |  |  |  |  |
| 18th |  |  |  |  |  |  |  |
| 19th |  |  |  |  |  |  |  |
| 20th |  |  |  |  |  |  |  |
| 21st |  |  |  |  |  |  |  |
| 22nd |  |  |  |  |  |  |  |
| 23rd |  |  |  |  |  |  |  |
| 24th |  |  |  |  |  |  |  |
| 25th |  |  |  |  |  |  |  |
| 26th |  |  |  |  |  |  |  |
| 27th |  |  |  |  |  |  |  |
| 28th |  |  |  |  |  |  |  |
| 29th |  |  |  |  |  |  |  |
| 30th |  |  |  |  |  |  |  |
| 31st |  |  |  |  |  |  |  |

|        | Guilt | Anxious | Sadness | Shame | Guilt | Worthless |
|--------|-------|---------|---------|-------|-------|-----------|
| 1st    |       |         |         |       |       |           |
| 2nd    |       |         |         |       |       |           |
| 3rd    |       |         |         |       |       |           |
| 4th    |       |         |         |       |       |           |
| 5th    |       |         |         |       |       |           |
| 6th    |       |         |         |       |       |           |
| 7th    |       |         |         |       |       |           |
| 8th    |       |         |         |       |       |           |
| 9th    |       |         |         |       |       |           |
| 10th   |       |         |         |       |       |           |
| 11th   |       |         |         |       |       |           |
| 12th   |       |         |         |       |       |           |
| 13th   |       |         |         |       |       |           |
| 14th   |       |         |         |       |       |           |
| 15th   |       |         |         |       |       |           |
| 16th   |       |         |         |       |       |           |
| 17th   |       |         |         |       |       |           |
| 18th   |       |         |         |       |       |           |
| 19th   |       |         |         |       |       |           |
| 20th   |       |         |         |       |       |           |
| 21st   |       |         |         |       |       |           |
| 22nd   |       |         |         |       |       |           |
| 23rd   |       |         |         |       |       |           |
| 24th   |       |         |         |       |       |           |
| 25th   |       |         |         |       |       |           |
| 26th   |       |         |         |       |       |           |
| 27th   |       |         |         |       |       |           |
| 28th   |       |         |         |       |       |           |
| 29th   |       |         |         |       |       |           |
| 30th   |       |         |         |       |       |           |
| 31st   |       |         |         |       |       |           |

# Food Tracker

| | Healthy food | Junk food | Both | Didn't eat ☹ |
|---|---|---|---|---|
| 1st | | | | |
| 2nd | | | | |
| 3rd | | | | |
| 4th | | | | |
| 5th | | | | |
| 6th | | | | |
| 7th | | | | |
| 8th | | | | |
| 9th | | | | |
| 10th | | | | |
| 11th | | | | |
| 12th | | | | |
| 13th | | | | |
| 14th | | | | |
| 15th | | | | |
| 16th | | | | |
| 17th | | | | |
| 18th | | | | |
| 19th | | | | |
| 20th | | | | |
| 21st | | | | |
| 22nd | | | | |
| 23rd | | | | |
| 24th | | | | |
| 25th | | | | |
| 26th | | | | |
| 27th | | | | |
| 28th | | | | |
| 29th | | | | |
| 30th | | | | |
| 31st | | | | |

# Weight Tracker

**Month:**

| | Kgs/lbs | | Kgs/lbs |
|---|---|---|---|
| 1st | | 16th | |
| 2nd | | 17th | |
| 3rd | | 18th | |
| 4th | | 19th | |
| 5th | | 20th | |
| 6th | | 21st | |
| 7th | | 22nd | |
| 8th | | 23rd | |
| 9th | | 24th | |
| 10th | | 25th | |
| 11th | | 26th | |
| 12th | | 27th | |
| 13th | | 28th | |
| 14th | | 29th | |
| 15th | | 30th | |
| | | 31st | |

# Journal

Good Morning Sunshine!

Lets start the beginning of the month by noting down our details, so this way we can track changes every month

Age:
Weight:
Height:
Date of last menstrual cycle and time frame:

Did you...

o Get out of bed, woke      o Brush you teeth      o Eat breakfast
   up at:                   o Take a shower        o Take your meds
o Smile

Every little task is important sometimes we forget the silliest things so lets make a to-do list to keep track!

To-do list:

Good afternoon!

Did you...

o Eat lunch            o Finish your tasks?

Good evening love, how's your day so far?

Did you...

o Eat snacks           o Finish all that you had on    o Eat dinner
o Have a good day         your to do list              o Sleep early
o Have a bad day

Good night and sleep well

Good Morning Sunshine!

Lets start the beginning of the month by noting down our details, so this way we can track changes every month

Age:
Weight:
Height:
Date of last menstrual cycle and time frame:

Did you...

o Get out of bed, woke      o Brush you teeth        o Eat breakfast
   up at:                   o Take a shower          o Take your meds
o Smile

Every little task is important sometimes we forget the silliest things so lets make a to-do list to keep track!

To-do list:




Good afternoon!

Did you...

o Eat lunch                o Finish your tasks?

Good evening love, how's your day so far?

Did you...

o Eat snacks               o Finish all that you had on   o Eat dinner
o Have a good day             your to do list              o Sleep early
o Have a bad day

Good night and sleep well

Good Morning Sunshine!

Lets start the beginning of the month by noting down our details, so this way we can track changes every month

Age:
Weight:
Height:
Date of last menstrual cycle and time frame:

Did you…

- o Get out of bed, woke
  up at:
- o Smile

- o Brush you teeth
- o Take a shower

- o Eat breakfast
- o Take your meds

Every little task is important sometimes we forget the silliest things so lets make a to-do list to keep track!

To-do list:

Good afternoon!

Did you…

- o Eat lunch
- o Finish your tasks?

Good evening love, how's your day so far?

Did you…

- o Eat snacks
- o Have a good day
- o Have a bad day

- o Finish all that you had on
  your to do list

- o Eat dinner
- o Sleep early

Good night and sleep well

Good Morning Sunshine!

Lets start the beginning of the month by noting down our details, so this way we can track changes every month

Age:
Weight:
Height:
Date of last menstrual cycle and time frame:

Did you…

o Get out of bed, woke    o Brush you teeth    o Eat breakfast
   up at:                 o Take a shower      o Take your meds
o Smile

Every little task is important sometimes we forget the silliest things so lets make a to-do list to keep track!

To-do list:

Good afternoon!

Did you…

o Eat lunch              o Finish your tasks?

Good evening love, how's your day so far?

Did you…

o Eat snacks            o Finish all that you had on    o Eat dinner
o Have a good day          your to do list             o Sleep early
o Have a bad day

Good night and sleep well

Good Morning Sunshine!

Lets start the beginning of the month by noting down our details, so this way we can track changes every month

Age:
Weight:
Height:
Date of last menstrual cycle and time frame:

Did you…

o Get out of bed, woke          o Brush you teeth          o Eat breakfast
   up at:                          o Take a shower            o Take your meds
o Smile

Every little task is important sometimes we forget the silliest things so lets make a to-do list to keep track!

To-do list:

Good afternoon!

Did you…

o Eat lunch                      o Finish your tasks?

Good evening love, how's your day so far?

Did you…

o Eat snacks                     o Finish all that you had on      o Eat dinner
o Have a good day                   your to do list                 o Sleep early
o Have a bad day

Good night and sleep well

Good Morning Sunshine!

Lets start the beginning of the month by noting down our details, so this way we can track changes every month

Age:
Weight:
Height:
Date of last menstrual cycle and time frame:

Did you...

- o Get out of bed, woke up at:
- o Smile
- o Brush you teeth
- o Take a shower
- o Eat breakfast
- o Take your meds

Every little task is important sometimes we forget the silliest things so lets make a to-do list to keep track!

To-do list:

Good afternoon!

Did you...

- o Eat lunch
- o Finish your tasks?

Good evening love, how's your day so far?

Did you...

- o Eat snacks
- o Have a good day
- o Have a bad day
- o Finish all that you had on your to do list
- o Eat dinner
- o Sleep early

Good night and sleep well

Good Morning Sunshine!

Lets start the beginning of the month by noting down our details, so this way we can track changes every month

Age:
Weight:
Height:
Date of last menstrual cycle and time frame:

Did you...

- o Get out of bed, woke up at:
- o Smile

- o Brush you teeth
- o Take a shower

- o Eat breakfast
- o Take your meds

Every little task is important sometimes we forget the silliest things so lets make a to-do list to keep track!

To-do list:

Good afternoon!

Did you...

- o Eat lunch

- o Finish your tasks?

Good evening love, how's your day so far?

Did you...

- o Eat snacks
- o Have a good day
- o Have a bad day

- o Finish all that you had on your to do list

- o Eat dinner
- o Sleep early

Good night and sleep well

Good Morning Sunshine!

Lets start the beginning of the month by noting down our details, so this way we can track changes every month

Age:
Weight:
Height:
Date of last menstrual cycle and time frame:

Did you…

- o Get out of bed, woke up at:
- o Smile
- o Brush you teeth
- o Take a shower
- o Eat breakfast
- o Take your meds

Every little task is important sometimes we forget the silliest things so lets make a to-do list to keep track!

To-do list:

Good afternoon!

Did you…

- o Eat lunch
- o Finish your tasks?

Good evening love, how's your day so far?

Did you…

- o Eat snacks
- o Have a good day
- o Have a bad day
- o Finish all that you had on your to do list
- o Eat dinner
- o Sleep early

Good night and sleep well

Good Morning Sunshine!

Lets start the beginning of the month by noting down our details, so this way we can track changes every month

Age:
Weight:
Height:
Date of last menstrual cycle and time frame:

Did you…

- o Get out of bed, woke up at:
- o Smile
- o Brush you teeth
- o Take a shower
- o Eat breakfast
- o Take your meds

Every little task is important sometimes we forget the silliest things so lets make a to-do list to keep track!

To-do list:

Good afternoon!

Did you…

- o Eat lunch
- o Finish your tasks?

Good evening love, how's your day so far?

Did you…

- o Eat snacks
- o Have a good day
- o Have a bad day
- o Finish all that you had on your to do list
- o Eat dinner
- o Sleep early

Good night and sleep well

Good Morning Sunshine!

Lets start the beginning of the month by noting down our details, so this way we can track changes every month

Age:
Weight:
Height:
Date of last menstrual cycle and time frame:

Did you…

- o Get out of bed, woke
    up at:
- o Smile

- o Brush you teeth
- o Take a shower

- o Eat breakfast
- o Take your meds

Every little task is important sometimes we forget the silliest things so lets make a to-do list to keep track!

To-do list:

Good afternoon!

Did you…

- o Eat lunch

- o Finish your tasks?

Good evening love, how's your day so far?

Did you…

- o Eat snacks
- o Have a good day
- o Have a bad day

- o Finish all that you had on
    your to do list

- o Eat dinner
- o Sleep early

Good night and sleep well

Good Morning Sunshine!

Lets start the beginning of the month by noting down our details, so this way we can track changes every month

Age:
Weight:
Height:
Date of last menstrual cycle and time frame:

Did you…

o Get out of bed, woke    o Brush you teeth       o Eat breakfast
   up at:                 o Take a shower         o Take your meds
o Smile

Every little task is important sometimes we forget the silliest things so lets make a to-do list to keep track!

To-do list:

Good afternoon!

Did you…

o Eat lunch              o Finish your tasks?

Good evening love, how's your day so far?

Did you…

o Eat snacks             o Finish all that you had on   o Eat dinner
o Have a good day           your to do list              o Sleep early
o Have a bad day

Good night and sleep well

dd/mm/yy

Good Morning Sunshine!

Lets start the beginning of the month by noting down our details, so this way we can track changes every month

Age:
Weight:
Height:
Date of last menstrual cycle and time frame:

Did you...

o Get out of bed, woke      o Brush you teeth            o Eat breakfast
  up at:                    o Take a shower              o Take your meds
o Smile

Every little task is important sometimes we forget the silliest things so lets make a to-do list to keep track!

To-do list:

Good afternoon!

Did you...

o Eat lunch              o Finish your tasks?

Good evening love, how's your day so far?

Did you...

o Eat snacks            o Finish all that you had on    o Eat dinner
o Have a good day         your to do list              o Sleep early
o Have a bad day

Good night and sleep well

Good Morning Sunshine!

Lets start the beginning of the month by noting down our details, so this way we can track changes every month

Age:
Weight:
Height:
Date of last menstrual cycle and time frame:

Did you…

o Get out of bed, woke         o Brush you teeth         o Eat breakfast
   up at:                      o Take a shower           o Take your meds
o Smile

Every little task is important sometimes we forget the silliest things so lets make a to-do list to keep track!

To-do list:

Good afternoon!

Did you…

o Eat lunch                    o Finish your tasks?

Good evening love, how's your day so far?

Did you…

o Eat snacks                   o Finish all that you had on    o Eat dinner
o Have a good day                 your to do list              o Sleep early
o Have a bad day

Good night and sleep well

Good Morning Sunshine!

Lets start the beginning of the month by noting down our details, so this way we can track changes every month

Age:
Weight:
Height:
Date of last menstrual cycle and time frame:

Did you…

- o Get out of bed, woke up at:
- o Smile
- o Brush you teeth
- o Take a shower
- o Eat breakfast
- o Take your meds

Every little task is important sometimes we forget the silliest things so lets make a to-do list to keep track!

To-do list:

Good afternoon!

Did you…

- o Eat lunch
- o Finish your tasks?

Good evening love, how's your day so far?

Did you…

- o Eat snacks
- o Have a good day
- o Have a bad day
- o Finish all that you had on your to do list
- o Eat dinner
- o Sleep early

Good night and sleep well

Good Morning Sunshine!

Lets start the beginning of the month by noting down our details, so this way we can track changes every month

Age:
Weight:
Height:
Date of last menstrual cycle and time frame:

Did you…

- o Get out of bed, woke up at:
- o Smile

- o Brush you teeth
- o Take a shower

- o Eat breakfast
- o Take your meds

Every little task is important sometimes we forget the silliest things so lets make a to-do list to keep track!

To-do list:

Good afternoon!

Did you…

- o Eat lunch

- o Finish your tasks?

Good evening love, how's your day so far?

Did you…

- o Eat snacks
- o Have a good day
- o Have a bad day

- o Finish all that you had on your to do list

- o Eat dinner
- o Sleep early

Good night and sleep well

Good Morning Sunshine!

Lets start the beginning of the month by noting down our details, so this way we can track changes every month

Age:
Weight:
Height:
Date of last menstrual cycle and time frame:

Did you…

- o Get out of bed, woke up at:
- o Smile
- o Brush you teeth
- o Take a shower
- o Eat breakfast
- o Take your meds

Every little task is important sometimes we forget the silliest things so lets make a to-do list to keep track!

To-do list:

Good afternoon!

Did you…

- o Eat lunch
- o Finish your tasks?

Good evening love, how's your day so far?

Did you…

- o Eat snacks
- o Have a good day
- o Have a bad day
- o Finish all that you had on your to do list
- o Eat dinner
- o Sleep early

Good night and sleep well

Good Morning Sunshine!

Lets start the beginning of the month by noting down our details, so this way we can track changes every month

Age:
Weight:
Height:
Date of last menstrual cycle and time frame:

Did you…

- o Get out of bed, woke up at:
- o Smile
- o Brush you teeth
- o Take a shower
- o Eat breakfast
- o Take your meds

Every little task is important sometimes we forget the silliest things so lets make a to-do list to keep track!

To-do list:

Good afternoon!

Did you…

- o Eat lunch
- o Finish your tasks?

Good evening love, how's your day so far?

Did you…

- o Eat snacks
- o Have a good day
- o Have a bad day
- o Finish all that you had on your to do list
- o Eat dinner
- o Sleep early

Good night and sleep well

Good Morning Sunshine!

Lets start the beginning of the month by noting down our details, so this way we can track changes every month

Age:
Weight:
Height:
Date of last menstrual cycle and time frame:

Did you...

- o Get out of bed, woke up at:
- o Smile
- o Brush you teeth
- o Take a shower
- o Eat breakfast
- o Take your meds

Every little task is important sometimes we forget the silliest things so lets make a to-do list to keep track!

To-do list:

Good afternoon!

Did you...

- o Eat lunch
- o Finish your tasks?

Good evening love, how's your day so far?

Did you...

- o Eat snacks
- o Have a good day
- o Have a bad day
- o Finish all that you had on your to do list
- o Eat dinner
- o Sleep early

Good night and sleep well

Good Morning Sunshine!

Lets start the beginning of the month by noting down our details, so this way we can track changes every month

Age:
Weight:
Height:
Date of last menstrual cycle and time frame:

Did you…

o Get out of bed, woke       o Brush you teeth       o Eat breakfast
   up at:                    o Take a shower         o Take your meds
o Smile

Every little task is important sometimes we forget the silliest things so lets make a to-do list to keep track!

To-do list:

Good afternoon!

Did you…

o Eat lunch              o Finish your tasks?

Good evening love, how's your day so far?

Did you…

o Eat snacks             o Finish all that you had on    o Eat dinner
o Have a good day           your to do list              o Sleep early
o Have a bad day

Good night and sleep well

Good Morning Sunshine!

Lets start the beginning of the month by noting down our details, so this way we can track changes every month

Age:
Weight:
Height:
Date of last menstrual cycle and time frame:

Did you...

- o Get out of bed, woke up at:
- o Smile
- o Brush you teeth
- o Take a shower
- o Eat breakfast
- o Take your meds

Every little task is important sometimes we forget the silliest things so lets make a to-do list to keep track!

To-do list:

Good afternoon!

Did you...

- o Eat lunch
- o Finish your tasks?

Good evening love, how's your day so far?

Did you...

- o Eat snacks
- o Have a good day
- o Have a bad day
- o Finish all that you had on your to do list
- o Eat dinner
- o Sleep early

Good night and sleep well

Good Morning Sunshine!

Lets start the beginning of the month by noting down our details, so this way we can track changes every month

Age:
Weight:
Height:
Date of last menstrual cycle and time frame:

Did you…

o Get out of bed, woke        o Brush you teeth        o Eat breakfast
   up at:                     o Take a shower          o Take your meds
o Smile

Every little task is important sometimes we forget the silliest things so lets make a to-do list to keep track!

To-do list:



Good afternoon!

Did you…

o Eat lunch                o Finish your tasks?

Good evening love, how's your day so far?

Did you…

o Eat snacks               o Finish all that you had on   o Eat dinner
o Have a good day             your to do list             o Sleep early
o Have a bad day

Good night and sleep well

Good Morning Sunshine!

Lets start the beginning of the month by noting down our details, so this way we can track changes every month

Age:
Weight:
Height:
Date of last menstrual cycle and time frame:

Did you…

- o Get out of bed, woke up at:
- o Smile
- o Brush you teeth
- o Take a shower
- o Eat breakfast
- o Take your meds

Every little task is important sometimes we forget the silliest things so lets make a to-do list to keep track!

To-do list:

Good afternoon!

Did you…

- o Eat lunch
- o Finish your tasks?

Good evening love, how's your day so far?

Did you…

- o Eat snacks
- o Have a good day
- o Have a bad day
- o Finish all that you had on your to do list
- o Eat dinner
- o Sleep early

Good night and sleep well

Good Morning Sunshine!

Lets start the beginning of the month by noting down our details, so this way we can track changes every month

Age:
Weight:
Height:
Date of last menstrual cycle and time frame:

Did you…

o Get out of bed, woke          o Brush you teeth          o Eat breakfast
   up at:                       o Take a shower            o Take your meds
o Smile

Every little task is important sometimes we forget the silliest things so lets make a to-do list to keep track!

To-do list:

Good afternoon!

Did you…

o Eat lunch                     o Finish your tasks?

Good evening love, how's your day so far?

Did you…

o Eat snacks                    o Finish all that you had on    o Eat dinner
o Have a good day                  your to do list              o Sleep early
o Have a bad day

Good night and sleep well

Good Morning Sunshine!

Lets start the beginning of the month by noting down our details, so this way we can track changes every month

Age:
Weight:
Height:
Date of last menstrual cycle and time frame:

Did you…

- o Get out of bed, woke up at:
- o Smile
- o Brush you teeth
- o Take a shower
- o Eat breakfast
- o Take your meds

Every little task is important sometimes we forget the silliest things so lets make a to-do list to keep track!

To-do list:

Good afternoon!

Did you…

- o Eat lunch
- o Finish your tasks?

Good evening love, how's your day so far?

Did you…

- o Eat snacks
- o Have a good day
- o Have a bad day
- o Finish all that you had on your to do list
- o Eat dinner
- o Sleep early

Good night and sleep well

Good Morning Sunshine!

Lets start the beginning of the month by noting down our details, so this way we can track changes every month

Age:
Weight:
Height:
Date of last menstrual cycle and time frame:

Did you…

- o Get out of bed, woke up at:
- o Smile
- o Brush you teeth
- o Take a shower
- o Eat breakfast
- o Take your meds

Every little task is important sometimes we forget the silliest things so lets make a to-do list to keep track!

To-do list:

Good afternoon!

Did you…

- o Eat lunch
- o Finish your tasks?

Good evening love, how's your day so far?

Did you…

- o Eat snacks
- o Have a good day
- o Have a bad day
- o Finish all that you had on your to do list
- o Eat dinner
- o Sleep early

Good night and sleep well

Good Morning Sunshine!

Lets start the beginning of the month by noting down our details, so this way we can track changes every month

Age:
Weight:
Height:
Date of last menstrual cycle and time frame:

Did you…

- o Get out of bed, woke up at:
- o Smile
- o Brush you teeth
- o Take a shower
- o Eat breakfast
- o Take your meds

Every little task is important sometimes we forget the silliest things so lets make a to-do list to keep track!

To-do list:

Good afternoon!

Did you…

- o Eat lunch
- o Finish your tasks?

Good evening love, how's your day so far?

Did you…

- o Eat snacks
- o Have a good day
- o Have a bad day
- o Finish all that you had on your to do list
- o Eat dinner
- o Sleep early

Good night and sleep well

Good Morning Sunshine!

Lets start the beginning of the month by noting down our details, so this way we can track changes every month

Age:
Weight:
Height:
Date of last menstrual cycle and time frame:

Did you...

o Get out of bed, woke    o Brush you teeth      o Eat breakfast
  up at:                  o Take a shower        o Take your meds
o Smile

Every little task is important sometimes we forget the silliest things so lets make a to-do list to keep track!

To-do list:

Good afternoon!

Did you...

o Eat lunch              o Finish your tasks?

Good evening love, how's your day so far?

Did you...

o Eat snacks             o Finish all that you had on   o Eat dinner
o Have a good day          your to do list             o Sleep early
o Have a bad day

Good night and sleep well

Good Morning Sunshine!

Lets start the beginning of the month by noting down our details, so this way we can track changes every month

Age:
Weight:
Height:
Date of last menstrual cycle and time frame:

Did you...

- o Get out of bed, woke up at:
- o Smile
- o Brush you teeth
- o Take a shower
- o Eat breakfast
- o Take your meds

Every little task is important sometimes we forget the silliest things so lets make a to-do list to keep track!

To-do list:

Good afternoon!

Did you...

- o Eat lunch
- o Finish your tasks?

Good evening love, how's your day so far?

Did you...

- o Eat snacks
- o Have a good day
- o Have a bad day
- o Finish all that you had on your to do list
- o Eat dinner
- o Sleep early

Good night and sleep well

Good Morning Sunshine!

Lets start the beginning of the month by noting down our details, so this way we can track changes every month

Age:
Weight:
Height:
Date of last menstrual cycle and time frame:

Did you...

o Get out of bed, woke        o Brush you teeth        o Eat breakfast
   up at:                     o Take a shower          o Take your meds
o Smile

Every little task is important sometimes we forget the silliest things so lets make a to-do list to keep track!

To-do list:

Good afternoon!

Did you...

o Eat lunch                   o Finish your tasks?

Good evening love, how's your day so far?

Did you...

o Eat snacks                  o Finish all that you had on    o Eat dinner
o Have a good day                your to do list              o Sleep early
o Have a bad day

Good night and sleep well

Good Morning Sunshine!

Lets start the beginning of the month by noting down our details, so this way we can track changes every month

Age:
Weight:
Height:
Date of last menstrual cycle and time frame:

Did you…

- o Get out of bed, woke up at:
- o Smile
- o Brush you teeth
- o Take a shower
- o Eat breakfast
- o Take your meds

Every little task is important sometimes we forget the silliest things so lets make a to-do list to keep track!

To-do list:

Good afternoon!

Did you…

- o Eat lunch
- o Finish your tasks?

Good evening love, how's your day so far?

Did you…

- o Eat snacks
- o Have a good day
- o Have a bad day
- o Finish all that you had on your to do list
- o Eat dinner
- o Sleep early

Good night and sleep well

Good Morning Sunshine!

Lets start the beginning of the month by noting down our details, so this way we can track changes every month

Age:
Weight:
Height:
Date of last menstrual cycle and time frame:

Did you...

- o Get out of bed, woke up at:
- o Smile
- o Brush you teeth
- o Take a shower
- o Eat breakfast
- o Take your meds

Every little task is important sometimes we forget the silliest things so lets make a to-do list to keep track!

To-do list:

Good afternoon!

Did you...

- o Eat lunch
- o Finish your tasks?

Good evening love, how's your day so far?

Did you...

- o Eat snacks
- o Have a good day
- o Have a bad day
- o Finish all that you had on your to do list
- o Eat dinner
- o Sleep early

Good night and sleep well

# This Month...

o I tried something new by…

o I helped somebody by…

o I become a better person by…

o I lost ____ kgs by…

o I gained ____kgs by…

o

o

o

# Habit Tracker

**Month:**

|  | 1st | 2nd | 3rd | 4th | 5th |  |
|---|---|---|---|---|---|---|
| Sleep | | | | | | |
| Caffeine | | | | | | |
| Alcohol | | | | | | |
| Cigarettes | | | | | | |
| Exercise | | | | | | |
|  | 6th | 7th | 8th | 9th | 10th | |
| Sleep | | | | | | |
| Caffeine | | | | | | |
| Alcohol | | | | | | |
| Cigarettes | | | | | | |
| Exercise | | | | | | |
|  | 11th | 12th | 13th | 14th | 15th | |
| Sleep | | | | | | |
| Caffeine | | | | | | |
| Alcohol | | | | | | |
| Cigarettes | | | | | | |
| Exercise | | | | | | |
|  | 16th | 17th | 18th | 19th | 20th | |
| Sleep | | | | | | |
| Caffeine | | | | | | |
| Alcohol | | | | | | |
| Cigarettes | | | | | | |
| Exercise | | | | | | |
|  | 21th | 22th | 23th | 24th | 25th | |
| Sleep | | | | | | |
| Caffeine | | | | | | |
| Alcohol | | | | | | |
| Cigarettes | | | | | | |
| Exercise | | | | | | |
|  | 26th | 27th | 28th | 29th | 30th | 31st |
| Sleep | | | | | | |
| Caffeine | | | | | | |
| Alcohol | | | | | | |
| Cigarettes | | | | | | |
| Exercise | | | | | | |

# Emotion tracker

*How are you felling today? It is important to be in touch with yourself and your emotions.*

| | Anger | Hurt/Pain | Disappointment | Upset | Happy | Blah! | Lazy |
|---|---|---|---|---|---|---|---|
| 1st | | | | | | | |
| 2nd | | | | | | | |
| 3rd | | | | | | | |
| 4th | | | | | | | |
| 5th | | | | | | | |
| 6th | | | | | | | |
| 7th | | | | | | | |
| 8th | | | | | | | |
| 9th | | | | | | | |
| 10th | | | | | | | |
| 11th | | | | | | | |
| 12th | | | | | | | |
| 13th | | | | | | | |
| 14th | | | | | | | |
| 15th | | | | | | | |
| 16th | | | | | | | |
| 17th | | | | | | | |
| 18th | | | | | | | |
| 19th | | | | | | | |
| 20th | | | | | | | |
| 21st | | | | | | | |
| 22nd | | | | | | | |
| 23rd | | | | | | | |
| 24th | | | | | | | |
| 25th | | | | | | | |
| 26th | | | | | | | |
| 27th | | | | | | | |
| 28th | | | | | | | |
| 29th | | | | | | | |
| 30th | | | | | | | |
| 31st | | | | | | | |

|        | Guilt | Anxious | Sadness | Shame | Guilt | Worthless |
|--------|-------|---------|---------|-------|-------|-----------|
| 1st    |       |         |         |       |       |           |
| 2nd    |       |         |         |       |       |           |
| 3rd    |       |         |         |       |       |           |
| 4th    |       |         |         |       |       |           |
| 5th    |       |         |         |       |       |           |
| 6th    |       |         |         |       |       |           |
| 7th    |       |         |         |       |       |           |
| 8th    |       |         |         |       |       |           |
| 9th    |       |         |         |       |       |           |
| 10th   |       |         |         |       |       |           |
| 11th   |       |         |         |       |       |           |
| 12th   |       |         |         |       |       |           |
| 13th   |       |         |         |       |       |           |
| 14th   |       |         |         |       |       |           |
| 15th   |       |         |         |       |       |           |
| 16th   |       |         |         |       |       |           |
| 17th   |       |         |         |       |       |           |
| 18th   |       |         |         |       |       |           |
| 19th   |       |         |         |       |       |           |
| 20th   |       |         |         |       |       |           |
| 21st   |       |         |         |       |       |           |
| 22nd   |       |         |         |       |       |           |
| 23rd   |       |         |         |       |       |           |
| 24th   |       |         |         |       |       |           |
| 25th   |       |         |         |       |       |           |
| 26th   |       |         |         |       |       |           |
| 27th   |       |         |         |       |       |           |
| 28th   |       |         |         |       |       |           |
| 29th   |       |         |         |       |       |           |
| 30th   |       |         |         |       |       |           |
| 31st   |       |         |         |       |       |           |

# Food Tracker

| | Healthy food | Junk food | Both | Didn't eat ☹ |
|---|---|---|---|---|
| 1st | | | | |
| 2nd | | | | |
| 3rd | | | | |
| 4th | | | | |
| 5th | | | | |
| 6th | | | | |
| 7th | | | | |
| 8th | | | | |
| 9th | | | | |
| 10th | | | | |
| 11th | | | | |
| 12th | | | | |
| 13th | | | | |
| 14th | | | | |
| 15th | | | | |
| 16th | | | | |
| 17th | | | | |
| 18th | | | | |
| 19th | | | | |
| 20th | | | | |
| 21st | | | | |
| 22nd | | | | |
| 23rd | | | | |
| 24th | | | | |
| 25th | | | | |
| 26th | | | | |
| 27th | | | | |
| 28th | | | | |
| 29th | | | | |
| 30th | | | | |
| 31st | | | | |

# Weight Tracker

**Month:**

| | Kgs/lbs | | Kgs/lbs |
|---|---|---|---|
| 1st | | 16th | |
| 2nd | | 17th | |
| 3rd | | 18th | |
| 4th | | 19th | |
| 5th | | 20th | |
| 6th | | 21st | |
| 7th | | 22nd | |
| 8th | | 23rd | |
| 9th | | 24th | |
| 10th | | 25th | |
| 11th | | 26th | |
| 12th | | 27th | |
| 13th | | 28th | |
| 14th | | 29th | |
| 15th | | 30th | |
| | | 31st | |

# Journal

dd/mm/yy

Good Morning Sunshine!

Lets start the beginning of the month by noting down our details, so this way we can track changes every month

Age:
Weight:
Height:
Date of last menstrual cycle and time frame:

Did you…

o Get out of bed, woke      o Brush you teeth       o Eat breakfast
   up at:                  o Take a shower         o Take your meds
o Smile

Every little task is important sometimes we forget the silliest things so lets make a to-do list to keep track!

To-do list:

Good afternoon!

Did you…

o Eat lunch                  o Finish your tasks?

Good evening love, how's your day so far?

Did you…

o Eat snacks                 o Finish all that you had on    o Eat dinner
o Have a good day               your to do list              o Sleep early
o Have a bad day

Good night and sleep well

Good Morning Sunshine!

Lets start the beginning of the month by noting down our details, so this way we can track changes every month

Age:
Weight:
Height:
Date of last menstrual cycle and time frame:

Did you…

o Get out of bed, woke       o Brush you teeth       o Eat breakfast
   up at:                      o Take a shower        o Take your meds
o Smile

Every little task is important sometimes we forget the silliest things so lets make a to-do list to keep track!

To-do list:

Good afternoon!

Did you…

o Eat lunch                  o Finish your tasks?

Good evening love, how's your day so far?

Did you…

o Eat snacks                 o Finish all that you had on    o Eat dinner
o Have a good day               your to do list            o Sleep early
o Have a bad day

Good night and sleep well

Good Morning Sunshine!

Lets start the beginning of the month by noting down our details, so this way we can track changes every month

Age:
Weight:
Height:
Date of last menstrual cycle and time frame:

Did you…

- o Get out of bed, woke up at:
- o Smile
- o Brush you teeth
- o Take a shower
- o Eat breakfast
- o Take your meds

Every little task is important sometimes we forget the silliest things so lets make a to-do list to keep track!

To-do list:

Good afternoon!

Did you…

- o Eat lunch
- o Finish your tasks?

Good evening love, how's your day so far?

Did you…

- o Eat snacks
- o Have a good day
- o Have a bad day
- o Finish all that you had on your to do list
- o Eat dinner
- o Sleep early

Good night and sleep well

Good Morning Sunshine!

Lets start the beginning of the month by noting down our details, so this way we can track changes every month

Age:
Weight:
Height:
Date of last menstrual cycle and time frame:

Did you...

o Get out of bed, woke       o Brush you teeth        o Eat breakfast
   up at:                    o Take a shower          o Take your meds
o Smile

Every little task is important sometimes we forget the silliest things so lets make a to-do list to keep track!

To-do list:

Good afternoon!

Did you...

o Eat lunch                o Finish your tasks?

Good evening love, how's your day so far?

Did you...

o Eat snacks               o Finish all that you had on   o Eat dinner
o Have a good day             your to do list              o Sleep early
o Have a bad day

Good night and sleep well

Good Morning Sunshine!

Lets start the beginning of the month by noting down our details, so this way we can track changes every month

Age:
Weight:
Height:
Date of last menstrual cycle and time frame:

Did you…

o Get out of bed, woke    o Brush you teeth        o Eat breakfast
   up at:                 o Take a shower          o Take your meds
o Smile

Every little task is important sometimes we forget the silliest things so lets make a to-do list to keep track!

To-do list:

Good afternoon!

Did you…

o Eat lunch                o Finish your tasks?

Good evening love, how's your day so far?

Did you…

o Eat snacks               o Finish all that you had on   o Eat dinner
o Have a good day             your to do list             o Sleep early
o Have a bad day

Good night and sleep well

Good Morning Sunshine!

Lets start the beginning of the month by noting down our details, so this way we can track changes every month

Age:
Weight:
Height:
Date of last menstrual cycle and time frame:

Did you…

o Get out of bed, woke    o Brush you teeth        o Eat breakfast
   up at:                 o Take a shower          o Take your meds
o Smile

Every little task is important sometimes we forget the silliest things so lets make a to-do list to keep track!

To-do list:

Good afternoon!

Did you…

o Eat lunch              o Finish your tasks?

Good evening love, how's your day so far?

Did you…

o Eat snacks             o Finish all that you had on    o Eat dinner
o Have a good day           your to do list              o Sleep early
o Have a bad day

Good night and sleep well

Good Morning Sunshine!

Lets start the beginning of the month by noting down our details, so this way we can track changes every month

Age:
Weight:
Height:
Date of last menstrual cycle and time frame:

Did you…

o Get out of bed, woke          o Brush you teeth          o Eat breakfast
   up at:          o Take a shower          o Take your meds
o Smile

Every little task is important sometimes we forget the silliest things so lets make a to-do list to keep track!

To-do list:

Good afternoon!

Did you…

o Eat lunch          o Finish your tasks?

Good evening love, how's your day so far?

Did you…

o Eat snacks          o Finish all that you had on          o Eat dinner
o Have a good day          your to do list          o Sleep early
o Have a bad day

Good night and sleep well

Good Morning Sunshine!

Lets start the beginning of the month by noting down our details, so this way we can track changes every month

Age:
Weight:
Height:
Date of last menstrual cycle and time frame:

Did you…

o Get out of bed, woke        o Brush you teeth          o Eat breakfast
   up at:                     o Take a shower            o Take your meds
o Smile

Every little task is important sometimes we forget the silliest things so lets make a to-do list to keep track!

To-do list:

Good afternoon!

Did you…

o Eat lunch                   o Finish your tasks?

Good evening love, how's your day so far?

Did you…

o Eat snacks                  o Finish all that you had on    o Eat dinner
o Have a good day                your to do list               o Sleep early
o Have a bad day

Good night and sleep well

Good Morning Sunshine!

Lets start the beginning of the month by noting down our details, so this way we can track changes every month

Age:
Weight:
Height:
Date of last menstrual cycle and time frame:

Did you…

- o Get out of bed, woke up at:
- o Smile
- o Brush you teeth
- o Take a shower
- o Eat breakfast
- o Take your meds

Every little task is important sometimes we forget the silliest things so lets make a to-do list to keep track!

To-do list:

Good afternoon!

Did you…

- o Eat lunch
- o Finish your tasks?

Good evening love, how's your day so far?

Did you…

- o Eat snacks
- o Have a good day
- o Have a bad day
- o Finish all that you had on your to do list
- o Eat dinner
- o Sleep early

Good night and sleep well

Good Morning Sunshine!

Lets start the beginning of the month by noting down our details, so this way we can track changes every month

Age:
Weight:
Height:
Date of last menstrual cycle and time frame:

Did you…

- o Get out of bed, woke up at:
- o Smile

- o Brush you teeth
- o Take a shower

- o Eat breakfast
- o Take your meds

Every little task is important sometimes we forget the silliest things so lets make a to-do list to keep track!

To-do list:

Good afternoon!

Did you…

- o Eat lunch

- o Finish your tasks?

Good evening love, how's your day so far?

Did you…

- o Eat snacks
- o Have a good day
- o Have a bad day

- o Finish all that you had on your to do list

- o Eat dinner
- o Sleep early

Good night and sleep well

Good Morning Sunshine!

Lets start the beginning of the month by noting down our details, so this way we can track changes every month

Age:
Weight:
Height:
Date of last menstrual cycle and time frame:

Did you…

- o Get out of bed, woke up at:
- o Smile
- o Brush you teeth
- o Take a shower
- o Eat breakfast
- o Take your meds

Every little task is important sometimes we forget the silliest things so lets make a to-do list to keep track!

To-do list:

Good afternoon!

Did you…

- o Eat lunch
- o Finish your tasks?

Good evening love, how's your day so far?

Did you…

- o Eat snacks
- o Have a good day
- o Have a bad day
- o Finish all that you had on your to do list
- o Eat dinner
- o Sleep early

Good night and sleep well

Good Morning Sunshine!

Lets start the beginning of the month by noting down our details, so this way we can track changes every month

Age:
Weight:
Height:
Date of last menstrual cycle and time frame:

Did you…

- o Get out of bed, woke
  up at:
- o Smile

- o Brush you teeth
- o Take a shower

- o Eat breakfast
- o Take your meds

Every little task is important sometimes we forget the silliest things so lets make a to-do list to keep track!

To-do list:

Good afternoon!

Did you…

- o Eat lunch

- o Finish your tasks?

Good evening love, how's your day so far?

Did you…

- o Eat snacks
- o Have a good day
- o Have a bad day

- o Finish all that you had on
  your to do list

- o Eat dinner
- o Sleep early

Good night and sleep well

Good Morning Sunshine!

Lets start the beginning of the month by noting down our details, so this way we can track changes every month

Age:
Weight:
Height:
Date of last menstrual cycle and time frame:

Did you…

o Get out of bed, woke       o Brush you teeth       o Eat breakfast
  up at:                          o Take a shower          o Take your meds
o Smile

Every little task is important sometimes we forget the silliest things so lets make a to-do list to keep track!

To-do list:

Good afternoon!

Did you…

o Eat lunch                   o Finish your tasks?

Good evening love, how's your day so far?

Did you…

o Eat snacks                  o Finish all that you had on    o Eat dinner
o Have a good day               your to do list               o Sleep early
o Have a bad day

Good night and sleep well

Good Morning Sunshine!

Lets start the beginning of the month by noting down our details, so this way we can track changes every month

Age:
Weight:
Height:
Date of last menstrual cycle and time frame:

Did you...

- o Get out of bed, woke up at:
- o Smile
- o Brush you teeth
- o Take a shower
- o Eat breakfast
- o Take your meds

Every little task is important sometimes we forget the silliest things so lets make a to-do list to keep track!

To-do list:

Good afternoon!

Did you...

- o Eat lunch
- o Finish your tasks?

Good evening love, how's your day so far?

Did you...

- o Eat snacks
- o Have a good day
- o Have a bad day
- o Finish all that you had on your to do list
- o Eat dinner
- o Sleep early

Good night and sleep well

Good Morning Sunshine!

Lets start the beginning of the month by noting down our details, so this way we can track changes every month

Age:
Weight:
Height:
Date of last menstrual cycle and time frame:

Did you...

o Get out of bed, woke          o Brush you teeth          o Eat breakfast
   up at:                          o Take a shower            o Take your meds
o Smile

Every little task is important sometimes we forget the silliest things so lets make a to-do list to keep track!

To-do list:

Good afternoon!

Did you...

o Eat lunch                    o Finish your tasks?

Good evening love, how's your day so far?

Did you...

o Eat snacks                   o Finish all that you had on    o Eat dinner
o Have a good day                 your to do list                o Sleep early
o Have a bad day

Good night and sleep well

Good Morning Sunshine!

Lets start the beginning of the month by noting down our details, so this way we can track changes every month

Age:
Weight:
Height:
Date of last menstrual cycle and time frame:

Did you…

o Get out of bed, woke        o Brush you teeth         o Eat breakfast
   up at:                     o Take a shower           o Take your meds
o Smile

Every little task is important sometimes we forget the silliest things so lets make a to-do list to keep track!

To-do list:

Good afternoon!

Did you…

o Eat lunch                   o Finish your tasks?

Good evening love, how's your day so far?

Did you…

o Eat snacks                  o Finish all that you had on    o Eat dinner
o Have a good day                your to do list               o Sleep early
o Have a bad day

Good night and sleep well

Good Morning Sunshine!

Lets start the beginning of the month by noting down our details, so this way we can track changes every month

Age:
Weight:
Height:
Date of last menstrual cycle and time frame:

Did you…

o Get out of bed, woke     o Brush you teeth     o Eat breakfast
   up at:                  o Take a shower       o Take your meds
o Smile

Every little task is important sometimes we forget the silliest things so lets make a to-do list to keep track!

To-do list:

Good afternoon!

Did you…

o Eat lunch               o Finish your tasks?

Good evening love, how's your day so far?

Did you…

o Eat snacks              o Finish all that you had on   o Eat dinner
o Have a good day            your to do list             o Sleep early
o Have a bad day

Good night and sleep well

Good Morning Sunshine!

Lets start the beginning of the month by noting down our details, so this way we can track changes every month

Age:
Weight:
Height:
Date of last menstrual cycle and time frame:

Did you...

o Get out of bed, woke        o Brush you teeth          o Eat breakfast
   up at:                     o Take a shower            o Take your meds
o Smile

Every little task is important sometimes we forget the silliest things so lets make a to-do list to keep track!

To-do list:

Good afternoon!

Did you...

o Eat lunch              o Finish your tasks?

Good evening love, how's your day so far?

Did you...

o Eat snacks             o Finish all that you had on    o Eat dinner
o Have a good day           your to do list               o Sleep early
o Have a bad day

Good night and sleep well

Good Morning Sunshine!

Lets start the beginning of the month by noting down our details, so this way we can track changes every month

Age:
Weight:
Height:
Date of last menstrual cycle and time frame:

Did you…

o Get out of bed, woke    o Brush you teeth    o Eat breakfast
   up at:                 o Take a shower      o Take your meds
o Smile

Every little task is important sometimes we forget the silliest things so lets make a to-do list to keep track!

To-do list:

Good afternoon!

Did you…

o Eat lunch             o Finish your tasks?

Good evening love, how's your day so far?

Did you…

o Eat snacks            o Finish all that you had on    o Eat dinner
o Have a good day          your to do list             o Sleep early
o Have a bad day

Good night and sleep well

Good Morning Sunshine!

Lets start the beginning of the month by noting down our details, so this way we can track changes every month

Age:
Weight:
Height:
Date of last menstrual cycle and time frame:

Did you…

- o Get out of bed, woke up at:
- o Smile
- o Brush you teeth
- o Take a shower
- o Eat breakfast
- o Take your meds

Every little task is important sometimes we forget the silliest things so lets make a to-do list to keep track!

To-do list:

Good afternoon!

Did you…

- o Eat lunch
- o Finish your tasks?

Good evening love, how's your day so far?

Did you…

- o Eat snacks
- o Have a good day
- o Have a bad day
- o Finish all that you had on your to do list
- o Eat dinner
- o Sleep early

Good night and sleep well

Good Morning Sunshine!

Lets start the beginning of the month by noting down our details, so this way we can track changes every month

Age:
Weight:
Height:
Date of last menstrual cycle and time frame:

Did you…

o Get out of bed, woke up at:
o Smile

o Brush you teeth
o Take a shower

o Eat breakfast
o Take your meds

Every little task is important sometimes we forget the silliest things so lets make a to-do list to keep track!

To-do list:

Good afternoon!

Did you…

o Eat lunch

o Finish your tasks?

Good evening love, how's your day so far?

Did you…

o Eat snacks
o Have a good day
o Have a bad day

o Finish all that you had on your to do list

o Eat dinner
o Sleep early

Good night and sleep well

Good Morning Sunshine!

Lets start the beginning of the month by noting down our details, so this way we can track changes every month

Age:
Weight:
Height:
Date of last menstrual cycle and time frame:

Did you...

o Get out of bed, woke    o Brush you teeth         o Eat breakfast
   up at:                 o Take a shower           o Take your meds
o Smile

Every little task is important sometimes we forget the silliest things so lets make a to-do list to keep track!

To-do list:

Good afternoon!

Did you...

o Eat lunch              o Finish your tasks?

Good evening love, how's your day so far?

Did you...

o Eat snacks             o Finish all that you had on   o Eat dinner
o Have a good day           your to do list             o Sleep early
o Have a bad day

Good night and sleep well

Good Morning Sunshine!

Lets start the beginning of the month by noting down our details, so this way we can track changes every month

Age:
Weight:
Height:
Date of last menstrual cycle and time frame:

Did you…

- o Get out of bed, woke up at:
- o Smile

- o Brush you teeth
- o Take a shower

- o Eat breakfast
- o Take your meds

Every little task is important sometimes we forget the silliest things so lets make a to-do list to keep track!

To-do list:

Good afternoon!

Did you…

- o Eat lunch

- o Finish your tasks?

Good evening love, how's your day so far?

Did you…

- o Eat snacks
- o Have a good day
- o Have a bad day

- o Finish all that you had on your to do list

- o Eat dinner
- o Sleep early

Good night and sleep well

Good Morning Sunshine!

Lets start the beginning of the month by noting down our details, so this way we can track changes every month

Age:
Weight:
Height:
Date of last menstrual cycle and time frame:

Did you…

- o Get out of bed, woke up at:
- o Smile
- o Brush you teeth
- o Take a shower
- o Eat breakfast
- o Take your meds

Every little task is important sometimes we forget the silliest things so lets make a to-do list to keep track!

To-do list:

Good afternoon!

Did you…

- o Eat lunch
- o Finish your tasks?

Good evening love, how's your day so far?

Did you…

- o Eat snacks
- o Have a good day
- o Have a bad day
- o Finish all that you had on your to do list
- o Eat dinner
- o Sleep early

Good night and sleep well

Good Morning Sunshine!

Lets start the beginning of the month by noting down our details, so this way we can track changes every month

Age:
Weight:
Height:
Date of last menstrual cycle and time frame:

Did you…

o Get out of bed, woke     o Brush you teeth        o Eat breakfast
   up at:                          o Take a shower        o Take your meds
o Smile

Every little task is important sometimes we forget the silliest things so lets make a to-do list to keep track!

To-do list:

Good afternoon!

Did you…

o Eat lunch                o Finish your tasks?

Good evening love, how's your day so far?

Did you…

o Eat snacks              o Finish all that you had on   o Eat dinner
o Have a good day          your to do list              o Sleep early
o Have a bad day

Good night and sleep well

Good Morning Sunshine!

Lets start the beginning of the month by noting down our details, so this way we can track changes every month

Age:
Weight:
Height:
Date of last menstrual cycle and time frame:

Did you…

- o Get out of bed, woke
  up at:
- o Smile

- o Brush you teeth
- o Take a shower

- o Eat breakfast
- o Take your meds

Every little task is important sometimes we forget the silliest things so lets make a to-do list to keep track!

To-do list:

Good afternoon!

Did you…

- o Eat lunch

- o Finish your tasks?

Good evening love, how's your day so far?

Did you…

- o Eat snacks
- o Have a good day
- o Have a bad day

- o Finish all that you had on
  your to do list

- o Eat dinner
- o Sleep early

Good night and sleep well

dd/mm/yy

Good Morning Sunshine!

Lets start the beginning of the month by noting down our details, so this way we can track changes every month

Age:
Weight:
Height:
Date of last menstrual cycle and time frame:

Did you…

- o Get out of bed, woke up at:
- o Smile
- o Brush you teeth
- o Take a shower
- o Eat breakfast
- o Take your meds

Every little task is important sometimes we forget the silliest things so lets make a to-do list to keep track!

To-do list:

Good afternoon!

Did you…

- o Eat lunch
- o Finish your tasks?

Good evening love, how's your day so far?

Did you…

- o Eat snacks
- o Have a good day
- o Have a bad day
- o Finish all that you had on your to do list
- o Eat dinner
- o Sleep early

Good night and sleep well

Good Morning Sunshine!

Lets start the beginning of the month by noting down our details, so this way we can track changes every month

Age:
Weight:
Height:
Date of last menstrual cycle and time frame:

Did you...

o Get out of bed, woke          o Brush you teeth          o Eat breakfast
   up at:                       o Take a shower            o Take your meds
o Smile

Every little task is important sometimes we forget the silliest things so lets make a to-do list to keep track!

To-do list:

Good afternoon!

Did you...

o Eat lunch                    o Finish your tasks?

Good evening love, how's your day so far?

Did you...

o Eat snacks                   o Finish all that you had on    o Eat dinner
o Have a good day                 your to do list              o Sleep early
o Have a bad day

Good night and sleep well

Good Morning Sunshine!

Lets start the beginning of the month by noting down our details, so this way we can track changes every month

Age:
Weight:
Height:
Date of last menstrual cycle and time frame:

Did you…

| | | |
|---|---|---|
| o Get out of bed, woke up at: | o Brush you teeth | o Eat breakfast |
| o Smile | o Take a shower | o Take your meds |

Every little task is important sometimes we forget the silliest things so lets make a to-do list to keep track!

To-do list:

Good afternoon!

Did you…

o Eat lunch          o Finish your tasks?

Good evening love, how's your day so far?

Did you…

| | | |
|---|---|---|
| o Eat snacks | o Finish all that you had on your to do list | o Eat dinner |
| o Have a good day | | o Sleep early |
| o Have a bad day | | |

Good night and sleep well

Good Morning Sunshine!

Lets start the beginning of the month by noting down our details, so this way we can track changes every month

Age:
Weight:
Height:
Date of last menstrual cycle and time frame:

Did you…

- o Get out of bed, woke up at:
- o Smile
- o Brush you teeth
- o Take a shower
- o Eat breakfast
- o Take your meds

Every little task is important sometimes we forget the silliest things so lets make a to-do list to keep track!

To-do list:

Good afternoon!

Did you…

- o Eat lunch
- o Finish your tasks?

Good evening love, how's your day so far?

Did you…

- o Eat snacks
- o Have a good day
- o Have a bad day
- o Finish all that you had on your to do list
- o Eat dinner
- o Sleep early

Good night and sleep well

Good Morning Sunshine!

Lets start the beginning of the month by noting down our details, so this way we can track changes every month

Age:
Weight:
Height:
Date of last menstrual cycle and time frame:

Did you...

o Get out of bed, woke    o Brush you teeth    o Eat breakfast
   up at:    o Take a shower    o Take your meds
o Smile

Every little task is important sometimes we forget the silliest things so lets make a to-do list to keep track!

To-do list:

Good afternoon!

Did you...

o Eat lunch    o Finish your tasks?

Good evening love, how's your day so far?

Did you...

o Eat snacks    o Finish all that you had on    o Eat dinner
o Have a good day      your to do list    o Sleep early
o Have a bad day

Good night and sleep well

# This Month...

o I tried something new by...

o I helped somebody by...

o I become a better person by...

o I lost ____ kgs by...

o I gained ____kgs by...

o

o

o

# Habit Tracker

**Month:**

| | 1st | 2nd | 3rd | 4th | 5th | |
|---|---|---|---|---|---|---|
| Sleep | | | | | | |
| Caffeine | | | | | | |
| Alcohol | | | | | | |
| Cigarettes | | | | | | |
| Exercise | | | | | | |
| | 6th | 7th | 8th | 9th | 10th | |
| Sleep | | | | | | |
| Caffeine | | | | | | |
| Alcohol | | | | | | |
| Cigarettes | | | | | | |
| Exercise | | | | | | |
| | 11th | 12th | 13th | 14th | 15th | |
| Sleep | | | | | | |
| Caffeine | | | | | | |
| Alcohol | | | | | | |
| Cigarettes | | | | | | |
| Exercise | | | | | | |
| | 16th | 17th | 18th | 19th | 20th | |
| Sleep | | | | | | |
| Caffeine | | | | | | |
| Alcohol | | | | | | |
| Cigarettes | | | | | | |
| Exercise | | | | | | |
| | 21th | 22th | 23th | 24th | 25th | |
| Sleep | | | | | | |
| Caffeine | | | | | | |
| Alcohol | | | | | | |
| Cigarettes | | | | | | |
| Exercise | | | | | | |
| | 26th | 27th | 28th | 29th | 30th | 31st |
| Sleep | | | | | | |
| Caffeine | | | | | | |
| Alcohol | | | | | | |
| Cigarettes | | | | | | |
| Exercise | | | | | | |

# Emotion tracker

*How are you felling today? It is important to be in touch with yourself and your emotions.*

| | Anger | Hurt/Pain | Disappointment | Upset | Happy | Blah! | Lazy |
|---|---|---|---|---|---|---|---|
| 1st | | | | | | | |
| 2nd | | | | | | | |
| 3rd | | | | | | | |
| 4th | | | | | | | |
| 5th | | | | | | | |
| 6th | | | | | | | |
| 7th | | | | | | | |
| 8th | | | | | | | |
| 9th | | | | | | | |
| 10th | | | | | | | |
| 11th | | | | | | | |
| 12th | | | | | | | |
| 13th | | | | | | | |
| 14th | | | | | | | |
| 15th | | | | | | | |
| 16th | | | | | | | |
| 17th | | | | | | | |
| 18th | | | | | | | |
| 19th | | | | | | | |
| 20th | | | | | | | |
| 21st | | | | | | | |
| 22nd | | | | | | | |
| 23rd | | | | | | | |
| 24th | | | | | | | |
| 25th | | | | | | | |
| 26th | | | | | | | |
| 27th | | | | | | | |
| 28th | | | | | | | |
| 29th | | | | | | | |
| 30th | | | | | | | |
| 31st | | | | | | | |

|        | Guilt | Anxious | Sadness | Shame | Guilt | Worthless |
|--------|-------|---------|---------|-------|-------|-----------|
| 1st    |       |         |         |       |       |           |
| 2nd    |       |         |         |       |       |           |
| 3rd    |       |         |         |       |       |           |
| 4th    |       |         |         |       |       |           |
| 5th    |       |         |         |       |       |           |
| 6th    |       |         |         |       |       |           |
| 7th    |       |         |         |       |       |           |
| 8th    |       |         |         |       |       |           |
| 9th    |       |         |         |       |       |           |
| 10th   |       |         |         |       |       |           |
| 11th   |       |         |         |       |       |           |
| 12th   |       |         |         |       |       |           |
| 13th   |       |         |         |       |       |           |
| 14th   |       |         |         |       |       |           |
| 15th   |       |         |         |       |       |           |
| 16th   |       |         |         |       |       |           |
| 17th   |       |         |         |       |       |           |
| 18th   |       |         |         |       |       |           |
| 19th   |       |         |         |       |       |           |
| 20th   |       |         |         |       |       |           |
| 21st   |       |         |         |       |       |           |
| 22nd   |       |         |         |       |       |           |
| 23rd   |       |         |         |       |       |           |
| 24th   |       |         |         |       |       |           |
| 25th   |       |         |         |       |       |           |
| 26th   |       |         |         |       |       |           |
| 27th   |       |         |         |       |       |           |
| 28th   |       |         |         |       |       |           |
| 29th   |       |         |         |       |       |           |
| 30th   |       |         |         |       |       |           |
| 31st   |       |         |         |       |       |           |

# Food Tracker

| | Healthy food | Junk food | Both | Didn't eat ☹ |
|---|---|---|---|---|
| 1st | | | | |
| 2nd | | | | |
| 3rd | | | | |
| 4th | | | | |
| 5th | | | | |
| 6th | | | | |
| 7th | | | | |
| 8th | | | | |
| 9th | | | | |
| 10th | | | | |
| 11th | | | | |
| 12th | | | | |
| 13th | | | | |
| 14th | | | | |
| 15th | | | | |
| 16th | | | | |
| 17th | | | | |
| 18th | | | | |
| 19th | | | | |
| 20th | | | | |
| 21st | | | | |
| 22nd | | | | |
| 23rd | | | | |
| 24th | | | | |
| 25th | | | | |
| 26th | | | | |
| 27th | | | | |
| 28th | | | | |
| 29th | | | | |
| 30th | | | | |
| 31st | | | | |

# Weight Tracker

**Month:**

| | Kgs/lbs | | Kgs/lbs |
|---|---|---|---|
| 1st | | 16th | |
| 2nd | | 17th | |
| 3rd | | 18th | |
| 4th | | 19th | |
| 5th | | 20th | |
| 6th | | 21st | |
| 7th | | 22nd | |
| 8th | | 23rd | |
| 9th | | 24th | |
| 10th | | 25th | |
| 11th | | 26th | |
| 12th | | 27th | |
| 13th | | 28th | |
| 14th | | 29th | |
| 15th | | 30th | |
| | | 31st | |

# Journal

dd/mm/yy

Good Morning Sunshine!

Lets start the beginning of the month by noting down our details, so this way we can track changes every month

Age:
Weight:
Height:
Date of last menstrual cycle and time frame:

Did you...

o Get out of bed, woke          o Brush you teeth          o Eat breakfast
   up at:                       o Take a shower            o Take your meds
o Smile

Every little task is important sometimes we forget the silliest things so lets make a to-do list to keep track!

To-do list:

Good afternoon!

Did you...

o Eat lunch                o Finish your tasks?

Good evening love, how's your day so far?

Did you...

o Eat snacks               o Finish all that you had on    o Eat dinner
o Have a good day             your to do list               o Sleep early
o Have a bad day

Good night and sleep well

Good Morning Sunshine!

Lets start the beginning of the month by noting down our details, so this way we can track changes every month

Age:
Weight:
Height:
Date of last menstrual cycle and time frame:

Did you…

o Get out of bed, woke      o Brush you teeth       o Eat breakfast
   up at:                   o Take a shower         o Take your meds
o Smile

Every little task is important sometimes we forget the silliest things so lets make a to-do list to keep track!

To-do list:

Good afternoon!

Did you…

o Eat lunch                 o Finish your tasks?

Good evening love, how's your day so far?

Did you…

o Eat snacks                o Finish all that you had on    o Eat dinner
o Have a good day              your to do list             o Sleep early
o Have a bad day

Good night and sleep well

Good Morning Sunshine!

Lets start the beginning of the month by noting down our details, so this way we can track changes every month

Age:
Weight:
Height:
Date of last menstrual cycle and time frame:

Did you...

o Get out of bed, woke    o Brush you teeth       o Eat breakfast
   up at:                 o Take a shower         o Take your meds
o Smile

Every little task is important sometimes we forget the silliest things so lets make a to-do list to keep track!

To-do list:

Good afternoon!

Did you...

o Eat lunch              o Finish your tasks?

Good evening love, how's your day so far?

Did you...

o Eat snacks             o Finish all that you had on    o Eat dinner
o Have a good day           your to do list             o Sleep early
o Have a bad day

Good night and sleep well

dd/mm/yy

Good Morning Sunshine!

Lets start the beginning of the month by noting down our details, so this way we can track changes every month

Age:
Weight:
Height:
Date of last menstrual cycle and time frame:

Did you...

o Get out of bed, woke    o Brush you teeth    o Eat breakfast
  up at:    o Take a shower    o Take your meds
o Smile

Every little task is important sometimes we forget the silliest things so lets make a to-do list to keep track!

To-do list:

Good afternoon!

Did you...

o Eat lunch    o Finish your tasks?

Good evening love, how's your day so far?

Did you...

o Eat snacks    o Finish all that you had on    o Eat dinner
o Have a good day    your to do list    o Sleep early
o Have a bad day

Good night and sleep well

dd/mm/yy

Good Morning Sunshine!

Lets start the beginning of the month by noting down our details, so this way we can track changes every month

Age:
Weight:
Height:
Date of last menstrual cycle and time frame:

Did you...

o Get out of bed, woke up at:
o Smile

o Brush you teeth
o Take a shower

o Eat breakfast
o Take your meds

Every little task is important sometimes we forget the silliest things so lets make a to-do list to keep track!

To-do list:

Good afternoon!

Did you...

o Eat lunch

o Finish your tasks?

Good evening love, how's your day so far?

Did you...

o Eat snacks
o Have a good day
o Have a bad day

o Finish all that you had on your to do list

o Eat dinner
o Sleep early

Good night and sleep well

Good Morning Sunshine!

Lets start the beginning of the month by noting down our details, so this way we can track changes every month

Age:
Weight:
Height:
Date of last menstrual cycle and time frame:

Did you...

o Get out of bed, woke     o Brush you teeth      o Eat breakfast
   up at:                  o Take a shower        o Take your meds
o Smile

Every little task is important sometimes we forget the silliest things so lets make a to-do list to keep track!

To-do list:

Good afternoon!

Did you...

o Eat lunch               o Finish your tasks?

Good evening love, how's your day so far?

Did you...

o Eat snacks              o Finish all that you had on    o Eat dinner
o Have a good day            your to do list             o Sleep early
o Have a bad day

Good night and sleep well

Good Morning Sunshine!

Lets start the beginning of the month by noting down our details, so this way we can track changes every month

Age:
Weight:
Height:
Date of last menstrual cycle and time frame:

Did you…

o Get out of bed, woke          o Brush you teeth          o Eat breakfast
   up at:                            o Take a shower            o Take your meds
o Smile

Every little task is important sometimes we forget the silliest things so lets make a to-do list to keep track!

To-do list:

Good afternoon!

Did you…

o Eat lunch                    o Finish your tasks?

Good evening love, how's your day so far?

Did you…

o Eat snacks                   o Finish all that you had on    o Eat dinner
o Have a good day                 your to do list               o Sleep early
o Have a bad day

Good night and sleep well

Good Morning Sunshine!

Lets start the beginning of the month by noting down our details, so this way we can track changes every month

Age:
Weight:
Height:
Date of last menstrual cycle and time frame:

Did you…

- o Get out of bed, woke up at:
- o Smile

- o Brush you teeth
- o Take a shower

- o Eat breakfast
- o Take your meds

Every little task is important sometimes we forget the silliest things so lets make a to-do list to keep track!

To-do list:

Good afternoon!

Did you…

- o Eat lunch

- o Finish your tasks?

Good evening love, how's your day so far?

Did you…

- o Eat snacks
- o Have a good day
- o Have a bad day

- o Finish all that you had on your to do list

- o Eat dinner
- o Sleep early

Good night and sleep well

Good Morning Sunshine!

Lets start the beginning of the month by noting down our details, so this way we can track changes every month

Age:
Weight:
Height:
Date of last menstrual cycle and time frame:

Did you...

o Get out of bed, woke    o Brush you teeth      o Eat breakfast
   up at:              o Take a shower        o Take your meds
o Smile

Every little task is important sometimes we forget the silliest things so lets make a to-do list to keep track!

To-do list:

Good afternoon!

Did you...

o Eat lunch                  o Finish your tasks?

Good evening love, how's your day so far?

Did you...

o Eat snacks                 o Finish all that you had on    o Eat dinner
o Have a good day              your to do list              o Sleep early
o Have a bad day

Good night and sleep well

Good Morning Sunshine!

Lets start the beginning of the month by noting down our details, so this way we can track changes every month

Age:
Weight:
Height:
Date of last menstrual cycle and time frame:

Did you…

o Get out of bed, woke        o Brush you teeth        o Eat breakfast
   up at:                                o Take a shower          o Take your meds
o Smile

Every little task is important sometimes we forget the silliest things so lets make a to-do list to keep track!

To-do list:

Good afternoon!

Did you…

o Eat lunch                     o Finish your tasks?

Good evening love, how's your day so far?

Did you…

o Eat snacks                    o Finish all that you had on    o Eat dinner
o Have a good day                  your to do list              o Sleep early
o Have a bad day

Good night and sleep well

Good Morning Sunshine!

Lets start the beginning of the month by noting down our details, so this way we can track changes every month

Age:
Weight:
Height:
Date of last menstrual cycle and time frame:

Did you…

o Get out of bed, woke       o Brush you teeth        o Eat breakfast
   up at:                    o Take a shower          o Take your meds
o Smile

Every little task is important sometimes we forget the silliest things so lets make a to-do list to keep track!

To-do list:

Good afternoon!

Did you…

o Eat lunch                  o Finish your tasks?

Good evening love, how's your day so far?

Did you…

o Eat snacks                 o Finish all that you had on    o Eat dinner
o Have a good day               your to do list             o Sleep early
o Have a bad day

Good night and sleep well

Good Morning Sunshine!

Lets start the beginning of the month by noting down our details, so this way we can track changes every month

Age:
Weight:
Height:
Date of last menstrual cycle and time frame:

Did you…

- o Get out of bed, woke up at:
- o Smile
- o Brush you teeth
- o Take a shower
- o Eat breakfast
- o Take your meds

Every little task is important sometimes we forget the silliest things so lets make a to-do list to keep track!

To-do list:

Good afternoon!

Did you…

- o Eat lunch
- o Finish your tasks?

Good evening love, how's your day so far?

Did you…

- o Eat snacks
- o Have a good day
- o Have a bad day
- o Finish all that you had on your to do list
- o Eat dinner
- o Sleep early

Good night and sleep well

Good Morning Sunshine!

Lets start the beginning of the month by noting down our details, so this way we can track changes every month

Age:
Weight:
Height:
Date of last menstrual cycle and time frame:

Did you…

- o Get out of bed, woke up at:
- o Smile
- o Brush you teeth
- o Take a shower
- o Eat breakfast
- o Take your meds

Every little task is important sometimes we forget the silliest things so lets make a to-do list to keep track!

To-do list:

Good afternoon!

Did you…

- o Eat lunch
- o Finish your tasks?

Good evening love, how's your day so far?

Did you…

- o Eat snacks
- o Have a good day
- o Have a bad day
- o Finish all that you had on your to do list
- o Eat dinner
- o Sleep early

Good night and sleep well

Good Morning Sunshine!

Lets start the beginning of the month by noting down our details, so this way we can track changes every month

Age:
Weight:
Height:
Date of last menstrual cycle and time frame:

Did you…

o Get out of bed, woke        o Brush you teeth         o Eat breakfast
   up at:                     o Take a shower           o Take your meds
o Smile

Every little task is important sometimes we forget the silliest things so lets make a to-do list to keep track!

To-do list:

Good afternoon!

Did you…

o Eat lunch                 o Finish your tasks?

Good evening love, how's your day so far?

Did you…

o Eat snacks           o Finish all that you had on    o Eat dinner
o Have a good day          your to do list             o Sleep early
o Have a bad day

Good night and sleep well

Good Morning Sunshine!

Lets start the beginning of the month by noting down our details, so this way we can track changes every month

Age:
Weight:
Height:
Date of last menstrual cycle and time frame:

Did you…

o Get out of bed, woke       o Brush you teeth       o Eat breakfast
   up at:                    o Take a shower         o Take your meds
o Smile

Every little task is important sometimes we forget the silliest things so lets make a to-do list to keep track!

To-do list:

Good afternoon!

Did you…

o Eat lunch                o Finish your tasks?

Good evening love, how's your day so far?

Did you…

o Eat snacks               o Finish all that you had on    o Eat dinner
o Have a good day             your to do list              o Sleep early
o Have a bad day

Good night and sleep well

Good Morning Sunshine!

Lets start the beginning of the month by noting down our details, so this way we can track changes every month

Age:
Weight:
Height:
Date of last menstrual cycle and time frame:

Did you...

- o Get out of bed, woke up at:
- o Smile

- o Brush you teeth
- o Take a shower

- o Eat breakfast
- o Take your meds

Every little task is important sometimes we forget the silliest things so lets make a to-do list to keep track!

To-do list:

Good afternoon!

Did you...

- o Eat lunch

- o Finish your tasks?

Good evening love, how's your day so far?

Did you...

- o Eat snacks
- o Have a good day
- o Have a bad day

- o Finish all that you had on your to do list

- o Eat dinner
- o Sleep early

Good night and sleep well

Good Morning Sunshine!

Lets start the beginning of the month by noting down our details, so this way we can track changes every month

Age:
Weight:
Height:
Date of last menstrual cycle and time frame:

Did you...

o Get out of bed, woke          o Brush you teeth          o Eat breakfast
  up at:                        o Take a shower            o Take your meds
o Smile

Every little task is important sometimes we forget the silliest things so lets make a to-do list to keep track!

To-do list:

Good afternoon!

Did you...

o Eat lunch                     o Finish your tasks?

Good evening love, how's your day so far?

Did you...

o Eat snacks                    o Finish all that you had on     o Eat dinner
o Have a good day                 your to do list                o Sleep early
o Have a bad day

Good night and sleep well

dd/mm/yy

Good Morning Sunshine!

Lets start the beginning of the month by noting down our details, so this way we can track changes every month

Age:
Weight:
Height:
Date of last menstrual cycle and time frame:

Did you...

- Get out of bed, woke up at:
- Smile
- Brush you teeth
- Take a shower
- Eat breakfast
- Take your meds

Every little task is important sometimes we forget the silliest things so lets make a to-do list to keep track!

To-do list:

Good afternoon!

Did you...

- Eat lunch
- Finish your tasks?

Good evening love, how's your day so far?

Did you...

- Eat snacks
- Have a good day
- Have a bad day
- Finish all that you had on your to do list
- Eat dinner
- Sleep early

Good night and sleep well

Good Morning Sunshine!

Lets start the beginning of the month by noting down our details, so this way we can track changes every month

Age:
Weight:
Height:
Date of last menstrual cycle and time frame:

Did you…

o Get out of bed, woke      o Brush you teeth        o Eat breakfast
   up at:                   o Take a shower          o Take your meds
o Smile

Every little task is important sometimes we forget the silliest things so lets make a to-do list to keep track!

To-do list:

Good afternoon!

Did you…

o Eat lunch                  o Finish your tasks?

Good evening love, how's your day so far?

Did you…

o Eat snacks                 o Finish all that you had on    o Eat dinner
o Have a good day               your to do list               o Sleep early
o Have a bad day

Good night and sleep well

Good Morning Sunshine!

Lets start the beginning of the month by noting down our details, so this way we can track changes every month

Age:
Weight:
Height:
Date of last menstrual cycle and time frame:

Did you...

- o Get out of bed, woke    o Brush you teeth      o Eat breakfast
  up at:                    o Take a shower        o Take your meds
- o Smile

Every little task is important sometimes we forget the silliest things so lets make a to-do list to keep track!

To-do list:

Good afternoon!

Did you...

- o Eat lunch               o Finish your tasks?

Good evening love, how's your day so far?

Did you...

- o Eat snacks              o Finish all that you had on    o Eat dinner
- o Have a good day           your to do list               o Sleep early
- o Have a bad day

Good night and sleep well

Good Morning Sunshine!

Lets start the beginning of the month by noting down our details, so this way we can track changes every month

Age:
Weight:
Height:
Date of last menstrual cycle and time frame:

Did you…

- o Get out of bed, woke up at:
- o Smile
- o Brush you teeth
- o Take a shower
- o Eat breakfast
- o Take your meds

Every little task is important sometimes we forget the silliest things so lets make a to-do list to keep track!

To-do list:

Good afternoon!

Did you…

- o Eat lunch
- o Finish your tasks?

Good evening love, how's your day so far?

Did you…

- o Eat snacks
- o Have a good day
- o Have a bad day
- o Finish all that you had on your to do list
- o Eat dinner
- o Sleep early

Good night and sleep well

Good Morning Sunshine!

Lets start the beginning of the month by noting down our details, so this way we can track changes every month

Age:
Weight:
Height:
Date of last menstrual cycle and time frame:

Did you…

- o Get out of bed, woke
    up at:
- o Smile

- o Brush you teeth
- o Take a shower

- o Eat breakfast
- o Take your meds

Every little task is important sometimes we forget the silliest things so lets make a to-do list to keep track!

To-do list:

Good afternoon!

Did you…

- o Eat lunch

- o Finish your tasks?

Good evening love, how's your day so far?

Did you…

- o Eat snacks
- o Have a good day
- o Have a bad day

- o Finish all that you had on
    your to do list

- o Eat dinner
- o Sleep early

Good night and sleep well

Good Morning Sunshine!

Lets start the beginning of the month by noting down our details, so this way we can track changes every month

Age:
Weight:
Height:
Date of last menstrual cycle and time frame:

Did you...

o Get out of bed, woke    o Brush you teeth        o Eat breakfast
   up at:                 o Take a shower          o Take your meds
o Smile

Every little task is important sometimes we forget the silliest things so lets make a to-do list to keep track!

To-do list:

Good afternoon!

Did you...

o Eat lunch              o Finish your tasks?

Good evening love, how's your day so far?

Did you...

o Eat snacks             o Finish all that you had on    o Eat dinner
o Have a good day           your to do list              o Sleep early
o Have a bad day

Good night and sleep well

Good Morning Sunshine!

Lets start the beginning of the month by noting down our details, so this way we can track changes every month

Age:
Weight:
Height:
Date of last menstrual cycle and time frame:

Did you...

- o Get out of bed, woke
  up at:
- o Smile

- o Brush you teeth
- o Take a shower

- o Eat breakfast
- o Take your meds

Every little task is important sometimes we forget the silliest things so lets make a to-do list to keep track!

To-do list:

Good afternoon!

Did you...

- o Eat lunch

- o Finish your tasks?

Good evening love, how's your day so far?

Did you...

- o Eat snacks
- o Have a good day
- o Have a bad day

- o Finish all that you had on
  your to do list

- o Eat dinner
- o Sleep early

Good night and sleep well

Good Morning Sunshine!

Lets start the beginning of the month by noting down our details, so this way we can track changes every month

Age:
Weight:
Height:
Date of last menstrual cycle and time frame:

Did you...

o Get out of bed, woke    o Brush you teeth    o Eat breakfast
   up at:    o Take a shower    o Take your meds
o Smile

Every little task is important sometimes we forget the silliest things so lets make a to-do list to keep track!

To-do list:

Good afternoon!

Did you...

o Eat lunch      o Finish your tasks?

Good evening love, how's your day so far?

Did you...

o Eat snacks    o Finish all that you had on    o Eat dinner
o Have a good day    your to do list    o Sleep early
o Have a bad day

Good night and sleep well

Good Morning Sunshine!

Lets start the beginning of the month by noting down our details, so this way we can track changes every month

Age:
Weight:
Height:
Date of last menstrual cycle and time frame:

Did you...

- o Get out of bed, woke
    up at:
- o Smile
- o Brush you teeth
- o Take a shower
- o Eat breakfast
- o Take your meds

Every little task is important sometimes we forget the silliest things so lets make a to-do list to keep track!

To-do list:

Good afternoon!

Did you...

- o Eat lunch
- o Finish your tasks?

Good evening love, how's your day so far?

Did you...

- o Eat snacks
- o Have a good day
- o Have a bad day
- o Finish all that you had on
    your to do list
- o Eat dinner
- o Sleep early

Good night and sleep well

Good Morning Sunshine!

Lets start the beginning of the month by noting down our details, so this way we can track changes every month

Age:
Weight:
Height:
Date of last menstrual cycle and time frame:

Did you...

o Get out of bed, woke       o Brush you teeth        o Eat breakfast
   up at:                    o Take a shower          o Take your meds
o Smile

Every little task is important sometimes we forget the silliest things so lets make a to-do list to keep track!

To-do list:

Good afternoon!

Did you...

o Eat lunch              o Finish your tasks?

Good evening love, how's your day so far?

Did you...

o Eat snacks             o Finish all that you had on   o Eat dinner
o Have a good day           your to do list             o Sleep early
o Have a bad day

Good night and sleep well

Good Morning Sunshine!

Lets start the beginning of the month by noting down our details, so this way we can track changes every month

Age:
Weight:
Height:
Date of last menstrual cycle and time frame:

Did you…

o Get out of bed, woke     o Brush you teeth     o Eat breakfast
  up at:                    o Take a shower     o Take your meds
o Smile

Every little task is important sometimes we forget the silliest things so lets make a to-do list to keep track!

To-do list:

Good afternoon!

Did you…

o Eat lunch               o Finish your tasks?

Good evening love, how's your day so far?

Did you…

o Eat snacks           o Finish all that you had on    o Eat dinner
o Have a good day        your to do list           o Sleep early
o Have a bad day

Good night and sleep well

dd/mm/yy

Good Morning Sunshine!

Lets start the beginning of the month by noting down our details, so this way we can track changes every month

Age:
Weight:
Height:
Date of last menstrual cycle and time frame:

Did you...

o Get out of bed, woke   o Brush you teeth        o Eat breakfast
   up at:                o Take a shower          o Take your meds
o Smile

Every little task is important sometimes we forget the silliest things so lets make a to-do list to keep track!

To-do list:

Good afternoon!

Did you...

o Eat lunch              o Finish your tasks?

Good evening love, how's your day so far?

Did you...

o Eat snacks             o Finish all that you had on   o Eat dinner
o Have a good day           your to do list            o Sleep early
o Have a bad day

Good night and sleep well

Good Morning Sunshine!

Lets start the beginning of the month by noting down our details, so this way we can track changes every month

Age:
Weight:
Height:
Date of last menstrual cycle and time frame:

Did you…

o Get out of bed, woke      o Brush you teeth        o Eat breakfast
   up at:                   o Take a shower          o Take your meds
o Smile

Every little task is important sometimes we forget the silliest things so lets make a to-do list to keep track!

To-do list:

Good afternoon!

Did you…

o Eat lunch               o Finish your tasks?

Good evening love, how's your day so far?

Did you…

o Eat snacks              o Finish all that you had on   o Eat dinner
o Have a good day            your to do list             o Sleep early
o Have a bad day

Good night and sleep well

Good Morning Sunshine!

Lets start the beginning of the month by noting down our details, so this way we can track changes every month

Age:
Weight:
Height:
Date of last menstrual cycle and time frame:

Did you...

o Get out of bed, woke        o Brush you teeth        o Eat breakfast
  up at:                      o Take a shower          o Take your meds
o Smile

Every little task is important sometimes we forget the silliest things so lets make a to-do list to keep track!

To-do list:

Good afternoon!

Did you...

o Eat lunch              o Finish your tasks?

Good evening love, how's your day so far?

Did you...

o Eat snacks             o Finish all that you had on    o Eat dinner
o Have a good day          your to do list               o Sleep early
o Have a bad day

Good night and sleep well

# This Month...

o I tried something new by…

o I helped somebody by…

o I become a better person by…

o I lost ____ kgs by…

o I gained ____kgs by…

o

o

o

# Having a bad day?

Its okay, we all have days that are good and not too good that's just life. We have to learn to deal with its ups and downs. If everything in life was sunshine and roses, well as good as that sounds it would just be boring. You'll never be able to see the rainbow after the storm. So just remember, even though you can't see it now, everything has an upside just try to have some faith.

How to make yourself feel better…

Its quite easy to drown into a bad mood but difficult to get yourself up and about again. So here are a few things that cheer me up or help me feel better.

- Listen to peppy songs, when you listen to a song with a rapid beat you feel pumped up, well it takes a while to kick in but when it does you'll be dancing around in your underwear singing even when you don't know the lyrics.

- Cook, or distract yourself any other way. Trust me you don't need to be a master-chef to enter to kitchen you don't even need to stay all day long in front of the hot stove just make a microwaveable cake which literally takes 10mins tops and is supper easy

- Have a movie night, call some friends, family, sister, brother, your neighbor just anyone over and watch a fun movie.

# Things I am Grateful for...

- 
- 
- 
- 
- 
- 
- 
- 
-

# Things I want to improve...

- 
- 
- 
- 
- 
- 
-

# Things I love about myself...

- 
- 
- 
- 
- 
- 
-

# Things that make me proud of myself...

- 
- 
- 
- 
- 
- 
- 
-

*Rant here!*

So this is the end of our journey of three hundred and sixty five days. Congratulations! I am extremely proud of you, you have successfully been in touch with yourself for an entire year. I know its really difficult to stay constant and write down for 365 days, you must have skipped a few days or cheated a little in the between but that's okay. Remember taking care of yourself should be your number one priority. It is okay to be selfish sometimes because your needs and important too. Don't always slug around for other people. It is crucial to know the value of yourself and respect yourself. If you are unable to do that, others won't either. It starts with you.

Contact information:

Email: dristiswritings@gmail.com
Facebook Page: facebook.com/dristiswritings
Instagram: dristi98

All suggestions, feedbacks and/or complaints are welcome.

# My inspirations:

- Beau Taplin
- Lang Leav
- MVDarkLight
- R.M. Drake
- Rune Cazuli
- Rupi Kaur
- R.H. Sin
- Samantha King